BROOKINGS TRADE FORUM

—— 2006 ——

GLOBAL LABOR MARKETS?

Susan M. Collins and Carol Graham

EDITORS

BROOKINGS INSTITUTION PRESS
Washington, D.C.

ISSN 1520-5479
ISBN-13: 978-0-8157-1296-1
ISBN-10: 0-8157-1296-0

For information on subscriptions, standing orders, and individual copies, contact Brookings Institution Press, P.O. Box 465, Hanover, PA 17331-0465. Or call 866-698-0010. E-mail brookings@tsp.sheridan.com. Visit Brookings online at www.brookings.edu/press/bookstore.htm.

Brookings periodicals are available online through Online Computer Library Center (contact the OCLC subscriptions department at 800-848-5878, ext. 6251) and Project Muse (http://muse.jhu.edu).

BROOKINGS
TRADE FORUM
——— 2006 ———

GLOBAL
LABOR MARKETS?

฿ THE BROOKINGS INSTITUTION

The Brookings Institution is a private nonprofit organization devoted to research, education, and publication on important issues of domestic and foreign policy. Its principal purpose is to bring the highest quality independent research and analysis to bear on current and emerging policy problems. The Institution was founded on December 8, 1927, to merge the activities of the Institute for Government Research, founded in 1916, the Institute of Economics, founded in 1922, and the Robert Brookings Graduate School of Economics and Government, founded in 1924. Interpretations or conclusions in Brookings publications should be understood to be solely those of the authors.

BROOKINGS TRADE FORUM is a series of annual volumes that provide authoritative and in-depth analysis on current and emerging issues in international economics. The series aims to explore questions on international trade and macroeconomics in an interdisciplinary fashion with both practitioners and academics and seeks to gather in one place papers that provide a thorough look at a particular topic affecting international economic policy. Leading experts in the field will contribute to each volume. This ninth issue contains edited versions of the papers and comments presented at a conference held at the Brookings Institution, May 11–12, 2006. This year's forum focused on broadening and deepening our understanding of the extent and implications of increasing globalization of labor markets.

The conference and journal have benefited from the support of the William and Flora Hewlett Foundation, the Ewing Marion Kauffman Foundation, the GE Foundation, and the Tokyo Club Foundation for Global Studies.

Carmen Pagés, *World Bank*
Arvind Panagariya, *Columbia University*
Nina Pavcnik, *Dartmouth College*
Lant Pritchett, *Harvard University and World Bank*
Carmen Reinhart, *University of Maryland*
Mark R. Rosenzweig, *Yale University*
Isabel Sawhill, *Brookings Institution*
Stefano Scarpetta, *World Bank*
Andrew M. Warner, *Millennium Challenge Corporation*
Jeffrey G. Williamson, *Harvard University*

<table>
<tr><td>Conference
participants</td><td>Susan Aaronson, Kenan Institute, University of North Carolina
Jennifer Baumert, US International Trade Commission
Robert Blecker, American University
Barry Bosworth, Brookings Institution
Renee Bowen, Georgetown University
Lael Brainard, Brookings Institution
Ralph Bryant, Brookings Institution
Michael Clemens, Center for Global Development
Sydney F. Collins, University of Miami
I. M. Destler, University of Maryland & Institute for International Economics
William Dickens, Brookings Institution
Rebecca Dillender, Bureau of Internal Labor Affairs
Howard Dobson, United States Department of Labor
William Frenzel, Brookings Institution
Matthew Hoover, University of Maryland
Ergys Islamaj, Georgetown University
Kyle Johnson, US International Trade Commission
Melissa Kearney, Brookings Institution and University of Maryland
Robert Koopman, US International Trade Commission
Johannes Linn, Brookings Institution
Mario Marazzi, Federal Reserve Board
Camilo Mondragon, Georgetown University
Theodore Moran, Georgetown University
Zsolt Nyiri, Gallup World Poll
Scott Otteman, Commission for Labor Cooperation
Gregory Schoepfle, Department of Labor
Charles Schultze, Brookings Institution
Paula Stern, The Stern Group
Kenneth Swinnerton, Department of Labor
Beth Anne Wilson, Federal Reserve Board</td></tr>
</table>

SUSAN M. COLLINS
CAROL GRAHAM

Editors' Summary

An important feature of globalization is the increasing cross-national integration of labor markets. Yet there is little consensus on the implications of that integration, or on the costs and benefits for the many very different groups involved. While there is agreement—at least among most economists—that there are likely to be aggregate welfare gains from increased integration, it is clear that there are losers as well as winners in both developed and developing countries. For example, politically contentious debates about the effects of immigration on the wages of low-skilled workers have proliferated in the advanced industrial economies while poor developing countries have become embroiled in equally contentious debates about the effects of out-migration of skilled workers on their human capital base. Untangling the myriad effects is made even more complex by intermediate arrangements, such as the offshoring of various productive activities by developed country firms to emerging-market economies. This creates new opportunities for skilled workers in the latter, but at the same time offshoring may alter employment opportunities for skilled workers in the advanced economies, and the wage distributions in both.

This ninth issue of the *Brookings Trade Forum* brought together some of the foremost experts on migration, representing diverse perspectives and backgrounds. New research commissioned for each session launched an interrelated series of lively discussions during the conference, held on May 11 and 12, 2006. The objective was not to attempt to reach consensus, but to broaden and deepen our understanding of the extent and implications of the integration of global labor markets. Thus the forum addressed a wide range of topics—from the welfare effects of immigration on labor markets in both developing and developed economies, to the relationship between education systems in sending countries and labor market outcomes in recipient countries, to the merits and demerits of proposals that would drastically reduce restrictions against cross-border labor migration.

ix

Despite the wide range of topics, a number of themes emerged from the analyses. We highlight four. Perhaps the most obvious was the difficulty in drawing general conclusions about the welfare effects of global labor market integration. Various papers and discussions highlighted some of the many critical mediating factors. These include the skill set of the particular group(s) under discussion, the labor market composition in the recipient countries, the relative returns to different types of labor in the sending and receiving countries, the nature of the contractual arrangements relevant for immigrants' work, and more general macroeconomic and financial market trends.

A second theme was that the investments that developing countries make in higher education are no guarantee of retaining their best and brightest. Indeed those very investments may increase the likelihood of out-migration, particularly when the returns to skilled labor are much lower in developing than in the advanced economies.

Third, if international labor markets were more flexible, participants stressed that cross-border labor mobility would likely skyrocket relative to current levels—even if that flexibility entailed only temporary migration. On balance, that increased mobility would have positive effects for poverty reduction worldwide, but its effects on particular nations and on recipient country labor markets would be more mixed. Finally, the discussion made quite clear that, while the economic effects of proposals to increase international labor mobility are themselves difficult enough to measure, the related questions of political rights and citizenship for temporary workers are daunting and have implications for international as well as national norms and standards.

This volume presents the revised papers, invited commentary, and general discussions from the conference. One paper in the volume explicitly examines flows of skilled migrants across countries and how such flows are affected by education investments in the sending countries and by differential returns to skilled labor across countries. Another focuses on the evolution of wage dynamics during development and how those dynamics are affected by global labor market integration. A third paper examines mobility between formal- and informal-sector jobs in emerging market and transition economies and how those trends are affected by the nature of each country's integration into the global economy. Two papers focus explicitly on the potential effects of significant reductions in international labor market mobility, from temporary work permits for migrant workers.

A final panel was asked to reflect broadly on these topics. The first panelist questioned the adequacy of the traditional Heckscher-Ohlin framework for explaining developments in a world where trade patterns do not conform to the underlying assumptions. He suggests an alternative in which productivity differentials can lead to the matching of skilled workers from advanced economies with skilled workers from developing countries—and the potential for increased inequality between skilled and unskilled workers in both. A second panelist discussed costs and benefits of international labor migration within the classic Heckscher-Olin framework and then assessed how that framework has been altered by the increase in offshoring. The final panelist explicitly addressed the effects of increasing immigration on wage inequality in the United States, as well as the broader implications for a growth model based on significant labor and capital inflow but a fragile prosperity based on high levels of indebtedness, increasing poverty and inequality, and limited mobility and opportunity. In the remainder of this introduction, we summarize the main points that emerged in each of these sessions.

LANT PRITCHETT BEGINS his stimulating paper by asking why there are such large discrepancies in wages across countries if labor and capital markets are as mobile—and policies and institutions are as similar—as most traditional models suggest. He notes that even with the increase in the number of sovereign states in the post–World War II years, there should be more economic integration than there actually is. Instead, differential productivity shocks have led to permanent divergence between countries and, in the most extreme cases, the existence of what he calls "ghost" countries and "zombies."

Pritchett argues that region-specific shocks can lead to long-run shifts in labor demand, even after other factors have adjusted. If there is population mobility, for example, between regions within a country, one should expect to see population drop sharply in the region experiencing a negative shock (hence the term ghost towns), with little variability in wages across regions over the medium to long run. However, if populations are immobile, which is typically the case across sovereign borders, the adjustment occurs via a decrease in wages. Instead of ghost countries, the results are "zombies": living dead economies, with wages and incomes falling over time—a situation that characterizes many countries in sub-Saharan Africa. Even if policies and institutions matter a lot, which they do, geography can still also matter. Thus lack of mobility results in countries with many more people than they should otherwise have, regardless of their domestic policies and institutions.

To test his proposition, Pritchett looks at a number of episodes of labor migration and population and wage change across states, provinces, and regions within countries, and across countries—both when mobility is restricted and during an era of open borders. He finds that the variability in per capita income growth rates is spectacularly larger among countries than among regions within countries. At the same time, the variability in population growth across countries in the world is absolutely smaller than the variability across regions within countries. For example, he shows that there has been huge variability in population growth across regions in the United States. He also cites the contrasting examples of Ireland, where the population shrunk dramatically following the potato shock of 1871, and Bolivia, where the population is 90 percent higher than it was in 1972 despite huge economic shocks.

Pritchett identifies a number of countries that are hardcore geographic zombies (such as Zambia) contrasted with those that he labels as policy zombies (such as Cuba). Zambia is a classic case. He concludes that if its population had fallen in accordance with the economic shocks at the same rate that Ireland's population fell, then it would now be just 18 percent of its current level. If it had fallen at the same rate as in some U.S. regions that suffered negative shocks, then it would now be at just 25 percent of its current level.

He concludes by noting that all aid is based on the presumption that countries can increase their income levels. His analysis points to an inconvenient fact—even in fully integrated economies, there can be big changes in desired population. Without population mobility, geographic shocks create a different dynamic: one of falling wages and outputs. If labor supply cannot be elastic, it is prices that must adjust. However, aid policies focus on *national* development strategies, not the well-being of populations—for example, on Zambia rather than on Zambians. He concludes that a policy that dramatically increased labor mobility—perhaps through temporary work permits and strong penalties for exceeding stay limits—would do much more to reduce world poverty than millions of dollars of foreign assistance to national governments.

Both discussants found Pritchett's results on population and wage trends compelling, and his arguments and proposal thought provoking. Cliff Gaddy highlights the extent to which Pritchett's interest is in zombies—where the actual population significantly exceeds the desired one—rather than in ghosts and in spatial zombies rather than in institutional ones. He notes that spatial zombies are worse than policy zombies because policies can be fixed, while geography in most instances cannot.

Gaddy applies Pritchett's framework to Russia, where his own research is based. However, instead of geographic shocks and mobility constrained by national borders, Russia provides examples in which people are forced to live in places that geographic features make very unattractive. He compares cities in Russia with those in free economies that have similar climate and resource endowments (including distance from the market). For example, consider Perm,

Russia, and Duluth, Minnesota. While the current population in Duluth is about the same as it was in 1920, Perm's population quadrupled over the same time period. Based on the relative distribution of pre-Bolshevik Russia, when the population was more concentrated in the European part of the country, Gaddy estimates that many populations in large Russian cities are now two to four times their desired size.

He concludes that Russia is a case in which policies prevent cities that should be ghosts from becoming ghosts, so they remain zombies, and where resources (oil and gas) subsidize economic activity in those zombie cities that would otherwise be defunct.

Simon Johnson commends Pritchett for yet another innovative paper that breaks new ground and will prompt a great deal of further investigation. He agrees with the core point motivating Pritchett's analysis. Since 1945 cross-border migrations are not only on a much-reduced scale compared with the past, they are also asymmetric. It is much easier to move into boom areas than it is to move out of bust areas. And, perhaps most important, migrations out of small, poor countries are now quite difficult. In addition, Johnson identifies a major risk that is only hinted at in the paper: economic depression may lead to deadlock and conflict, exacerbating the income decline.

Johnson finds Pritchett's analogy to ghost towns a provocative but productive way to think about some of the problems in relatively poor countries today, from Haiti (whose economy was previously based on sugar) to parts of West Africa (where commodity booms come and go). However, he notes that when people cannot leave becoming a zombie is not the only possible outcome. The inhabitants may find something else to do. Perhaps they have skills that are useful for other activities or they can attract other kinds of investment. Barbados, for example, has managed to achieve a much higher level of income than Guyana, despite the fact that both have strong heritages of sugar, slavery and other forms of forced labor, and deep ethnic divisions.

He concludes by noting that almost none of the great successes of the past fifty years (that is, rapid sustained growth, starting with weak or very weak institutions) have been based on commodity price booms. Instead, the catalyst has been figuring out how to better integrate into global manufacturing production chains. Low wages are not a sufficient solution, but they are also not necessarily an obstacle to initiating a sustained growth process.

MARK ROSENZWEIG EMPIRICALLY analyzes the cross-country migration of students. This group has received surprisingly little prior attention among researchers, despite its importance. For instance, the flow of students to the

United States far outpaces flows of other immigration categories, such as skilled workers or legal unskilled workers. Using data on student visas, Rosenzweig examines the direction of migration, the returns to various skill levels, and differences across different countries. He notes that most migration models fail to account for either different skill levels of migrants or differences in returns to skills across countries. He exploits a new data set from the New Immigrant Survey to examine the flow of students to the United States, the stock of U.S. foreign-born students, and the number of U.S. foreign-born students who become permanent residents. His paper extends beyond the standard focus on the GDP of the sending countries and looks at rewards to skills across countries.

He tests two separate models of migration. One is a schooling constraint model, in which migrants come from countries with high rewards to skills but low opportunities to obtain additional schooling at home. The second is a model in which migrants acquire skills at home, where the skill price is low. However, expanded schooling opportunities at home actually increase migrant outflows because the domestic rewards to skills remain much lower than in the developed countries.

Rosenzweig first notes that the direction of migration flows is very clear. The lion's share of the world's student migration goes to the United States, followed by the United Kingdom, and then to Australia and Canada. At the same time, (purchasing power parity) PPP-adjusted earnings of high school and college graduates vary tremendously across countries. In countries such as Nigeria, college graduates earn as little as $1,000 per year; in Korea, college graduates still earn less than $10,000 per year, while in the United States, high school and college graduates earn $35,000 and $50,000 per year, respectively.

The main sending countries are in Asia. Topping the list are countries with high economic growth rates, but with low skills prices (China and India). They are also far away from the United States, have at least one university ranked in the top 200 in the world, and have very large populations. Rosenzweig finds that growth rates and per capita GDP both affect the capacity of countries to send student migrants. The number of U.S. student visas issued annually, the stock of U.S. foreign students, and the number of foreign-born students who remain permanently in the United States are all higher for countries with lower skill prices and for countries with a larger number of universities per capita.

It is interesting that Rosenzweig finds that an increase in the number of home universities increases the number of student stayers in the United States. This suggests a story of educated students coming to graduate school in the United States, seeing huge wage differentials, and thus choosing to stay. It also suggests that some kinds of developing country investments in education can exacerbate brain drain. Thus higher skill prices in the home country are negatively correlated with student outflows; when controlling for skill prices, greater domestic investment in education is associated with more out-migration. As he notes, a better understand of these linkages will be important for determining the optimal distribution of additional investments in schooling. Somewhat less surprisingly, he also shows that those migrants who have come to the United States with prior student visas and have been able to become permanent residents (that is, they acquire green cards) are much more likely to get a job and to get married. This is in part because they are more likely to meet someone while in school.

In concluding, Rosenzweig also cautions readers that his data select only one kind of migrant—those with relatively high educational attainment. Other types of immigration may also have important implications for schooling. For instance, remittances from unskilled migrants may contribute to better education in the home countries.

In his discussion, Douglas Irwin notes that the paper sets up a horse race of sorts between the "school constrained" and the "migration" models. Rosenzweig finds overwhelming evidence for the migration model because of the huge gaps in wage levels—regardless of skill level—between developing and OECD (Organization for Economic Cooperation and Development) countries.

Irwin finds the framework in the paper compelling, but he is skeptical of the conclusions for two reasons. First, he is puzzled why so many migrants return home if wage differences are really so large. In this context, he highlights the large variation in the propensity of students to stay in the United States who come from sending countries with similar wage levels.

Second, Irwin argues that an analysis based on time series data might provide more compelling support for a school constrained model that the cross-country results reported in the paper. For example, in Korea, rewards to higher skills increased over time, but so did demand for foreign higher education, as domestic education became inadequate.

In his extensive commentary, the second discussant, Jeffrey Williamson, both highlights a number of important contributions of the paper and makes a variety of suggestions for extending the analysis. He notes that the brain drain debate would be better served if we spent more time understanding foreign student migration. The United States today admits two to three times as many foreign students as those already-schooled foreign born who are admitted on the basis of their skills. Further, it is much easier for potential immigrants as students to get permanent skilled jobs in the United States than any other way.

Williamson highlights two very important findings in the paper. Student migration is positively correlated with gaps in skill wages. More and better schools at home are correlated with more student emigration, not less, ceteris paribus, where the ceteris paribus that matters most is low skill wages at home. This is a powerful finding, which might suggest that investment in the quantity and quality of educational institutions in poor countries will serve to push more students abroad, rather than retain more at home.

However, Williamson stresses that both findings speak to *correlations* only. The critical next steps should focus on establishing *causation*. He then discusses three potential flaws in the paper that might influence these inferences: selectivity, omitted variables, and causality. On the selectivity front, Williamson points out that good students go to "good" schools in host countries *and* at home. Although the analysis controls for average schooling quality at home, a country with low average school quality can still have a number of excellent schools from which the emigrants are selected.

In terms of omitted variables, one concern is lack of a "friends and relatives" effect. Long-distance migration is expensive, and contacts in the host country are key to help with finance, job search, and assimilation. He posits that the addition of stocks of foreign born to the regressions will dramatically change the results. He also worries that the population size variable may pick up effects of the spectacular demographic transition underway in many developing economies. An alternative would be the share of the university-aged population.

He then turns to causality. The paper reports that more and better schools at home are correlated with low skill wages at home. Why? Similarly, tables 5 to 7 report that more and better schools at home are associated with more students abroad. Is this because more and better schools lower the cost of migration? Or does the emigration serve to encourage schooling demand by the next cohort? Williamson cites the need for the author to reconcile his results with the brain drain–gain literature.

Finally, Williamson uses his economic historian hat to note that Rosenzweig misses four great opportunities to deal with the past and the future, which could help confirm or deny his conclusions. First, when did foreign students start arriving in big numbers at Australian, Canadian, British, and American universities? Second, how will student migration flows play out over the next few decades? Third, how do host countries compete for students? Fourth and finally, the analysis should allow for increased skilled immigration from poor countries to reduce the OECD skilled wage gap, thereby increasing skill scarcity at home. During the great mass migrations before 1913, European emigration contributed to wage convergence in the Atlantic economy. Why should we expect things to be different in the twenty-first century?

ANDREW WARNER'S PAPER presents and analyzes new data on wages by occupation for fifty-eight countries. The paper also provides empirical evidence from a number of sources on how wage levels correlate with GDP—both across countries and across time within countries—and explores determinants of cross-country wage levels.

The paper begins with a useful overview of strengths and limitations of the available international wage data. A key problem is lack of consistency, both across countries and over time. Further, most of the data focus only on manufacturing, and breakdowns are often not available by occupation. Historically, data sets also tended to include very few of the poorer countries. Recently, the well-known Freeman-Oostendorp data set provided a major advance by estimating standardized wages and earnings from the large data set of the International Labor Organization (ILO). Thus an important advantage of the data presented here is that they were all collected using the same methodology and during the same time period (January–February 1999). This implies a high degree of comparability across countries.

The data come from collaboration with the World Economic Forum's executive opinion survey. Samples were chosen to be proportional to the sectoral distribution of nonagricultural workers. Data on typical 1998 monthly wages and salaries for five occupations were collected through personal interviews (in principle with a top manager in each enterprise). The occupational categories were office cleaner, driver, secretary (with five-years experience), mid-level manager, and senior manager. Warner reports that adjusting the wages for observable differences in firm characteristics across countries has little impact on his results.

Warner highlights two notes of caution relevant for interpreting the empirical results he presents. First, at a sufficiently aggregated level, wages will necessarily be strongly correlated with GDP per worker. However, wages of specific occupations that represent fractions of an economy can behave quite differently from economy-wide GDP. Second, wages and GDP are both clearly endogenous. Thus the relationships presented in the paper should be viewed as descriptive, not causal. The analysis at the end of the paper attempts to address this issue by controlling for the capital-labor ratio—a key factor that simultaneously affects both wage levels and GDP per worker.

Warner presents three major sets of results. He provides a wealth of charts as well as simple regressions to explore correlations between wages and per capita GDP. Focusing on results using his new data, wages in less-skilled occupations tend to rise proportionately with real GDP as expected. But it is interesting that managerial wages (the most-skilled occupations) are found to rise less than proportionately. Consistent with existing literature, he also finds that dispersion of average wages across occupations (for example, managers compared with drivers) declines as GDP rises, both between and within countries.

The second set of empirical results clearly indicates the importance of capital-labor ratios in explaining differences in wages for similar work (occupation) across countries. Finally, the paper also relates average occupational wages to variation across countries in skill abundance, labor market institutions, product market competition, and exposure to globalization, controlling for capital per worker. Globalization is measured with a subjective variable (on a 1 to 7 scale) of the extent to which managers in a country speak a foreign language. The author finds that the positive association between average wages of managers and GDP per capita is weaker in countries with higher share of managers who are proficient in English. He finds negative effects of average levels of skill accumulation across countries on wages in high-skilled occupations. The paper also shows some evidence of roles for minimum wage rules, market competition, and a greater degree of openness in the market for managerial occupations.

Warner concludes by noting that differences in the quantity of capital around the world, coupled with still significant barriers to mobility of labor, capital, and goods and services, are the major reasons for vastly different wage levels for similar occupations around the world. He offers two possible explanations for the finding that the gap between wages of managers and office cleaners (an indicator of the skill premium) tends to narrow as countries become wealthier. One is that relative skill supplies tend to increase, reducing the skill premium. The second is that pay for managers in poorer countries may be pulled up toward global pay scales if workers in these occupations have acquired language and other skills that make them competitive in a global market for managers.

Both discussants, Nina Pavcnik and Harry Holzer, stressed that an important contribution of the paper is to bring a useful new data set to bear on the analysis of cross-country differences in the returns to labor. Advantages of the data are that they overcome some of the comparability problems that typically plague cross-country data sets and that they provide detailed information about firms. In terms of limitations, Pavcnik mentioned the absence of information over time and expressed concerns that the relatively small samples taken in each country may not be nationally representative.

Pavcnik is reassured by Warner's finding that average occupational wages are strongly positively correlated with GDP per capita for all occupations. Yet she finds it striking that this positive correlation is smaller for higher-paying occupational groups such as managers and that the positive association between average wages of managers and GDP per capita is weaker in countries where a higher share of managers are proficient in the English language.

A recurring theme in Warner's paper, which Pavcnik highlights, is the extent to which the weaker correlation between occupational wages and GDP per capita observed for managers reflects a labor market for managers that is more influenced by global factors than are the labor markets for lower-skill occupations such as janitors or office cleaners and drivers. Yet she questions the use of the foreign language variable as a measure of globalization, as it likely reflects country characteristics such as the country's colonial ties and the quality of domestic institutions. She suggests that the paper would benefit by focusing on a particular aspect of globalization, enabling the analysis to pinpoint the channels through which that aspect of globalization might affect wages. The implicit assumption underlying the paper's argument is that globalization should make average wages less dependent on local economic conditions. However, theory does not necessarily predict whether trade liberalization will cause wages to equalize across countries. If trade is driven by differences in relative factor abundance, wages could equalize if the countries produce the same goods (that is, are in the same cone of diversification) and use the same production technology. But if trade is driven by relative productivity differences, cross-country real wage differences might persist—even with free trade.

Pavcnik emphasizes that it is very difficult to establish the link between globalization and aggregated wages. Recent work in international trade, including her own with Penelope Goldberg, has moved beyond looking at cross-country averages and instead uses microlevel surveys of workers and firms to emphasize the importance of heterogeneity in the impact of globalization within a country. These recent studies show that, following changes in industry tariffs, trade affects individuals with similar observable characteristics differentially depending on their industry affiliation. She concludes by noting that future work will make additional use of Warner's detailed data to further our understanding of determinants of wages in a globalized world.

In addition to commending Warner on his interesting new data set, Holzer also notes the importance of the questions the paper raises. To what extent do different groups of workers in different countries share in the economic growth associated with international trade? To what extent are they compensated for the higher risks and growing inequality that trade often generates? Overall, he finds Warner's main results—relating wages to real per capita GDP and to capital-labor ratios, as well as a variety of market and institutional characteristics—to be broadly consistent with expectations. However, he notes that Warner's finding that wage responsiveness to real GDP declines with the rise in skill level of the job is somewhat contradicted by the other studies that Warner cites, such as those by Freeman and Oostendorp and Ashenfelter and Jurajda.

Holzer encourages Warner to further explore the role of capital-labor ratios in explaining wages across countries within each occupation. He wants to know more about the partial contribution of this variable to the results, and about its use as an instrument variable. He raises questions about several additional variables. The indicator measuring a respondent's perception of the intensity of competition does not specify any kind of reference point, making it difficult to interpret in a cross-country context. The foreign language variable arbitrarily assigns a value of 6 on a scale of 7 to countries where the use of English is widespread. Such a measure could be a proxy for many different characteristics of countries in the regressions that are estimated.

Holzer concludes by noting that his specific criticisms do not detract from the fact that Warner has addressed some of the most important questions in international labor markets, generated a potentially important new set of data, and produced some descriptive findings that are very useful.

DEVESH KAPUR AND JOHN MCHALE in the fourth paper provide a general critique of Lant Pritchett's Plan B, which would allow massive flows of temporary migrants across borders. They do not focus on the specifics of this proposal but on the general case for using migration as a poverty-alleviation tool. The idea is "if you cannot bring good institutions to the poor, allow the poor to move to the good institutions."

They make five basic points. First, differences in institutional quality are significant determinants of differences in living standards, but institutional improvement is very hard to "buy" without high levels of foreign aid, and even then it can be an elusive objective. Second, there is potential for large income gains through institutional arbitrage as economically debilitating institutional structures are left behind because of high levels of out-migration. Third, there may be negative effects for host countries that include distributional harm to the incomes of the less skilled, fiscal harm from attracting individuals who impose net costs, and harm to civic capital arising from reduced cohesiveness within communities. Fourth, to the extent that rich countries target the highly skilled, institutional development in developing countries may be hurt by the loss of human capital. Finally, given weak institutions in sending countries, it is critical to design any program to ensure that the benefits of expanded migration accrue to the intended beneficiaries and not to rent seekers.

Kapur and McHale frame their discussion with a debate in political philosophy between nationalists and cosmopolitans. Focusing on the concept of "partial cosmopolitans," they apply Amartya Sen's concept of consequence-based evaluation to assess Plan B. This allows the evaluator—for example, the rich country—to consider both the interests of co-nationals and the interests of foreign-born individuals, with the weight on the latter increasing, the worse off their starting point is.

Kapur and McHale note that standard development strategies often fail because they focus on poor countries rather than poor people, resulting in a continuation of high levels of poverty. If you accept partial cosmopolitanism, however, then the case for Plan B is largely empirical and based on the answers to such questions as: How much would the migrants benefit? Would rich country natives be hurt (and if so, which ones and how much)? Would those left behind be hurt? (On the one hand they gain from remittances, but on the other they and the home country lose through skill loss, a problem that is worse for small countries).

The authors then review the evidence. They note extreme divergence in income levels among countries due to institutions and physical capital per worker, and they argue that these income gaps are due more to places than to people. Their evidence for this is that, while human capital is lower in poor countries, there are still huge gains from migration. The impact on rich countries from reasonable levels of skilled migrants is on balance good: increased innovation, knowledge spillovers, specialized skills, scale economies, and the fiscal benefits from more well-paid earners. Not surprisingly, many rich countries seek to attract mobile talent.

There is much more skepticism about the benefits of unskilled migration, as suggested by the work of George Borjas documenting the negative effects on the wages of U.S. unskilled workers (that is, native born). Yet the authors note that these findings are disputed by many other researchers, some of whom conclude that the effects of immigration on wages wane over time. Also, immigrants and natives are not always perfect substitutes, as the standard models suggest. However, Kapur and McHale also state that the fiscal rights of migrants should not impose fiscal burdens on natives.

Finally, the impact on the sending countries appears to be very sensitive to the skill composition of emigration, with skilled emigration posing the greatest risk of harm. Not all of the effects are bad, however, as skilled emigrants may return later and become positive forces for institutional change. The risks are greatest, meanwhile, for small countries, for whom the pool of skilled individuals that can generate momentum for institutional change is very small.

The authors conclude by noting that the devil will be in the details. Implementing such a plan, which would inevitably include a smaller supply of visas than have been requested by poor country citizens so far, would provide huge potential opportunities for rent seeking. It would be critical to ensure that the beneficiaries of the plan were the emigrating citizens. While endorsing Plan B in principle, they caution that much more needs to be done before it could be implemented.

In his comments, Gary Burtless began by noting the very persuasive evidence in Lant Pritchett's paper showing that cross-regional differences in average incomes are much narrower where the legal impediments to migration flows are small. Pritchett's message is that, while cross-border mobility may not be an engine of development in lagging areas, it is a driver of cross-regional income equalization. Yet he notes that the paper by Kapur and McHale makes a different point: that cross-regional income differences are not only due to economic shocks but also are due to regional and national differences in institutions. Burtless would add to this list differences in social norms, including trust and honest dealing in the market place. He sees institutions and norms as essentially stuck in place. To change them, citizens can either make a revolution or move somewhere else. The latter is what usually happens.

However, modern nation-states tend to regard cross-border mobility with suspicion—particularly mobility by those who want to compete with native workers. Rich democracies do not make distinctions between those migrants who want to work for a few years and those who want to stay indefinitely.

Burtless points out that Kapur and McHale's discussion of political philosophy leads them to conclude that it is a good idea for nation-states to take the interests of people—and particularly poor people—in other countries into account in addition to the interest of their own citizens. Although this perspective may not be particularly radical to employees of universities, international institutions, or nongovermental organizarions, he doubted that it was typical of the median rich country voter. He stressed that the political viability of Plan B depends on what the median voter thinks, and in particular on how she or he would weight welfare gains to immigrants against the distribution of gains and losses among fellow citizens.

In Burtless's view, the essential fact—made clear in the Rosenzweig paper— is that most Third World workers would benefit tremendously if they could enter the United States freely to work. Gains and losses for everyone else are less clear and hard to estimate reliably. Some home-country residents benefit through remittances. At the same time, no one knows whether out-migration hurts or helps local governance, entrepreneurship, education, or public health in developing countries. Burtless noted that the authors' own conclusions about the welfare effects on unskilled native workers are imprecise. While some of these losses can be ameliorated by transfer programs, it is difficult to reliably identify the losers. When social protection programs are more generally available, as in many European countries, voters may be even more suspicious about benefits accruing to migrants.

Burtless concludes that immigration has most likely improved the welfare of both migrants and of native-born individuals in the United States. But identifying those gains precisely is very difficult. And in the long run, the political feasibility of Plan B depends crucially on persuading rich-country voters that they ought to accept more migrants for moral reasons or that they are very likely to derive economic benefits from doing so. In his view, the current political debate in the rich countries reflects little consensus on either of these propositions.

THE FIFTH PAPER switched gears to focus on labor mobility within, instead of among, countries. Suzanne Duryea, Gustavo Marquéz, Carmen Pagés, and Stefano Scarpetta report on their ongoing empirical analysis of job and earnings mobility in low- and middle-income countries. As they note, developing countries are often observed to experience even larger rates of labor market mobility than do developed economies, as jobs are created and destroyed and as workers move among jobs and change their labor market status. While this dynamism can promote economic efficiency and growth by moving resources into more productive activities, the welfare losses associated with high job insecurity can be considerable. Furthermore, the limited social safety nets in developing economies are less able to insulate workers against economic risks. Their findings highlight that mobility is indeed very high both across jobs as well as in and out of the labor market and that there appears to be significant earning consequences associated with some types of mobility.

The work analyzes experiences in nine countries. Three are in Latin America (Argentina, Mexico, and Venezuela). The remaining six are in eastern Europe and the former Soviet Union (Albania, Georgia, Hungary, Poland, Russia, and Ukraine). This sample is quite heterogeneous, with per capita incomes ranging from less than $2,000 in Georgia to more than $12,000 in Argentina. The period of study varies across countries, from two to twelve years from 1990 to 2004, depending on data availability. While countries such as Venezuela experienced almost no GDP growth during the period of study, others such as Albania and especially Ukraine grew rapidly. Most of the countries opened up more to trade. The Latin American economies all experienced considerable volatility, including the peso crisis in Mexico and the beginning of the crisis in Argentina. The economies of eastern Europe and the former Soviet Union were all undergoing transitions toward more market-oriented economies, although restructuring proceeded at different paces. The data enable the authors to consider six distinct labor market statuses: out of the labor force, unemployed, farmer, self-employed, and wage employee in either the formal or the informal sector.

Their analysis uncovers a complex picture of labor mobility. Although there is considerable cross-country heterogeneity, some broad themes emerge. All nine countries exhibit a high degree of mobility both in and out of the labor market and among types of jobs. Wage jobs in the informal sector tend to be less secure than those in the formal sector, and there is much more movement between wage jobs in the formal and informal sectors than there is between wage jobs and self-employment. Those who leave self-employment are more likely to move into the informal sector, become unemployed, or leave the labor force than they are to secure formal sector jobs. Although limited social safety nets imply that workers typically cannot afford long periods of unemployment, the authors find greater unemployment persistence in transition economies.

This labor mobility has implications for earnings. While moving from the formal to the informal sector tends to reduce earnings in Latin America, it had the opposite effect in some transition economies. Switching from informal employment to self-employment tends to be associated with increased earnings. However, the authors find evidence that switching is associated with worker characteristics that are likely related to their productivity, suggesting selection biases that are important for interpreting their results.

In her discussion of the paper, Carmen Reinhart focuses on three main issues. She stresses that her background caused her to think about a country's economic performance from the macroeconomic perspective. During the period studied, some countries in the sample had experienced large output swings, while others were just emerging from a severe recession. Exchange-rate or banking crises characterized some of the episodes. In many cases, there were large changes in key relative prices, such as between traded and nontraded goods. These developments would all be expected to have labor market implications, such as displacing workers from formal sector jobs. Furthermore, crisis periods within a country and countries that are crisis-prone may not be representative experiences from which to draw general lessons about labor market dynamics. Thus, she thinks that it would be very important for the authors to control for macroeconomic variables in their future analyses.

Reinhart encourages the authors to enrich their analysis by also studying transitions within labor market groupings. For instance, in many of the economies, she believes that there had been significant shifts of labor from agriculture and industry into the financial sector. Much of this would have taken place within the formal sector and thus not classified as a transition. It would also be interesting to know how much of the formal sector dynamics could be associated with downsizing of state-owned enterprises, especially in transition economics.

Finally, she expresses some concerns about the data. In particular, she cautions that the data for the informal sector may be of relatively low quality. It would be helpful for the authors to discuss potential measurement errors and to explore ways to check the robustness of their conclusions. However, she also stresses that despite its limitations the type of econometric analysis these authors are using is very valuable for helping us understand labor market dynamics within developing countries.

OUR THREE PANELISTS were asked to think more broadly about global labor market and migration issues. Michael Kremer examined two new ways of modeling trade and immigration that have different implications from those of the traditional Heckscher-Ohlin (H-O) trade model. Standard versions of the H-O model predict that inequality will tend to decline in poor countries that open up to trade but rise in rich countries that allow increased immigration of low-skilled workers. In contrast, Kremer's models shows that, under some sets of assumptions, trade can increase inequality in poor countries, while migration can raise the relative wages of low-skilled workers.

Kremer first surveys the evidence that higher levels of trade lead to declining inequality in developing countries. He finds that most empirical studies have concluded that inequality and openness are in fact positively correlated, particularly in Latin America. These studies suggest the need to move beyond the factor endowment basis for trade contained in the Hecksher-Ohlin framework.

One of the trade models proposed by Kremer captures the globalization of the production process. A key feature is that workers of varying skill levels maximize output by working together only when the relative difference between their skill levels is not too great. Globalization enables workers in rich and poor countries to work together. However, it is only the higher-skilled workers in developing countries who have sufficient skills (such as speaking English) to join the global supply chain. Thus trade benefits the better-off in developing countries while leaving low-skilled workers unaffected, thereby worsening inequality.

Kremer's second model approximates a type of immigration that has become prevalent in many newly rich countries such as Hong Kong and Singapore. These countries have instituted programs that encourage foreigners to immigrate and work as private household workers (nannies) for a limited period of time. This frees up higher-skilled natives, mostly women, to leave domestic work and enter the labor force. The taxes paid by the migrant women constitute a pure gain for the host society, while increased participation of high-skilled women may reduce the skill wage premium.

Kremer uses his model to calibrate the effects a Hong Kong–type program would be likely to have in the United States. In contrast to the negative distributional impact and small increase in welfare implied by the Hecksher-Ohlin framework, Kremer finds that a foreign private worker program could cause the relative wage of low-skilled workers to rise by 10 percent and welfare to increase by 1.84 percent of GDP. Furthermore, his model suggests that wage inequality would decrease, even if three-fifths of the immigrants leaked into the general economy to compete with native low-skilled workers.

Arvind Panagariya explores some of the recent issues in the migration debate in the context of the conventional trade literature on the "brain-drain." This literature typically analyzes implications of migration for each of the three entities involved: the migrant, the source country, and the destination country.

Because migration enables the migrant to earn a higher wage in the destination country, the traditional literature sees him as an unambiguous beneficiary. Some question this view in the context of Third World mothers who emigrate to care for First World children, leaving their own children behind. However, Panagariya argues that the traditional conclusion is correct: Migrating mothers make the choice voluntarily; the income they earn improves life for their children (cared for by family back home); they bring loving care to the First World children (perhaps unavailable from super-busy First World mothers).

The effects of emigration on the source country are more complex and controversial. The traditional literature shows that if the migrant does not own any other factors of production before or after emigration, his departure hurts those left behind. However, remittances could more than make up for the decline in their income.

Since remittances are more likely and larger if migration is temporary, some economists suggest temporary migration as an alternative development strategy. Panagariya is skeptical. Examples of developing countries experiencing rapidly rising living standards on a sustained basis through emigration in the last fifty years are few and far between. He stresses that virtually every successful growth experience has taken place in the presence of rapidly expanding trade and either low or declining trade barriers. More important, world markets are open to international trade, so a strategy based on outward-oriented trade policies is readily available. In contrast, opening rich country markets to migration—be it temporary or permanent—on a large enough scale to make a dent in global poverty is a fantasy at present.

For small developing countries, however, there is some evidence that skilled emigration has reduced the welfare of those left behind despite remittances. In particular, in some African and Caribbean countries, the proportion of emigrants who are skilled has exceeded 45 percent—in some instances reaching as high as 80 percent.

Panagariya argues that skilled emigration may benefit larger developing countries, even if remittances per migrant are relatively low. At 4.3 percent, the proportion of skilled workers emigrating from India is less likely to have created a serious shortage of such workers at home. Further, the conventional welfare losses have been more than offset by faster development of the information technology industry, increased incentives to seek technical education, and a variety of "diaspora effects," such as improved political and economic links between the United States and India.

There is a large literature on the effects of immigration on the destination country, principally the United States. The dominant theme has been that immigration depressed wages, worsened the income distribution, and imposed fiscal costs on the native population. However, Panagariya finds that the theoretical and empirical bases for these propositions are rather fragile. He argues that most existing studies fail to account for the interaction of immigration and trade on wages and that increased supply of labor from immigration is likely to be offset by reduced supply of labor through trade. Immigration expands those sectors that use the migrating factor more intensively, reducing the need for imports of these goods and services.

Panagariya also argues that the adverse impact on natives from immigrants' access to welfare programs and public services has been overstated. In his view, typical calculations consider only the cost side of the equation. Immigrants also provide services such as gardening, housework, and child care that either generate surplus for native consumers or allow them to earn much higher incomes through participation in the labor force. A balanced evaluation must take both sides of the equation into account.

Isabel Sawhill focuses on developments in rich-country labor markets and the extent to which these are affected by migration issues. She notes that much of the debate on immigration in the United States focuses on wage inequality, which, similar to the number of individuals in poverty, has been rising. Clearly, the United States has a strong economy that attracts a great deal of labor and capital from abroad (thereby providing numerous opportunities for migrants of all skill sets). However, she sees its prosperity as fragile, both because of its reliance on high levels of foreign debt and because the strong growth was, rather ironically, accompanied by more inequality and poverty and by low mobility rates compared with other OECD countries.

Sawhill's comments focus on three sets of new research results. The first was work by William Dickens and Erica Groshen examining trends in real wages across OECD countries. These authors found that the United States has less real wage rigidity than do most other wealthy economies, with levels comparable to those in Greece. Labor markets in the United States are characterized by high levels of flexibility, which is often cited as part of the reason for such strong U.S. rates of growth.

Another part of the story, though, is increasing levels of wage inequality. In exploring this dimension, Sawhill cites research by Melissa Kearney and others. From 1973 to 1990, wage inequality increased in the upper (as measured by the ratio in earnings between the ninetieth and fiftieth deciles) and lower (as measured by the ratio between the fiftieth and tenth deciles) tails of the income distribution. In the 1990s, however, wage inequality increased only in the upper tail. In other words, the distance between the wealthiest workers and the rest of the distribution increased, while trends in the lower tail remained the same. At least on the surface, this does not suggest that unskilled immigrants were the force driving changes in wage inequality. However, it is important to note that these official data do not include earnings of illegal immigrants.

Sawhill also cites recent work by Tom Hertz, which looks at trends in social mobility. Hertz examines intergenerational mobility as measured by the earnings elasticity between fathers and sons. In his sample of OECD economies, the United States has the lowest level of social mobility after the United Kingdom, a result that she argues defies the image of the United States as the land of opportunity.

Finally, Sawhill cites research by Carol Graham that examines happiness levels—and their relation to GDP levels—across countries. This work finds little correlation between per capita income levels and happiness in either developing or developed economies. It suggests that growth alone—without a broad base, with high levels of inequality and insecurity, and absent a broad base of opportunities for upward mobility—will not increase happiness.

Sawhill concludes that these bodies of research suggest that immigration is not to blame for trends in inequality in the United States. But at the same time, our current—and fragile—pattern of growth does not benefit the average citizen as much as it does the wealthier ones, nor does it increase happiness or subjective well-being.

IN SUM, the presentations and discussions at the conference raised a remarkably wide range of important policy issues—as well as questions for future research. While there was widespread agreement in some areas, many others were quite controversial, such as those highlighting normative questions about political rights as well as the empirical questions about welfare benefits for workers in both sending and recipient countries. Many of these issues will remain at the forefront of public and policy debates on migration and labor markets for years to come. It is our hope that the empirical and theoretical work presented in this volume can help to inform those debates and to provide impetus for the broad range of new research that will be necessary for a fuller understanding of our increasingly global labor markets.

LANT PRITCHETT
Kennedy School of Government and World Bank

Boom Towns and Ghost Countries: Geography, Agglomeration, and Population Mobility

The post–World War II period is a historically unique economic experiment that combines a "proliferation of sovereigns" with "everything but labor" globalization.[1] In 1940 there were only sixty-five independent countries. Twice that many—125 countries–have been created in the last 60 years.[2] The newly created states varied enormously in size (in both territory and population), resources, location, income levels, and politics. Each nation-state is sovereign within its own boundaries and can determine its own economic policies, laws, regulations, political systems, and, most important, who can cross its borders.

I would like to thank the LIEP (Lunches on International Economic Policy) and Development Lunch (Economic Development Lunch Series) groups at Harvard for helpful comments, in particular LIEP members Dani Rodrik for the idea of migration in the international system as an issue, Ricardo Hausmann for suggesting figure 6, and Mark Rosenzweig and Robert Lawrence for pushing on theory and interpretation. The paper was substantially revised in response to the comments made by Simon Johnson and Clifford Gaddy at the Brookings Trade Forum meetings and the insightful comments of the organizers Carol Graham and Susan Collins. Hannah Pritchett produced the data and figures on county population movements. Eliana Carranza assisted in the final stages.

1. See Braun, Hausmann, and Pritchett (2002) for a discussion on the proliferation of sovereigns; Pritchett (2006).

2. Other methods and sources give different numbers, but with the same direction. Alesina, Spolaore, and Wacziarg (2005) report 69 in 1920, 89 in 1950, and 192 in 1995. There have been three large waves of nation-state creations: the decolonized states in South and East Asia closely following WWII as both winners and losers lost colonies (for example, India from the British, Indonesia from the Dutch, Vietnam from the French, Korea from the Japanese); a second later wave of new states created from British and French decolonization; and the latest wave from dissolution of the Soviet Union that both created new nation-states from the Soviet Union and allowed new nation-states from the break-up of former satellites (for example, Yugoslavia, Czechoslovakia); but with many others in between these three waves (for example, the Portuguese colonies of Africa gained independence in the 1970s after a change in government in Portugal, Belize became independent only in 1981, and East Timor voted to separate from Indonesia in 1999).

The proliferation of sovereign states in the post-WWII period has been accompanied generally by a trend towards globalization of everything but labor. The postwar international system encouraged the reduction in the policy impediments to economic transactions across borders by regulating the means of payment (International Monetary Fund, IMF), providing a framework for negotiating reductions in trade barriers (General Agreement on Tariffs and Trade, or GATT, and World Trade Organization, or WTO), and providing for capital flows (World Bank), first directly by lending and more recently by encouraging financial liberalization. But unlike the first era of globalization from 1870 to 1914, which was an "age of mass migration," the post-WWII international system has, generally, tightly regulated movement of people across borders.[3] While international organizations have been established to encourage free and open economic activity, no such international organization or mechanism exists to encourage nation-states to adopt more liberal policies for labor mobility.

Economic theories have different predictions about the outcome of slicing geographic space into smaller and smaller units, each with potentially different economic policies and institutions (proliferation of sovereigns) combined with free mobility of goods, capital, ideas, but not labor (everything but labor globalization).[4] One collection of models predicts happy outcomes (at least conditionally). The Solow-Swan model of economic growth has constant returns to scale, has essentially no "geography," and when applied across nations often assumes diffusion of ideas and capital mobility and hence predicts that, if countries were to have identical policies and institutions, they would converge to equal levels of per worker income. Some simple trade models had even stronger predictions, showing that under certain conditions factor prices would converge without the mobility of either capital or labor.[5] Alesina and Spolaore argue that

3. For a discussion on "age of mass migration," see Hatton and Williamson (1998, 2006). There were virtually open borders between Europe and areas of recent settlement (what O'Rourke and Williamson [2001] call the "Atlantic Economy"), but there were also substantial "South-South" movements of population—for example, the movement of ethnic Indians to the Caribbean and eastern Africa and the Chinese around East Asia.

4. Elsewhere I have questioned whether the cliché that the post-WWII period is an era of globalization is accurate, as there are three phenomena: decolonization and proliferation of nation-states (which reduced or at least dramatically changed the nature of globalization), a failure to resume the pre-WWI open borders (even among advanced nations) in conjunction with increased barriers to labor movements across nation-states, and a modest move toward fewer policy restrictions to the movement of goods (and to a lesser extent capital). Only the last of these is unambiguously globalization, but it is by no means obvious that it is the most important of these three.

5. While, as with nearly any general theorem in economics, the formal conditions for the "factor price equalization theorem" were very stringent and unrealistic, the forces implied by the theorem—that compared with autarky the net factor supplies change with integration and hence should change relative prices—make a great deal of sense.

if the economic costs of sovereignty decline (say because of lower costs to trade across nations) and if there are political gains from sovereignty one would expect to see more and more sovereign nation-states, but each integrated economically more tightly into multinational agreements (for example, Czechoslovakia splitting into two nation-states, both of which join the European Union [EU], or the Baltic states splitting from the Soviet Union and joining the EU).[6]

But these relatively happy stories must confront the fact that neither income per capita across nation-states nor factor prices (wages) have converged.[7] The semihappy interpretation is that levels (or growth rates) of income and wages are determined by policies and institutions. If the observed divergence is the result of divergence of policies and institutions, then at least policy reform or institutional changes can equalize incomes potentially (although the feasibility of purposive action to induce institutional change is hotly debated).

There are, however, other economic models in which the proliferation of sovereigns and labor immobility would lead to permanently divergent or even diverging levels of incomes. Region-specific shocks to productivity can come in a variety of forms, both positive and negative:

—The depletion of a location-specific natural resource (mine, forest, soil quality, or water table) can lead to a fall in the *physical* productivity of factors applied and a fall in labor demand. Ghost towns near depleted mines are the classic examples.[8]

—Technological changes can raise the productivity of a given region. Seeds developed during the Green Revolution dramatically raised the productivity of areas conducive to their use (reliable water supply was crucial). For a more historical example, the advent of the potato in Ireland dramatically raised the caloric productivity of Irish soils (and the potato blight therefore induced a huge negative shock in productivity).

—A permanent fall in the relative price of a good produced with a location-specific natural resource leads to a fall in the *value* productivity of factors applied. The impact of new suppliers on existing coffee-growing regions might be a classic (ongoing) example; other examples include the decline in demand

6. Alesina and Spolaore (2003).
7. While a plausible reduction in the global *personal* distribution of income has occurred (Sala-i-Martin 2002) because the two largest nations, India and China, have done relatively well, especially since a transition to rapid growth in China in 1978 and in India in the early 1980s (Hausmann, Pritchett, and Rodrik 2005), the dispersion of GDP per capita across *nations* has widened, which is the relevant unit to policies.
8. For me, the origin of some of this thinking is that I grew up near a town, Idaho City, that was once a thriving frontier town (the largest in Idaho territory) and now has a population of 458 people (in 2000). Why? Simple. There used to be gold in the river nearby, and now there is not any commercially exploitable gold.

for sisal, jute, or rubber with the advent of technological substitutes; for a more historical example: the decline in food prices in England because of the lowering of transport costs from New World suppliers.

—Technological changes can increase or decrease the desirability of collocation. Historically textile industries were located near rivers because water power was used, whereas the advent of other power sources led the industry to migrate to other locations. Being close to coal was historically an important determinant of industrial location, but much less so now.

—Changes in transport costs and transport routes have an impact on cities and regions and industries. Some cities benefited from a prime position along overland trade routes—which disappeared with low-cost, reliable ocean transport. Others benefited from proximity to navigable rivers when this was the lowest-cost transport—which changed after the introduction of railways and effective road transport. A more modern example is the reduction in the "transport costs" of information, which has dramatically raised the productivity of English-speaking labor in places like India.

The impact of region-specific productivity changes on long-run labor demand depends on other features of the economic model. It is possible that regions are close substitutes in the production of some items, so that long-run labor demand could be very elastic as incipient decreases in the wages of one region would lead to an inflow of capital that would, over time, raise labor demand. But if one combines an economic model that incorporates region-specific productivity shocks with agglomeration economies, then the resulting changes in labor demand can be even more dramatic and the final shift in labor demand can be even larger than the initial shock. For instance, if a city requires a certain density of economic activity in its natural catchment area (determined by transport costs), then the declines in *regional* labor demand can be nonlinear with respect to shocks, if the region is no longer able to support a viable city within its borders.

Suppose there are region-specific shocks that lead to large long-run shifts in labor demand (even after all other factors such as capital and goods trade have been accommodated) then

—*If* population mobility across regions is allowed and hence the regional supply of labor is elastic, in the long run one should observe large variability in the growth rates of populations across regions and relatively small variability in the interregional growth of real wages and (conditional) convergence in levels of income.

—*If* population mobility is restricted and hence the regional supply of labor is inelastic, in the long run one should observe large variability in the growth of wages, little or no convergence in the level of incomes, and small variability in the growth of population.

This is a much less relentlessly happy story about the consequences of the proliferation of sovereigns and globalization of everything but labor. As geographic space is sliced into smaller nation-state units, some regions will experience large, persistent, positive shocks to labor demand and become "boom towns" with rapidly rising wages and incomes. But other regions may well experience large, persistent, negative, geographic-specific productivity shocks that reduce labor demand and lead to incipient "ghost countries." However, if outward labor mobility is limited, this will lead the adjustment to come not in changes in population but in wages, so countries will be "zombies"— the "living ghosts"—with falling wages and incomes.

The current conventional wisdom is that policies and institutions or perhaps just institutions are the key determinants of long-run levels of income.[9] In this view ghosts and zombies can be cured with the exorcism of bad policy. I think the consensus is correct that institutions or, to state it clearer, the performances of institutions in carrying out necessary functions are key to long-run prosperity. However, I argue here that there is some evidence that strongly suggests the existence of "hard-core geographic zombies"—countries whose current labor force far exceeds the quantity of labor demanded consistent with high (or adequate) wages even at the best imaginable policies and institutions.[10]

It is impossible to cleanly separate the effects of geography and institutions, not least because geography affects institutions. Indirect evidence of the importance of purely geographic factors comes from three examples of regions within countries (states, provinces, prefectures) that have completely integrated (or are integrating) markets for goods, capital, and labor and have identical, or nearly

9. See World Bank (2005) for the conventional wisdom concerning policies and institutions; Acemoglu, Johnson, and Robinson (2001); Rodrik, Subramanian and Trebbi (2002); Easterly and Levine (2001) concerning institutions; although see the dissenting view of Glaeser and colleagues (2004).

10. These two sentences (the primary importance of institutions and existence of ghost or zombie countries) are not a contradiction for three reasons. First, with large countries the ghosts will be ghost regions, not ghost countries, so cross-national data (which include spatially large countries, such as India, China, Argentina, and Indonesia) may not be driven by too many ghosts. Second, key issues are the opportunities for responding to shocks and the elasticity in long-run labor demand. A country such as Malaysia may experience a large, negative shock to its rubber industry but could respond by moving into low-wage manufactured exports. Thus not all initial spatial shocks will translate into "ghosthood" (the comparison with Chile and Zambia experiencing similar copper shocks is instructive). Third, in cross-national regressions, one does not horse race "geography" and "institutions"; the horse race is between specific measures of policies, specific measures of institutions, and specific measures of geography, such as being in the tropics, being landlocked, or having natural resources.

identical, policies and institutions. In the following sections, I examine the variations in populations and wages and incomes across

—States and provinces within countries,

—Counties and regions (agglomerations of counties) within the United States, and

—Countries during the era of open borders.

Analytical Framework

I start with the following question: "How much does the *desired* population of a given geographic region vary over time?" This, it turns out, is a very hard question to ask, because it has been largely ignored in the economic literature, for both theoretical and practical reasons. Theoretically, the implication of the Solow-Swan model and nearly all of its extensions is that the question of the "desired population" of countries never arose, because of several factors:

—With constant returns to scale, the location of production is formally indeterminate,[11]

—Within these growth models, there were no specifically geographic features at all, such as land or resources,

—If capital was fully and rapidly mobile, then any incipient differences in the marginal product of labor could be equalized by capital mobility,

—If knowledge of the production function diffused, then differences in technology could be eliminated by moving ideas, not people, and

—The models were about the evolution of aggregates within a set of boundaries that were assumed fixed.

Growth models typically assume zero labor mobility and even make population growth exogenous.[12]

However, two recent strands of research, the economics of increasing returns to scale and agglomeration economies and the empirical literature on the geo-

---

11. Basically, for technical reasons, it is just much easier to deal with models in which the aggregate production function has constant returns to scale—as in all generations of the Solow model. But the *literal* implication of constant returns to scale is that the distribution of economic activity across space is indeterminate; thus this is not a question that can be answered within the formal apparatus of a growth model. Practically, this was not such a great loss, since the first generation of growth theorists was interested in the source of persistent growth of output per capita in the already developed economies; and because nearly all of these countries are economically (and spatially) large and their economies did not have a strong resource component, simply ignoring the spatial allocation of economic activity was not crucial to those questions.

12. However, fertility has been made endogenous in more recent growth models.

graphic determinants of growth, are putting geography and population mobility back on the map (so to speak).

Trade economists have reintroduced increasing returns to scale into models of international trade and from there into spatial economics.[13] This combination has led to the use of the new formal apparatus for addressing fundamental questions such as "what determines the number and location of cities?"[14] A second element of this interest in agglomeration economies is the continued interest in regional economies and the rise and decline of populations of cities and regions within countries. Blanchard and Katz document state-level movements in employment in the United States and demonstrate convergence in real wages but large, persistent variability in population growth rates across states.[15] Recent papers have examined the role of changes in productivity and demand in simultaneously determining population sizes and real estate prices.[16] Moreover, authors reviewing the basic facts of economic growth are again emphasizing that the stylized facts of the spatial concentration of economic output require an important role of agglomeration economies.[17]

The empirical literature estimating growth regressions has rediscovered the notion that there are connections between the geographic characteristics of countries and their economic performance. In particular the work of Mellinger, Sachs, and Gallup emphasized spatial factors such as tropical location and transport costs (characterized as being landlocked or having navigable rivers) on economic potential and economic growth.[18] The work of Sachs and Warner introduced the notion of a "resource curse"—that countries richly endowed with natural resources had, on average, lower growth rates.[19] This work on resources has been followed by theoretical work on the causal linkages that explain these empirical regularities of geographic features on growth using a variety of causal paths that work through institutions or politics or both.[20]

13. For models of international trade, see Helpman and Krugman (1987); for spatial economics, see Krugman (1991a, 1991b). The "new growth" models *á la* Romer (1986) introduced the possibility of increasing returns to scale to some factors and hence reintroduced the possibility of agglomeration economies and scale economies. Many of the implications of the scale effects of the first generation of growth models were clearly counterfactual; the more recent vintages are at least arguably plausible, although Jones (2005) points out that the question of whether "scale effects" are "bug or a feature" of growth models is still open.

14. For example, Fujita, Krugman, Venables (1999).

15. Blanchard and Katz (1992).

16. For example, Glaeser and Gyourko (2005).

17. Easterly and Levine (2001).

18. Mellinger, Sachs, and Gallup (1999).

19. Sachs and Warner (2001).

20. There is a huge and ongoing debate about the sources of these results (for example, Auty 2001). Are they purely geographic (Sachs and Warner 2001), or are they the result of the impact

The weak link between these literatures is that the models of agglomeration usually assume labor mobility when examining the dynamics of populations within countries, and studies of the impact of geography focus on long-run *levels* of income rather than on the role of shocks on changes in growth rates, incomes, and population.

A General Set of Equations for Regional Growth

To discuss growth and regional population mobility—particularly geographic shifts—one needs a framework within which output, factors, and labor are simultaneously determined. At a minimum this framework needs to specify a production function, the level and evolution of productivity, the evolution of accumulated factors, and finally how population is distributed.

Suppose there are $i = 1,..., N$ spatially distinct regions—which could be either geographically arbitrary units or political or administrative subunits of countries (that is, districts, counties, states, provinces, or prefectures).[21]

Output determination. Output at any point in time is a function of productivity, A, and factors of production (I will only assume that the production function is separable), such that

(1) $$y_i = A_i f(K_i, L_i).$$

Productivity (A). The elements that affect the trajectory of the long-run equilibrium productivity of the ith region include geography, G; policy, P; institutions, I; technology, T; and agglomeration, M, such that

(2) $$A_{i*} = A(G_i, P_i, I_i, T_i, M_i).[22]$$

Some growth models often assumed that A represented exclusively something like technology—a set of blueprints for "netputs"—and assumed that this technology was freely available or diffused rapidly across regions so that all regions (within or across countries) shared the same A, while the approach proposed here is a much broader approach to the characterization of the productivity term.

---

of some (perhaps long-past) geographically based characteristics on subsequent institutions (for example, Sokoloff and Engerman 1994, 2002, 2003; Acemoglu, Johnson, and Robinson 2001), or are they the result of resource endowments on current politics (Isham and colleagues 2003).

21. For instance, the United States is divided for geological survey and cartographic purposes into "sections."

22. That is, as a matter of description at this stage, just think of these five headings as multidimensional lists of all possible factors that affect productivity and that whatever it is that anyone proposes (from existence of malaria to rule of law to usable "blueprints" for production) be classified under one of the five.

Production function. A general production function could exhibit constant returns to scale in all factors, or increasing returns in some or all factors, or external economies. If the production function has constant returns to scale, then it is impossible to discuss *formally* the spatial distribution of factors *within* any regional space that shares all other determinants of income in common. Increasing returns to scale or external economies of scale are able to predict the clustering of production into cities, but the additional complications in modeling are considerable. The spatial equilibrium across regions depends on the balance of centrifugal and centripetal forces.[23] Changes in the production function can make the forces stronger or weaker. The pressures for agglomeration are increased either by an increase in the returns to scale and external economies or by shifts in the composition of demand towards the scale-intensive activity.

Transport costs. The standard "iceberg" model of transport costs assumes that the production technology for transportation means that if one unit is shipped from the ith region to the jth region only $T_{ij} < 1$ units arrive, so that

$$(3) \qquad y_j = TC_{i,j}\, y_i.$$

Transport costs create a number of offsetting forces for concentration of production if there are intermediate goods and final goods. There are trade-offs between being near the intermediate inputs and being near the market for final demand. Krugman and Venables show that, starting from a very high level, a reduction in transport costs can cause increases in agglomeration (population movement towards cities) and increased differences in wages across regions, while continued decreases in transport costs to even lower levels can then cause spatial spreading of production in response to wage differences.[24] But these are not general results. Barriers to trade across regions can be modeled as increased transport costs (or vice versa), so that globalizing changes can come either through reductions in transport costs or through policy changes or both.

Accumulated factors of production. The desired capital stock in a given region depends on the returns to investors that are based on the *physical productivity* of additional capital in that region (which in turn is determined by general productivity, the production function, and transport costs) and the *appropriability* of those returns. In production functions with agglomeration effects, the returns to any one investor are contingent on the investment decisions of all other investors, which raises issues of multiple equilibrium. The appropriability of returns, $\varphi()$, depends on policies (for example, official tax rates) and on institutions (for example, legal and political risks). If one assumes that capital

23. Krugman (1998).
24. Krugman and Venables (1995).

markets are integrated, then a safe return, $\bar{r}$, is globally available, and optimal capital stock in the ith region, K_{i*}, equates the return in the region with the global return for the equilibrium labor force, L_{i*} such that

(4) $$\bar{r} = (1 - \varphi(P_i, I_i)) * \frac{\partial[A(G_i, P_i, I_i, T_i)f(K_{i*}, L_{i*})]}{\partial K}.$$

Given the long-run equilibrium capital stock, one also needs an equation of motion—the dynamics of the adjustment of the capital stock to its long-run value. I am agnostic about the specification, in particular because the usual linear dynamics imply symmetry to increases and decreases in the capital stock that is implausible for large deviations.

(5) $$\dot{k} = g_K(K_t^i - K_{i*}, AS_K).$$

Allocation of Population and Labor across Regions

The above formulation of output allows a definition of a region's "desired" population, the "constrained desired" population, and the "optimal" population. That is, one can imagine that the kth person living in region i can move into region j only by incurring some actual moving cost, $C_{i,j,k}$. The regions differ in attractiveness because of their income but also because of a set of other factors that affect utility and well-being for a person living in that region, Z_{ik} (for example, language, culture, ethnicity, temperature and climate, and congestion).

Also, over and above potential income and other features that determine utility, the de facto and de jure legal and administrative restrictions on population mobility create a set of individual and bilateral region-specific barriers to mobility. One can think of these as "virtual taxes," $\tau_{i,j,k}$ (I assume that the virtual tax on remaining in the region of one's birth is zero). These are virtual taxes because they are expressed as the price equivalent of what might be binding quantity constraints—that is, since borders are enforced using the compulsion of police and military power, the virtual tax could be large enough to prevent all movement.

This virtual tax formulation of the constraints on population mobility can encompass a range of alternatives.[25] One case is "free population mobility" with zero virtual taxes across all pairs of regions and for all persons. In this case, *utilities* are equalized across all regions (not necessarily per capita incomes,

25. This draws heavily on Neary and Roberts's (1980) formulation of "virtual prices" as a modeling technique for quantity constraints on allocations and trades.

even in real terms, because of Z). That is, one can expect differences in mobility across regions even within the same country to differ in response to wage differentials on the basis of, for instance, how homogeneous the culture is, how deep cultural ties to specific regions are, and so on. This will imply that labor mobility may well be less across countries than across regions of a country and that labor mobility will be less across regions of less homogenous countries than across more homogenous ones. But I am examining mostly how countries would respond to shocks so that even for a given level of Z one can predict the direction (if not magnitude or speed) of changes in desired populations—a point I return to several times in discussing the empirical results.

Another paradigm case is "full national mobility and zero international mobility." Assume that country C includes J_C regions (and the "rest of world" is J_{-C}) and is represented as having zero virtual taxes within the country $(\tau_{i,j,k} = 0, \forall i, j \in J_C)$. If person k is born within the boundaries of C and a virtual tax is infinity (as it can be with coercion), $(\tau_{i,j,k} = \infty, \forall j \in J_{-C})$ for all regions not in the country—both for people moving from country C to regions in other countries or moving from other countries to C—then the non–virtual tax inclusive utility is not being equalized across countries, and hence negative geographic shocks can produce widening differences in wages and incomes and utility across regions.

Of course, between these two extremes of "full national and no international" and "full global" labor movement, there are many possible variants. Some countries may not allow full internal mobility (an example being China). There may be full mobility across some countries and not others (for example, within the [core] EU but not between non-EU and EU countries). Finally, even if labor mobility is banned or limited de jure, the de facto situation conditional on current and anticipated enforcement of labor laws creates a very different set of virtual taxes.

Finally, the virtual taxes on labor mobility can be person specific, as immigration regimes of the jth region could allow high-skill but not low-skill immigration or family unification mobility or some other status that the legal regime wishes to recognize.

The *constrained desired population* of a region is simply the population of all individuals who prefer to live in region i—since they have higher perceived well-being, U—given the anticipated long-run equilibrium income of region i with its fully adjusted stocks of capital and labor *and* the set of virtual taxes in all other regions.[26]

---

26. An enormous problem with this approach is how exactly to make fertility endogenous. If $K(J)$ represents all people now alive, then the constrained desired population holds population as

(6) $\quad L_{i*} = \sum_{k=1}^{K(J)} I_k\{U_k(y_{i*}, Z_{i,k}, t_{i,j,k}) \geq U_k(y_{j*}, Z_{j,k}, C_{i,j,k}, \tau_{i,j,k}), \forall\ j \in \mathbf{J}\}.$

Finally, the labor force and population need an equation of motion for the adjustment of actual labor to the constrained desired level given the current aggregate stock of labor (AS):

(7) $\qquad\qquad\qquad l = g_L(L_t^i - L_{i*}, AS_L).$

This raises the obvious problem that the population within a given region depends on the rate of natural increase (the excess of births over deaths within the region) and on the mobility of persons across regions. While many researchers have made fertility and mortality behavior endogenous to economic growth and have assumed no labor mobility, I am going to do the opposite and assume, for now, that the rate of natural increase is exogenous so that I can focus on mobility.

The *unconstrained desired population* is the population with zero virtual taxes. The unconstrained desired population does take policies and institutions as given. So for instance, if a country is in a civil war or does not respect human rights or has hyperinflation, this could cause considerable variability in the desired population.

I define the *optimal population* as the *unconstrained desired population* when policies and institutions reach their best possible values. The distinction between unconstrained desired and optimal populations lies in the variability of the unconstrained desired population that might be due to negative consequences of poor policies (for example, hyperinflation or macroeconomic crashes), to consequences of poor institutional performance (for example, corruption or lack of freedoms), and to technological and geographic changes.[27]

This is an important distinction for policy. A "global policy maker" or even an altruistic population from a rich country or an international organization might respond differently to gaps between constrained and unconstrained desired populations than they would to gaps between the constrained and optimal populations. While in both instances there might be a demand for outward

---

fixed. However, over long periods, a country's fertility rate is dependent on opportunities for mobility and anticipated income prospects.

27. I do not model any impact of population movements on institutions, in part because there is not a definitive theory or any empirical evidence on what these impacts might be. Some argue that outward migration reduces pressure (and capacity) for institutional reform, since it is often the most motivated and entrepreneurial persons who move first. Others would argue that exposure of migrants to institutions elsewhere eventually brings back pressures and capacity for reform. Plausible narratives could be cited either way.

migration, the appropriate response depends on whether the unconstrained desired population can be quickly (if not easily) raised, for example, at the termination of a macroeconomic crisis, at the end of a civil war, because of improvements in economic policies or institutional reform, or because of a gap between the optimal population and existing population due to irremediable shocks.[28] If people are truly trapped in a nonviable geographic space, then restrictions on labor mobility are particularly pernicious, and as I argue elsewhere, they raise additional pressures on the international system for a fairer system for labor mobility.[29]

How much variability in output, how much variability in labor

How important are spatially specific (geographic or agglomeration or both) factors in determining growth rates of incomes and populations across regions? The above framework leads to a set of dynamic equations that specify the growth rates of per capita income and the labor force as jointly endogenous variables that are potentially driven by a whole host of determinants—among which are at least two that are spatially specific: geographic-specific elements of productivity and agglomeration economies in factor accumulation.

$$\dot{y}^i_{t,t-n} = y(G,P,I,T,TC,f,Z,AS_{K,L},\tau_{i,-i})$$
$$\dot{l}^i_{t,t-n} = l(G,P,I,T,TC,f,Z,AS_{K,L},Z,\tau_{i,-i}).$$

Each of the capital variables (for example, G and P) represents an entire *trajectory*, as observed growth rates over any given period ($t - n$ to t) can be caused by changes in the past leading to adjustments, by anticipated changes in the future, or even by steady-state differences in trajectories that depend on levels of output.

Theories modeling growth in a large advanced economy, such as that in the United States or Japan, usually assume away geographic factors for three good

---

28. I want to stress that my discussion on the desired population of regions has nothing to do with the usual "population pessimism"—that rapidly growing populations are per se a problem or that rapid population growth is a significant *independent cause* of slower growth in output per capita. In many ways that type of analysis gets it *exactly* backwards—it is not that populations are bad for output growth, it is that slow output growth is bad for the living standards of populations. The real "population crisis" is not when populations grow at 2 percent—all of the successful East Asian countries began their rapid growth with high rates of population growth—nor is the problem that a country's population is rising toward the desired level. The problem is when the desired population collapses to (or below) the actual population, because of exogenous shocks, technological changes, or bad governments. Since the fall in unconstrained desired population can be very large, this creates problems whether the population continues to grow or not.

29. Pritchett (2006).

reasons. First, in a spatially large economy that encompasses a large number of distinct regions, the likelihood of any one geographic factor, or even a set of factors, affecting aggregate growth is small, since regional shocks are smoothed out over space. Second, for advanced economies the share of directly natural resource–based industries (agriculture, mining, fisheries) is small. Third, fundamental geographic factors that do affect long-run *levels* of income or wages and that have not changed recently (climate, for example) could be assumed away when modeling *growth* as a dynamic of adjustment to long-run levels.

But none of these three reasons are true in general of the non-OECD (Organization for Economic Cooperation and Development) countries. First, the proliferation of sovereigns that has divided geographic space into smaller and smaller units increases the potential for geography-, policy-, or institution-induced variability in the income fundamentals (P, I, G, T). This is not to say that small is bad: boom towns like Hong Kong and Singapore are geographically very small. But it is to say that small is more likely to have regional shocks that are important. Second, production and exports in poorer countries are typically based more on natural resources and concentrated in many non-OECD countries. Third, there are natural and technological *changes* to spatial factors that strongly affect output.

Labor mobility is not important if desired populations do not change. Desired populations might not change (much) if *either* the fundamentals do not change or the mobility of other factors can compensate. The attractiveness of the regions might not change, because there are no changes in the interaction of geography and economics that cause people to first want to be in one place and then not want to be there. Thus labor mobility is not important for Antarctica because no substantial populations ever moved there—its attractiveness has not changed. But the classic counterexample is the movement to exploit nonrenewable natural resources—first people want to be there, and then when the extraction of the resource loses value people want to leave. The existence of ghost towns—places that once were booming and attracting migration and now have subsequently declined or even disappeared—suggests that there is variability to desired populations.

But even if regional shocks happen, large variations in the desired population might not occur if the mobility of other factors can compensate. Suppose a region attracts population because it relies on one type of economic activity, and then some natural or economic shock makes that activity no longer viable. There is no longer any reason for people to be *there* as opposed to any other place—but they are there. One possibility is that new activities are created, resources (capital) flow to that place, and people sustain roughly their same

Figure 1. Effects of Regional Shocks on Population and Wages

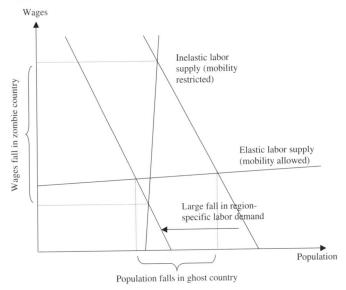

Population falls in ghost country

living standards despite changing their activities. Certainly in the story of many of the major cities of the world the original reason for the cities location has long since ceased to be relevant (for example, fortification or a transport link), but the city continues to thrive.

But there are two other possibilities. One is that new resources do not flow and people leave. In this case the labor supply curve is elastic, and large variations in population occur, with (smallish) observed differences in wage growth—which is a ghost region. The other possibility is that the desired population falls, perhaps dramatically, but people are not allowed to leave for attractive destinations (there could be "water in the virtual taxes" to use an import tariff analogy—the virtual tax imposed by coercion is very high). In this case the labor supply is inelastic, and hence all of the adjustment to the variability in the desired population of regions is forced onto real wages and living standards—which is a zombie (an unrealized ghost). The basic, embarrassingly basic, point is that if there are large region-specific shocks to labor demand then how that translates into changes in population and wage depends on the elasticity of labor supply (see figure 1).

Table 1 summarizes the possibilities between ghosts and zombies and whether they are determined by policies and institutions or spatial factors (which includes all types of location-specific shocks). In this framework the

Table 1. Classification into Ghost and Zombie Regions and into "Policy and Institutional" or "Hard-Core Spatial" Categories

	At existing policies and institutions	At optimal policies and institutions
$\tau_{i,j,k} \cong 0$ (Near free labor mobility between regions)	Unconstrained desired population $\hat{l}^i_{t,t-n} =$ $l(P,I,G,T,TC,f,Z,AS_{K,L},Z,\tau_{i,-i} \cong 0) << 0$ Result of large negative shock: **Ghosts—losing population**. Ghosts could be in either policy and institutional or hard-core spatial category.	Optimal population $\hat{l}^i_{t,t-n} =$ $l(P^*,I^*,G,T,TC,f,Z,AS_{K,L},Z,\tau_{i,-i} \cong 0) << 0$ Result of large negative shock: **Hard-core spatial ghosts—losing population** even at **optimal policies and institutions.**
$\tau_{i,j,k} \cong \infty$ (Closed borders to all people from countries i to all countries j $(-i)$)	Constrained population $\hat{y}^i_{t,t-n}(...) \le \hat{l}^i_{t,t-n}(.,\tau_{i,-i} \cong \infty)$ $\hat{l}^i_{t,t-n} = l(\cdot,\tau_{i,-i} \cong \infty) << l(\cdot,\tau_{i,-i} \cong 0)$ Result of large negative shock: **Zombies—falling output per worker (wages)** as population cannot adjust to desired level. Zombies could be in either policy and institutional or hard-core spatial category.	Constrained at optimal policies $\hat{y}^i_{t,t-n}(P^*,I^*,...) \le \hat{l}^i_{t,t-n}(P^*,I^*,...,\tau_{i,-i} \cong \infty)$ $\hat{l}^i_{t,t-n} = l(\cdot,\tau_{i,-i} \cong \infty) << l(\cdot,\tau_{i,-i} \cong 0)$ Result of large negative shock: **Hard-Core Spatial Zombies—falling output per worker (wages)** even at **optimal policies and institutions** (conditional on the shocks).

question of the paper is: Has the experiment of the proliferation of sovereigns and globalization of everything but labor led to hard-core spatial zombies? For instance, is Zambia a hard-core spatial zombie? People moved to Zambia, and to a particular region of Zambia, in part because a person could dig a hole in the ground and extract something of value, which was copper ore.[30] Technological changes in the world economy appear to have permanently reduced the profitability of copper mining. Currently around 10 million people live within the imaginary, and more or less arbitrary, borders of the nation-state of Zambia. Imagine if Zambians were free to move anywhere in the world, how many would still be within the current borders of Zambia? Alternatively, imagine that only 2 million people lived in Zambia and Zambia had the best possible policies and institutions; how many people would move there? The key question with countries with falling income is whether the country is a policy or institutional zombie or a hard-core spatial zombie. The next three sections provide empirical evidence that is suggestive of an important number of hard-core geographic zombies.

Size and Accommodation of Regional Shocks

This section examines the differences between changes in population and per capita income across provinces and states (where policies and institutions

30. I choose the example of Zambia and copper, again from personal experience, because I also spent some time living near the world's largest open pit copper mine, the Bingham mine about an hour outside of Salt Lake City, Utah. Since the fall of the price of copper, the mine has changed ownership three times.

are similar but geography varies and labor is mobile) and those changes in population and income per capita across countries (where policies and institutions and geography vary and labor is much less mobile). The four key points are illustrated with graphs, followed by a summary table.

—Even in countries with perfectly integrated markets for goods and capital and labor and similar policies and institutions, the variability of the growth rates of populations across regions (states and provinces) is large in absolute terms.

—The variability in the growth of income per capita across countries (when people cannot move freely) is large in absolute terms.

—The two facts above are consistent with large, spatially specific shocks to labor demand accommodated with elastic labor supply within countries and inelastic labor supply across countries.

—The difference across countries in labor mobility is smaller *in absolute terms by a factor multiple* across regions within countries.

Variability of Growth Rates of Income per Person and of Population within Countries

Barro and Sala-i-Martin have shown that regions within countries show a strong tendency for convergence (both absolutely and conditionally), so that the variability of the level of income per capita has declined.[31] I use the data from their book on income per capita and population within regions of countries (which could be states, provinces, prefectures, or regions) to illustrate a different point: the *absolute* variability of the *growth rates* of population and income per capita.

As outlined above in the framework on defining unconstrained desired population, with few or no constraints to population mobility $\tau_{i,j,k} \cong 0$, workers and households will move, at least in part, in response to economic opportunities. Within subregions of a fully integrated region or a larger unit, the variability in the rate of growth of output per worker should be very small, with powerful forces pushing toward convergence in the level of real incomes. But this convergence may or may not involve population movements, because a change in the unconstrained desired population of a region is due to a combination of shocks and to the fact that shocks are not being fully accommodated by movements in other factors such as capital or by trade. Theory alone does not provide an unambiguous prediction about the magnitude of interregional population

31. Barro and Sala-i-Martin (1997).

movements: jobs could move to people, or people to jobs, or any combination of those two.

The right picture is worth a thousand words, but nearly all standard software packages produce the wrong picture for our purposes as they display graphs that automatically scale the axes independently to roughly fill the visual space and do not maintain a 1 to 1 aspect ratio. While the standard approach makes it easiest to see the *covariances* of two variables, it is impossible to visually infer the respective *variances*. So here I do two things that are nonstandard. One, in all of the figures below, I scale the axes so that the range on the vertical (growth of income per capita) and horizontal (growth of population) axes are equal (note that the *axes* are not equal but the *ranges* [maximum less minimum] of the axes are equal) and force the figure to be visually square so that visually equal distances on the horizontal and vertical axes represent equal numerical differences. Second, I display percentile boxes that show the vertical and horizontal distances between the 10th and 90th percentiles.[32]

Figures 2 and 3 show three features of the growth of income per person and the growth of population for the continental United States (figure 2) and the prefectures of Japan (figure 3). First, the dispersion of growth rates of population is substantially larger than the dispersion of per capita income growth. In the United States the 10th–90th percentile range for the population is 2 percent per annum (henceforth ppa), from 0.6 ppa for Mississippi or Kansas to 2.6 ppa for Washington. The range for growth in income per capita is only 1.2 ppa—from 1.3 (California) to 2.5 ppa (Tennessee, Florida, Alabama). In Japan the 10th–90th percentile range is 1.9 ppa (–0.3 to 1.6) for population and only 1 ppa (4.8 to 5.8) for income.[33] As shown below (in figure 7 and table 1), other countries have absolutely smaller cross-regional variability in population growth; but in all of them the variability in population growth across regions is larger than the variability in growth of income per capita.

*Variability of Growth Rates of Income per Person
and of Population across Countries*

With a variety of shocks to the desired population and limited labor mobility in many sovereign states, one should expect to see wide variability across countries in growth rates of output per person and little variability of popula-

32. These boxes are orthogonal to the axes as I am not so interested in displaying the covariances as I am interested in comparing the differing variability in the two series. I am not displaying a range of the joint distribution, which would be a (perhaps tilted) ellipse.

33. The similar figures for all of the other countries with data in the Barro and Sala-i-Martin study (1997) (Canada, Spain, Italy, Germany, United Kingdom, and France) are in appendix 1 of an earlier working version of this paper.

Figure 2. Per Annum Growth of Income per Person and Population across States, 1900–90[a]

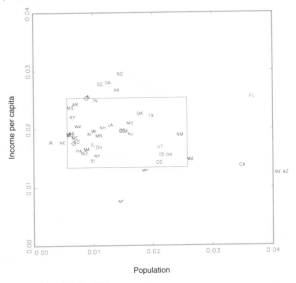

Source: Data from Barro and Sala-i-Martin (1997).
a. Data are for the contiguous United States. The box represents the 10th–90th percentile range for the population.

Figure 3. Per Annum Growth of Income per Person and Population across Japan, 1955–90[a]

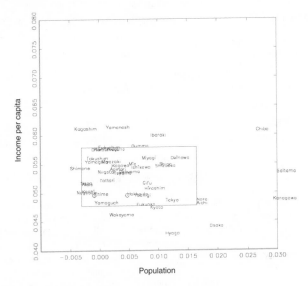

Source: Data from Barro and Sala-i-Martin (1997).
a. Data are for the prefectures of Japan. The box represents the 10th–90th percentile range for the population.

Figure 4. Per Annum Growth of GDP per Capita and Population for Non-OECD Countries, 1950–2000ª

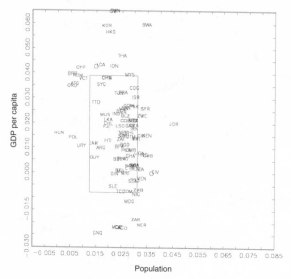

Source: Author's calculations based on data from the Penn World Tables v. 6.0 (Heston, Summers, and Aten 2002).
a. The box represents the 10th–90th percentile range for the population.

tion. That is, of course, exactly what one sees across the non-OECD countries in figure 4—many boom towns (high income growth) and zombies (zero or falling income) but few ghosts (losing population). The range of growth rates is more than 9 percentage points—from more than 6 ppa for Singapore and Taiwan to less than negative 2 ppa for the Democratic Republic of the Congo (formerly Zaïre), Niger, and Angola.[34] The 10th–90th difference is 4.6 ppa compared with only 1 percentage point across prefectures of Japan or only 0.9 across provinces of Canada.

The raw population growth rates shown in figure 4 substantially overstate the extent to which cross-national population mobility has played a role, since much of the cross-national variation in population is due to very different rates of natural increase. To compare cross-national variation with interregional

34. Per annum growth rates of GDP per capita are calculated as a least squares growth rate over the longest period available for each country in the data of the Penn World Table v. 6.0 (Heston, Summers, and Aten 2002) for all countries with at least 20 years of data. Per annum growth rates of population are calculated for the same period. For simplicity's sake this is reported as 1950–90, which is the availability of data for most of the countries but technically is "maximum availability of data from 1950 to 1990 for countries with at least 20 years of continuous data." I use this period (as opposed to many authors who drop the pre-1960 data) because the Barro and Sala-i-Martin data are only available for the period 1950–90 and I wanted to maximize comparability.

Figure 5. Per Annum Growth of GDP per Capita and Net Population for Non-OECD Countries, 1950–2000[a]

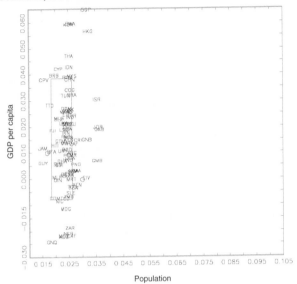

Population

Source: Author's calculations based on data from the Penn World Tables v. 6.0 (Heston, Summers, and Aten 2002).

a. The net population growth rate is the population growth rate minus the rate of natural increase. The box represents the 10th–90th percentile range for the population.

growth of populations within countries—where nearly all of the differences are due to mobility, since rates of natural increase are nearly equal within countries—I calculate the rate of population growth less the rate of natural increase (crude birth rates less crude death rates) as a proxy. But this almost certainly understates actual population mobility, because it is very difficult to get population estimates that do not, to a greater or lesser extent, depend on extrapolations based on the rate of natural increase. Thus one can question the reliability of the resulting estimates of net migration.[35] The compromise is to report both raw population growth rates and population growth net of natural increase (which I will call "net population growth" in a simple but awkward use of "net"); but I focus on net population growth as an indicator of labor mobility.

Figure 5 shows that the variability of growth of GDP per capita is enormously larger than the variability of net population growth rates. The 10th–90th per-

35. On the plus side, as seen in figure 5 at least, the results are quite plausible at the extremes, which show high rates of positive net migration in Israel, Jordan, Côte d' Ivoire, Hong Kong, and Singapore (all consistent with census evidence of estimated proportions of a foreign-born population) and large negative net migration in Jamaica and Guyana (consistent with estimates of U.S. Census estimates of immigrants from these countries).

centile range for net population growth rates is only 0.8 ppa—from –0.5 (Haiti or Mali) to 0.3 (Costa Rica). This is less than one-fifth (0.17) of the 10th–90th percentile range of growth of 4.6. Figure 5 displays the "tall and thin" distribution of cross-regional (in this case cross-national) growth rates of population and income per capita one would expect from the combination of large region-specific shocks to labor demand and inelastic labor supply (see figure 1).

Comparison of Across-Country with Within-Country Variability of Growth Rates

The variance in growth rates of populations across regions within countries with no barriers to mobility indicates how much unconstrained desired populations vary across geographic regions—even when goods and capital markets are perfectly integrated and policies and institutions are (more or less) the same. The question is whether variability is large in an absolute sense and in particular whether it is large relative to the observed variability in populations across countries. Moreover, if the variability of populations across countries is low, for which there are formal barriers to mobility, and if the variability of desired populations is large, one would expect the adjustment to happen through larger variability in output per person. Figure 6 illustrates the same point as Table 2 by showing the 10th–90th percentile boxes for growth of population and income per person on the same scale for regions within countries and across non-OECD countries for the three countries that display the largest cross-regional variation on population growth rates (United States, Canada, and Japan). Figure 7 shows the same figure for countries with smaller variance (Spain, Italy, France, United Kingdom, and Germany).[36] The graphically obvious point is that the 10–90 box for the non-OECD countries is very tall and thin (it is fatter in figures 6b and 7b that use total population, which incorporates differences in natural rates of increase) while the individual country boxes tend to be wider (in absolute terms) and much shorter—leaving fat, short boxes or, at best, squares. Table 2 gives the numerical versions of these graphical impressions, and together table 2 and figures 6 and 7 illustrate the four points of this section.

First, the absolute magnitude of labor mobility within countries that share similar policies and institutions appears to be quite large—graphically the within-country boxes are quite wide—but it varies considerably across coun-

36. The only reason for two figures is that with all eight countries one cannot make out the individual countries since the OECD countries tend to have similar economic and population growth rates. Also, these only show the rate of population growth rates adjusted for natural increase; those with raw population for the same sets of regions are in the working paper version.

Figure 6. Variability of Growth Rates of Output per Capita and Population within Regions of Countries and across Non-OECD Countries, for Various Years[a]

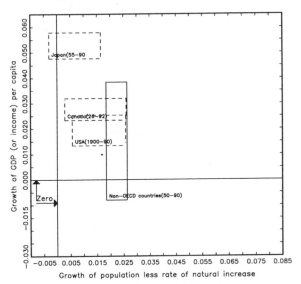

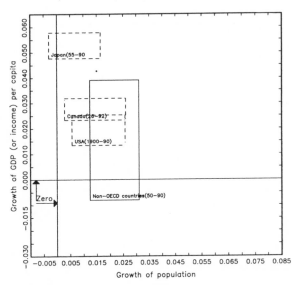

Sources: Author's calculations based on data from the Penn World Tables v. 6.0 (Heston, Summers, and Bettina 2002) for non-OECD countries and Barro and Sala-i-Martin (1997) for Japan, Canada, and the United States.

Figure 7. Variability of Growth Rates of Output per Capita and Population within Regions of Various European Countries and across Non-OECD Countries, for Various Years[a]

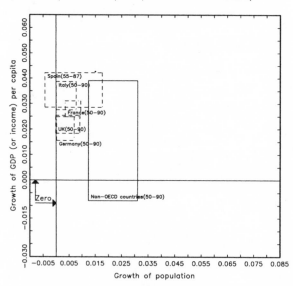

Sources: Author's calculations based on data from the Penn World Tables v. 6.0 (Heston, Summers, and Bettina 2002) for non-OECD countries and Barro and Sala-i-Martin (1997) for OECD countries.

Table 2. Variance in Growth of Population and Growth in GDP (or Income) per Capita across Countries and Regions

Region	Number of units	Period	10th–90th percentile difference in growth of		Ratio: 10th–90th percentile difference pop. growth to growth of	Standard deviations of per annum growth rates		$\frac{\sigma_P}{\sigma_{\frac{Y}{P}}}$
			Pop.	Y/P	Y/P	Pop.	Y/P	Ratio
I	II	III	IV	IV	V	VI	VII	VIII
Non-OECD countries								
Non-OECD countries[a] (pop. RNI)	91	1950–90	0.8	4.6	0.17	0.40	1.86	0.22
Regions of non-European industrialized countries[b]								
United States	48	1900–90	2.0	1.2	1.67	0.92	0.45	2.02
Canada	9	1926–92	2.3	0.9	2.56	0.78	0.33	2.37
Japan	47	1955–90	1.9	1.0	1.90	0.84	0.44	1.92
Regions of European countries								
United Kingdom	11	1950–90	0.9	0.7	1.29	0.37	0.32	1.14
France	21	1950–90	0.5	0.6	0.83	0.34	0.33	1.02
Spain	17	1955–87	2.2	1.3	1.69	0.80	0.67	1.20
Italy	20	1950–90	0.8	1.1	0.73	0.35	0.44	0.80
Germany	11	1950–90	0.7	0.9	0.78	0.34	0.39	0.82

Sources: Based on regional data from Barro and Sala-i-Martin (1997) and cross-national data from Penn World Tables v. 6.0 (Heston, Summers, and Aten 2002) on population and income, supplemented with data on crude birth and death rates from World Bank World Development Indicators to calculate rates of natural increase.

P, pop. = population; RNI = rate of natural increase; Y/P = GDP (or income) per capita.

a. For non-OECD countries, all available data from all countries with more than 20 years of data are used to calculate growth rates.

b. The United States, Canada, and Japan have the largest cross-regional variation on population growth rates.

tries. The 10th–90th difference in the United States is 2 ppa, in Japan 1.9 ppa, in Spain 2.2 ppa, and in the United Kingdom 0.9 ppa, while the lowest is 0.5 ppa in France. Since these differences occur during a forty-year period (or more, in the case of the United States or Canada), this difference in growth rates is impressive—a 2 ppa population growth differential between two initially equally sized regions would mean that the more rapidly growing region is twice the size of the slower growing region. Since the fact that large cross-regional population growth differentials exist is perhaps obvious (to American readers), it is worth stressing that most standard economic theories provide no predictions or intuition about the magnitude—in fact the usual intuition from standard growth or trade models is that capital or goods, being more mobile, would move, but not people. These cross-regional magnitudes have the advantage of controlling for policies and institutions, hence they reveal the magnitude of changes in unconstrained desired population that are likely truly spatial. However, they do not speak directly to the issue of spatial shocks to productivity, as demand-side factors that alter the utility affecting Z in the location decision (for example, air conditioning in the United States) explain some mobility as well.

Second, the box across non-OECD countries is very tall. The variability of growth rates of income per capita is spectacularly larger across countries than across regions within countries—10th–90th differences of 4.6 ppa across non-OECD countries and only around 1 ppa for the regions of the United States and Japan.

Third, very simple supply and demand analysis works: if demand is variable and if supply is elastic, then observed quantities should vary and prices less so, while if supply is inelastic, then prices should vary and quantities less so. Region-specific shocks to unconstrained labor demand should produce short, fat boxes with elastic labor supply and tall, thin boxes with inelastic labor supply. In table 2, column V (for 10th–90th percentiles) and column VIII (for standard deviations) show the ratio of the variability in the changes in populations to the variability of growth in income per capita. This ratio, a measure of whether a shock is accommodated with population mobility or income changes is roughly ten times larger for regions within the more mobile countries (for example, 1.69 for Spain versus 0.17 for non-OECD countries). But the point is not that labor supply is mobile within countries and less mobile across them—everyone knows that—nor is the point that demand-supply analysis works—all economists know that. The point is that supply and demand works and that data are consistent with the large variability in geographic-specific productivity, which is not eliminated by goods or capital movements, and that these shocks result in *either* large population movements (elastic labor supply) or large variability in income per capita (inelastic labor supply).

Fourth, the striking fact is that the variability in net population growth across developing countries is *absolutely smaller* than the variability in populations across regions within many countries. The difference between the 10th and 90th percentile population growth across the 91 non-OECD countries is only 0.8 ppa. Across the 47 prefectures of Japan the same gap is 1.9 ppa; across the 17 provinces of Spain, 2.2 ppa; and across the 48 (contiguous) states of the United States, the gap is 2.0 ppa. For instance, the net population decrease of Haiti or Mali is –0.5 ppa, while the net population increase of Hong Kong or Singapore is 0.7 ppa—a 1.2 ppa differential. Population growth in Kansas during the longest time frame was 0.6 ppa, and in California it was 3.4 ppa—a 2.8 percentage point differential. Here is the heuristic, and it is entirely heuristic, which is that the Kansas-California differential is not primarily due to policies and institutions; it is primarily due to geographic factors (such as access to coasts, innovations in irrigation, agglomeration economies, declining terms of trade for staples, among others). It is not difficult to believe that the geographic shocks (which include all technological and transport cost changes affecting the relative attractiveness of location) between places like Mali (landlocked with high transport costs, low rainfall) and Singapore are not of similar or larger magnitude compared with those between Kansas and California. And yet the net population growth differences, those driven by labor mobility, between Mali and Singapore are a small fraction of those between Kansas and California.

What is striking about figure 4 is not just the small absolute variance in net population growth (labor mobility) across countries, but that the vertical box roughly covers the data, implying that the people did not strikingly (meaning enough to be visually noticeable as a covariance) migrate toward rapid-growth countries. Perhaps this is different from regions, because migration behavior responds not only to *levels* of income but also to *growth rates*, and the levels of income across these non-OECD countries are not large, and growth is not strongly associated with initial levels of income (for example, richer countries did not also grow faster).[37] This requires some caution, because permanent mobility should be driven by differences in present discounted value of utility differences, which depend on levels of output and (anticipated) growth rates, while perhaps temporary mobility is driven almost exclusively by levels of wages.

37. I thank Susan Collins for this point.

Even so, the differences in growth rates implied by the vertical gaps imply that even countries that started nearly equal ended up with starkly different levels even by the 1980s or 1990s and certainly by the end of the period. Compare Chile and Bolivia. While Chile's income was only modestly higher than Bolivia's in 1955, by 2000 Chile's purchasing power parity (PPP) income per capita was three times higher than that of Bolivia. Yet Bolivia's rate of natural increase in the late 1990s was 2.4 ppa, and population growth in the 1990s was 2.33 ppa—so net population growth was only slightly smaller. In Chile, neighboring Bolivia and perhaps a natural labor mobility partner, the rate of natural increase was 1.4 and population growth 1.36—so the difference in net population growth between a pair of countries with threefold income differences was *three-hundredths* of a percentage point. The basic point is that the differences are quite small and are not associated with growth even if they may be associated with levels of output.

The four empirical results are sufficiently striking that I want to emphasize that they are *not* a trivial consequence of the obvious fact that people can move within regions and cannot move across national borders. There are many ways in which population mobility is allowed and yet cannot produce the above results. First, it is possible that geographic-specific shocks to the desired population are small. Using the within-country interregional results reduces the impact of location-specific policy, institution, or nongeographic technological shocks on desired populations. Second, it is possible that geographic-specific shocks to income do not result in changes in the desired population, as movements of goods or capital mitigate the impact of shocks on regional labor demand. It is not surprising that with *unrestricted* mobility there is convergence in incomes. Differences in population growth across spatially large regions within a (reasonably) homogenous policy and institutional environment in a fully integrated economy are absolutely and relatively large—as large or larger than existing cross-national differences that include both geographic and institutional components. This is a nontrivial empirical finding.

Ghost Regions of the United States

The previous section shows large differences in population growth across states of the United States as well as across regions (for example, prefectures, provinces) of other OECD countries. Results at the state level perhaps *understate* the degree of spatial population mobility by smoothing over large areas—some of which increased, while others decreased. Data across the roughly 3,000 counties in the United States illustrate the enormous degree of spatial variation in unconstrained desired populations even when policies and institutions are near identical. At the county level there are enormous changes in populations. While the population in the United States overall has doubled since 1930, there are counties that have been essentially depopulated between 1930 and 1990. Slope County in North Dakota has seen its population fall from 4,150 to only 907, Smith County in Kansas from 13,545 to only 5,078, Huerfano County in Colorado from 17,062 to only 6,009, and McDowell County in West Virginia from 90,479 to only 35,233. Of course there are counties with explosive growth in population.

One might think that these large population reductions are simply isolated cases and are not really of any consequence in a larger picture. In table 3, I illustrate that this is not the case, by assembling collections of counties of various sizes of initial population in 1930 that later had the largest percent reduction in population from 1930 to 1990. There were 612 counties that added up to 10 percent of the U.S. population in 1930 (around 12 million people), and they had the most rapid subsequent population reduction—losing 40 percent of their 1930 population. They are now only 30 percent as large as they would have been had they not experienced out-migration—these counties are legitimate ghosts. This also implies that had the population somehow continued to grow at the rate of natural increase their current population would potentially be *three times* their unconstrained desired level. As shown in table 3, the land area covered by these 612 counties is larger than the size of Bolivia. The 902 counties that contained 20 percent of the U.S. population in 1930 (24 million people) lost 27 percent of their population during the next sixty years and are only 36 percent of the counterfactual of no out-migration. The spatial area covered by these 902 counties is larger than all but about ten countries in the world.

Of course, adding up collections of counties sorted by their percent reduction maximizes the fall and is not directly analogous to countries, since these counties are not physically contiguous. A second exercise, shown in table 4, is to assemble counties that may cut across state boundaries but that are *contiguous*, such that it is at least conceivable that, had history been different, a plausibly shaped state (or country) could have been formed with these boundaries.[38] That is, while I deliberately constructed the areas to include counties losing population, I did not simply cut out cities or make dramatic detours to include or exclude a particular county. I assemble five regions of the United States that I name—*Texaklahoma* (northwest Texas and Oklahoma), *Heartland* (parts of

---

38. After all, national borders of existing countries were often drawn in pretty arbitrary ways and in the absence of much real information.

Table 3. Changes in Populations of Agglomerations of Counties in the United States

Agglomeration adds up to x in 1930[a]	Number of counties (out of 3,065)	Population 1930 (000s)	Percent change 1930–90	Current population relative to counter-factual at RNI (percent)	Total area (square miles)	Countries smaller in land area (total)
1 million	84	1,015.1	−64.0	17.8	89,111	Uganda, Syria (118)
5 million	321	5,006.4	−52.2	23.6	309,358	Turkey (160)
10 percent of U.S. population	612	12,140.2	−39.3	30.0	551,345	Bolivia, Mali (176)
20 percent of U.S. population	902	24,916.6	−27.5	35.9	774,539	Mexico, Indonesia (181)

Source: Author's calculations based on county population data.
RNI = rate of natural increase.
a. Counties collected were those with the highest percent reduction in population from 1930 to 1990.

Table 4. Population Change in Regions of the United States[a]

Region of the United States (contiguous counties)	Population 1930 (000s)	Percent change in population 1930–90	Ratio of current population to counter-factual at RNI	Area (square miles)	Countries smaller in land area (total)	Ratio of area per capita income to national average (percent)
Texaklahoma	835.8	−36.8	0.31	58,403	Nicaragua, Bangladesh (117)	92.2
Heartland	1,482.6	−34.0	0.33	59,708	(117)	85.2
Deep South	1,558.2	−27.9	0.36	36,284	Jordan, Austria, Sri Lanka (96)	62.6
Coal Pennsylvania	1,182.9	−27.9	0.36	2,972	Trinidad and Tobago, Mauritius (43)	84.5
Great Plains North	1,068.0	−27.7	0.36	100,920	Great Britain, Ghana, Ecuador (128)	85.4
Nation	123,202.6	101.9	...	3,536,278	...	100.0

Source: Author's calculations based on county population data.

... Does not apply.

RNI = rate of natural increase.

a. Regions are composed of contiguous collections of counties that cut across state borders.

Iowa, Missouri, Kansas, and Nebraska), *Deep South* (parts of Arkansas, Mississippi, and Alabama), *Coal Pennsylvania*, and *Great Plains North* (parts of Kansas and South Dakota).[39]

Even with the constraint of contiguity, one can assemble spatially large territories that have seen substantial population decline. The Great Plains North is a territory larger than Great Britain. Its population has declined 28 percent from 1930 to 1990 and is only a bit more than a third of what it would have been had population growth continued at the rate of natural increase. Texaklahoma is larger than Bangladesh and now has only 31 percent the population it would have had in the absence of out-migration. We use a few counties in the coal-producing region of Pennsylvania to illustrate that not all of these declines are explained by the decline of rural and agricultural populations; natural resource shocks also play a role.

Regions of counties within the United States can be seen as an experiment of what would happen in a fully globalized world—geographic units linked with fully integrated markets for land, capital, goods, *and* labor. In such a world one can expect that, since people would choose location so as to be indifferent between staying and moving, incomes would show some tendency to converge *in levels* (adjusting for nonincome dimensions, that is, the Z again). This does appear to be true since, with the exception of the Deep South, the incomes of the other four regions that are losing population are more than 84 percent of the national average—so these regions are poorer than the national average, but not dramatically so.

But one can ask—even with fully integrated markets with goods and capital and (roughly) equivalent policies and institutions—how much variability is there in desired populations within regions? Again the answer: "a lot." While it may be the case that population movements were less than they would have been because capital flowed to these regions and goods were mobile, it is still the case that the population shifts within the United States are huge. In particular, they are vastly larger than the population shifts one sees across the often equally arbitrary boundaries of countries in the world today.

To a large extent variability in regional population growth is a consequence of the well-known phenomena of urbanization, as everyone knows that the U.S. population went from rural to urban during this sixty-year period. Glaeser and Kohlhase showed a number of factors associated with the rise and decline of county populations—for example, having resource-based industries was "bad" and having sophisticated services was "good."[40]

39. The maps showing the regions and county-specific changes in population can be found in Pritchett (2006).
40. Glaeser and Kohlhase (2003).

But there is no guarantee that the boundaries of any given country contain a viable city. As urbanization proceeds and populations agglomerate into cities, there are areas of geographic space that do not contain a single "city" in equilibrium. In the simulations by Fujita, Krugman, and Venables of models with agglomeration economies, the number and location of cities in equilibrium can change dramatically, even with only smallish changes in parameters such as transport costs.[41] Boom towns attract enormous inflows of population. A ghost region might not contain, in a full mobility equilibrium, even a single city, because the initial negative shock is reinforced by a loss of agglomeration economies such that even with ideal policies and institutions the optimal population after a negative shock could be a small fraction of its current population.

Accommodating Shocks with Population Movements: Ireland

The third illustration of the importance of geographic shocks and their consquences for population depending on how the shocks are accommodated is the comparison of countries in the era of globalization with labor with adjustments in the era of globalization without labor. The nineteenth century was an age of mass migration, as many of the "areas of recent settlement" had open borders with respect to immigrants (at least to those of certain ethnic or national origin).[42] It was also an era of rapid reductions in transport costs and moves toward freer trade in goods and open capital markets (with massive movements in capital)—the first era of globalization. Hence this period is an interesting example of the question: "How would we expect geographic shocks to be accommodated in a globalizing world?"

The story of Ireland is an obvious, and dramatic, case in point. The introduction of the potato into Ireland has been a large positive shock, because it was a much cheaper source of calories per unit of land and was well adapted to the climate. This technological innovation allowed the population to grow without reducing the output per worker—population in 1841 was 2.5 times that of 1754. However, given the dependence of the Irish economy on the potato, the onset of the potato blight in the 1840s was an enormous negative shock. After the initial terrible period of the famine, the economy in fact did reasonably well by the standard measures—real unskilled wages relative to the United Kingdom *never* fell. The available aggregate figures show that GDP per capita in 1870 was more than 40 percent higher than it was in 1820.

41. Fujita, Krugman, and Venables (1999).
42. Hatton and Williamson (1998).

The obvious mechanism of adjustment was out-migration, which was substantial. Since one is used to seeing trends with steady exponential increases in population, the counterexample of Ireland is stunning. The recorded peak population of Ireland was more than 8 million (8,175,000), but by 1901 the population had fallen to only about 4.5 million (4,459,000)—a net loss of 3.7 million people. And of course this decrease happened despite rates of natural increase that would have led to increasing population. This contraction radically changed the relative size of countries—Canada's population in 1871 was less than half Ireland's peak, but by 1991 Canada's population was five times as large as Ireland's. Ireland was larger than Belgium in 1871 but only 60 percent as large by 1911. Even today with Ireland booming economically, Ireland's population is only 70 percent of its peak—and is at the same level as the population of *200 years ago.*

Ireland's experience with adjustment to negative shocks during an era of labor mobility can be compared with any number of countries in more recent times—I will use Bolivia first since it has comparable wage data over the same time frame.[43] Sometime in the late 1970s Bolivia's economic growth slowed, stopped, and reversed, in part because of negative shocks to Bolivia's extractive industries. How did Bolivians adjust to these shocks? Population today is almost 90 percent higher than that in 1972. In contrast, real industrial wages (at official exchange rates) have fallen from a peak of 14 percent of U.S. levels to only 8 percent. Real GDP per worker in 1992 was only 62 percent of its peak.

Comparing Ireland with Bolivia highlights the obvious: nearly all developing countries with negative shocks have seen their populations continue to expand rapidly while labor movements accommodated negative shocks, when there was freer labor mobility in the international system.

Existence of Hard-Core Geographic Zombies

On the one hand, one should rightly hesitate to declare that any particular territory is simply incapable of supporting its current population at acceptable standards of living. But, on the other hand, simply maintaining a fiction because it is politically convenient for the industrialized countries to do so is no better. I define *potential* zombie countries by two criteria: (1) countries where GDP

---

43. Although not quite; I had to extrapolate the wage data in the mid-1980s, since the raw wage data were anomalous, likely due to difficulties in exchange-rate comparisons at official exchange rates during rapid inflation.

per capita has fallen by more than 20 percent from peak to trough (where for data purposes the peak must come before 1990 to rule out recent zombies), and (2) GDP per capita today remains less than 90 percent of peak GDP. This produces a list of 33 countries that are potential zombies.

Of this list of potential zombies I have no systematic method for saying which are policy zombies and hence could spring to life tomorrow and which are hardcore geographic zombies that, even at optimal policies and institutions, would still have optimal populations far below their current actual population. Thus it could be that anticipated output fell because of disastrously bad politics or policies, which, if reversed, would cause the area to be enormously attractive. Perhaps the most obvious example is Cuba, where many people think an enormous boom will follow the end of Castro's regime. To document which countries are geographic ghosts, I would have to specify and parameterize some particular model of location, which would require grappling with the thorny issues of increasing returns to scale, among other things.

I conjecture four criteria to separate potential zombies from hard-core geographic zombies: (1) The decline is more likely due, or at least partly due, to geographic rather than to policy or institutional factors. While none of these countries has terrific policies or institutions, neither are they the "Zaïres" of the world that are "institutional ghosts." So I choose countries in which some identifiable negative shock has occurred (usually having to do with terms of trade of their export) that initiated the decline. (2) Landlocked countries are potentially hard-core, because substitution into other industries is more difficult. (3) "Small" populations (less than 20 million) imply that potential zombies will have a more difficult time smoothing over shocks. This also implies that in a locational equilibrium with population mobility and agglomeration there might not be sufficient economic activity for even one city, in which case the declines in desired population might be even more dramatic than those presented in the table below. (4) Countries that are in "bad" regions—that is, they are surrounded by other poor countries (for example, Luxemburg is a small, landlocked country that is in a good neighborhood; Cuba is much more likely to be an institutional rather than a geographic zombie).

Between the two economic criteria for potential zombies and these four criteria for hard-core geographic zombies, I identify countries and ask the question: "What is the gap between their current population and their *optimal* population?"

Since this question is impossible, I use two *hypothetical* questions (each with variants for a total of five scenarios) to illustrate some ranges. First, because output per person has fallen in all of these countries (by definition), I ask the question: If *optimal* population has received as large a negative shock relative to its peak as it has in the three counterfactuals [see the three options below], then what is the ratio of the postshock optimal population to the current population? The three counterfactual scenarios are—"What if optimal population in country Y relative to its population at peak GDP per capita has fallen by as much as the actual population

—Fell in Ireland in the nineteenth century (53 percent peak to trough)?

—Fell between 1930 and 1990 in three regions of the United States (Deep South, Great Plains North, Coal Pennsylvania; 28 percent)?

—Rose only as fast as the bottom 10th percentile [10th–90th] of the population growth in regions of the eight OECD countries in table 2 (at 0.01 percent per annum)?

This is obviously not proof that there have been changes in optimal populations of the countries, rather it is just a matter of exploring the implications of plausible counterfactual scenarios. In all of these regions in the counter-factual (Ireland, U.S. regions, and OECD regions), GDP per capita rose substantially while populations fell. In the zombie countries GDP per capita has fallen while populations rose. It is at least plausible these changes simply represent different adjustments to similar-sized shocks to geographic-specific maximal incomes—pushing the adjustment either into wages and capital stocks or into population movement.

Second, to investigate the gap between current and optimal population I ask the question: If the elasticity of GDP per person with respect to population is – 0.4, by how much would population have to fall to

—Restore previous peak GDP per capita, or

—Move GDP per capita to the level it would have been had it grown at 2 ppa since the peak (which is roughly the world's average growth rate and hence just avoids divergence)?

Since I began with the example of Zambia, let me use Zambia (first row in table 5) to illustrate the very simple way the five scenarios (three from counterfactual populations and two from income simulations) work and the results. Zambia's GDP per capita peaked in 1964 when its population was 3.5 million. Today, GDP per capita is only 59 percent of its peak and the population is 10.0 million. If Zambia's population had fallen from its 1964 level by as much as Ireland's actual population did (48 percent), then Zambia's population today would be only 1.86 million—18 percent of its current level. If Zambia's population had fallen from its 1964 level by as much as population in three of the ghost regions in the United States did (28 percent), then its population would only be 2.52 million—25 percent of its current level. If Zambia's population had grown at the 0.01 percent rate of the slow population growth (10th percentile) (10th–90th) regions of the eight OECD countries listed in table 2, its population would be about what it was in 1964, 3.52 million—but that is still only 35 percent of its current level.

The two output scenarios provide similarly striking ratios. Under the simple assumptions made, population and output per person, population would have to fall to 14 percent of its current level to raise GDP per person to the level of a nondivergent trend. This is consistent with a negative shock roughly the magnitude of Ireland's. To raise output per person just to its previous peak, population would have to fall to 36 percent of its current levels. Table 5 shows that the potential hard-core geographic zombies have optimal populations *very* much smaller than their current levels—sometimes only a third as large by the output calculations.

I am aware of how striking these numbers are. But it is not implausible that the desired population of Sahelian countries (for example, Niger and Chad) has fallen by as much as the desired population of the Great Plains North configuration of counties of the United States. In fact, there are many reasons to expect that the changes in desired population are probably larger in the Sahel. If this is so and if population mobility were not constrained, then three out of every four people would leave Niger, which might only be enough to restore output to its level of 1963. With the simple assumed elasticities, Chad would have to have seven of every ten people leave just to restore output to its previous peak GDP per capita in 1979.

Table 6 presents a variety of other countries. Some are possible institutional ghosts—which in some cases are countries in which output per person fell, at least initially, because of widespread armed conflict (for example, Mozambique, Nicaragua, El Salvador). To some extent these are the most hopeful ghosts, because it is possible that the desired population can recover very quickly. In others the fall in output is strongly associated with deterioration in the terms of trade, particularly for oil—(for example, Nigeria and Venezuela).

Jamaica is an interesting case, precisely because out-migration has already played such a large role in population dynamics. By the "OECD laggard" scenario, Jamaica's optimal population is 73 percent of its current population, because Jamaica's population has in fact grown so slowly, at only 1.2 ppa versus the 2.2 ppa of the rate of natural increase. It is already the case that there are nearly as many Jamaicans living outside of the national territory of Jamaica as within it.

Table 5. How Large is the Ghosthood? (Potential Hard-Core Ghosts)

Country	Year of peak GDP[b]	Ratio GDP per capita in 2000 to peak GDP	Current population (000s)	Ratio of what the population would be to the actual population if:				
				the shock were as large as the realized population changes			the labor force fell to restore GDP to x percent[a]	
				Ireland's 53 percent fall, 1841–1926	U.S. ghost regions' 28 percent fall, 1930–1990	OECD lagging regions[c]	Previous peak GDP (percent)	GDP[d] (percent)
Zambia	1964	0.59	10,089	0.18	0.25	0.35	36	14
Central African franc zone	1970	0.44	3,603	0.27	0.37	0.51	24	11
Niger	1963	0.50	10,832	0.17	0.23	0.32	29	11
Chad	1979	0.50	7,694	0.30	0.41	0.57	29	17
Rwanda	1981	0.75	8,508	0.33	0.45	0.63	55	30
Bolivia	1978	0.87	8,329	0.33	0.44	0.62	72	34
Romania	1986	0.74	22,435	0.54	0.74	1.03	54	34

Source: Author's calculations as described in text using population and GDP per capita data from *World Development Indicators*, World Bank (2006).

ppa = percent per annum.

a. Assuming an elasticity of GDP, or income, per capita to population of –0.4

b. GDP = GDP per capita.

c. Average population growth (0.01 ppa) of the regions in the 10th percentile in the eight OECD countries listed in table 2 (which shows only the 10th–90th differences).

d. Implying 2 ppa growth since peak (with no divergence).

Table 6. How Large Is the Ghosthood?

| Country | Year of peak GDP[b] | Ratio GDP per capita in 2000 to peak GDP | Current population (000s) | Ratio of what the population would be to the actual population if: | | | | |
| | | | | the shock were as large as the realized population changes | | | the labor force fell to restore GDP to x percent[a] | |
				Ireland's 53 percent fall, 1841–1926	U.S. ghost regions' 28 percent fall, 1930–1990	OECD lagging regions[c]	Previous peak GDP (percent)	GDP[d] (percent)
Burundi	1977	0.60	6,807	0.30	0.40	0.56	37%	20%
Togo	1969	0.61	4,527	0.23	0.31	0.43	39%	17%
Madagascar	1971	0.65	15,523	0.24	0.33	0.45	43%	19%
Namibia	1979	0.70	1,718	0.31	0.42	0.58	48%	25%
Congo	1984	0.80	3,018	0.33	0.45	0.62	61%	36%
Jamaica	1972	0.80	2,633	0.39	0.53	0.73	62%	26%
Gabon	1978	0.81	1,230	0.28	0.38	0.53	63%	30%
Gambia	1984	0.85	1,303	0.29	0.40	0.55	69%	39%
Jordan	1986	0.85	4,887	0.30	0.40	0.56	69%	42%
Senegal	1960	0.89	9,530	0.18	0.24	0.34	77%	21%
Côte d'Ivoire	1979	0.61	16,013	0.26	0.35	0.49	39%	21%
Cameroon	1986	0.67	14,876	0.37	0.50	0.69	45%	29%
Ghana	1972	0.87	19,306	0.25	0.34	0.47	73%	29%
Angola	1973	0.39	11,317	0.27	0.37	0.52	20%	11%
Mozambique	1973	0.49	17,691	0.30	0.41	0.57	28%	14%
Mauritania	1976	0.60	2,576	0.29	0.39	0.55	38%	19%
Sierra Leone	1970	0.62	4,630	0.30	0.41	0.58	39%	17%
El Salvador	1978	0.90	6,276	0.37	0.51	0.71	78%	36%

Table 6 (continued). How Large Is the Ghosthood?

| | | | | Ratio of what the population would be to the actual population if: | | | | |
| | | | | the shock were as large as the realized population changes | | | the labor force fell to restore GDP to x percent[a] | |
Country	Year of peak GDP[b]	Ratio GDP per capita in 2000 to peak GDP[b]	Current population (000s)	Ireland's 53 percent fall, 1841–1926	U.S. ghost regions' 28 percent fall, 1930–1990	OECD lagging regions[c]	Previous peak GDP (percent)	GDP[d] (percent)
Nicarauga	1977	0.40	5,071	0.28	0.38	0.53	21%	12%
Venezuela	1970	0.61	24,170	0.24	0.32	0.44	38%	17%
Tanzania	1987	0.64	33,696	0.36	0.50	0.69	41%	28%
Peru	1975	0.86	25,661	0.31	0.43	0.59	71%	31%
Zaïre	1970	0.27	46,754	0.23	0.31	0.43	13%	6%
Nigeria	1974	0.53	126,910	0.25	0.34	0.47	31%	16%

Source: Author's calculations as described in text using population and GDP per capita data from *World Development Indicators*, World Bank (2006).

ppa = percent per annum; Congo = Republic of the Congo; Zaïre = Democratic Republic of the Congo.

a. Assuming an elasticity of GDP, or income, per capita to population of –0.4

b. GDP = GDP per capita.

c. Average population growth (0.01 ppa) of the regions in the 10th percentile in the eight OECD countries listed in table 2 (which shows only the 10th–90th differences).

d. Implying 2 ppa growth since peak (with no divergence).

Conclusion

It would be convenient in many ways if the proposition that every country can achieve high and rising standards of living for its populations were factually true. One reason why it would be convenient is that the present international system and international organizations are, more or less, founded on this premise. That is, the proliferation of sovereigns and globalization of everything but labor are deeply embedded in the post-WWII international system. The premise that any country, were it only to adopt appropriate policies and institutions (whatever those might be, ranging from those of the Washington Consensus to Jeffrey Sachs's new agenda), would see its income levels, if not converge, at least rise to acceptable levels is reasonably central to nearly all discussions about foreign aid.

Hence this paper is a demonstration of an inconvenient fact and its implications. The inconvenient fact is that, at least in the three cases examined—regions within OECD countries, agglomerations of contiguous counties within the United States, and Ireland in the "Atlantic economy" (which are a proxy in some ways of globalization of labor even with equivalent policies and institutions)—when people are allowed to move they *do* move in massive numbers. This strongly suggests that even with fully integrated economies—far more integrated in fact than any feasible globalization on its current path could likely achieve—there are large changes in the unconstrained desired populations of areas over time. These changes in desired population can be accommodated with population movements and the equalization (or at least nondivergence) of incomes. These movements create rising populations in cities and in booming areas and relative and absolute population declines in other areas. The extreme is the creation of regions that are a "ghost" of their former self.

Without population mobility geographic-specific shocks create a different dynamic—one of falling wages and outputs. If labor supply cannot be elastic then prices must adjust, not quantities. The consequence is that it is plausible that even in a fully "everything but labor" globalized world and even with the best possible policies and institutions some countries will not succeed—they are potential ghost countries that are forced by restrictions on population mobility into an existence as zombies.

Why do I wish to stress this inconvenient fact and the uncomfortable idea that Zambia might be a zombie? Precisely because all current policy discussions focus only on Zambia—the nation-state—and not on Zambi*ans* the people. International organizations and international negotiations and international forums tend to be exactly that—inter*national* where the actors and agents all represent nation-states and their interests. There are structured organizations and institutions for bringing about reductions in the barriers to the movement of goods, thus enabling the movement of finance. There are organizations to bring about *national* development. But almost certainly the easiest way to improve the living standards of a Zambian is not to improve living standards in Zambia but to allow the person the choice to move out of Zambia. This issue of freer movement of the world's peoples needs to be more strongly addressed in the world's policy agenda.

Finally, in some discussions of this paper people have suggested that it was insensitive to suggest even the possibility that every single existing national boundary does not encompass a viable economy capable of sustaining their current population at anything like a decent standard of living. But this political correctness critique of doubting national viability is misguided—as it mistakes nations for something real. Who created the borders? Who created the nations? I would argue in fact that this view has it exactly backwards and that to insist on the interests of nation-states to control their borders over all other considerations—including the well-being of human beings who through no action or fault of their own are trapped in economically nonviable regions—is not a normatively attractive view.

Comments
and Discussion

Clifford G. Gaddy: Lant Pritchett has written a stimulating paper, rich in empirical observations and original insights and bold in its conclusions. His notion of economic "zombies" is especially attractive. I would like to suggest a way to extend its application.

What are zombies? We are familiar with ghost towns. These are places that have lost their populations as economic conditions shifted so fundamentally that the reason for their being has disappeared. People can vote with their feet: they leave and move elsewhere. This is healthy. What is unhealthy is when people want to move but cannot. When migration is ruled out as a response to the changed conditions, people may remain trapped in a region where living standards fall. The region should shrink but does not. It does not become an actual ghost. Rather, it is a potential ghost, or zombie. Zombie regions are populated by "the living dead with falling wages and incomes."

Despite the title of this paper, Lant's main concern is not ghosts but zombies. Moreover, his interest is in a particular kind of zombie—a spatial or geographic zombie. These are distinguished from institutional (or policy) zombies, which are potential institutional ghosts. The distinction has to do with the shock that should produce the ghost. Some regions or countries have been depopulated because the policies pursued, or the institutions pursued, or both are bad. But policies can be fixed (at least in principle). Spatial zombies are a worse case, because geography cannot be fixed.

Lant suspects that geographic zombies do exist and points to two things that make it likely that they do. First is the "proliferation of sovereigns." This has led to an increasing number of smaller states in the world. The second factor is a lack of mobility of labor across all national borders. When a geographic or spatial shock hits one of these smaller states in the absence of cross-border mobility, a zombie may result.

43

How does one know if a country is a zombie? A ghost is easy to identify: simply look for a large population loss over a relatively short period of time. Lant uses various historical examples to demonstrate that ghosts exist. Identifying a zombie is more difficult, however, because zombies involve a counterfactual. One has to see if the hypothetical desired population is less than the actual population. The challenge is to establish the benchmark, that is, the desired population. To show that a country is a zombie, one needs to show what *should* have happened in the presence of the negative geographic shock, if there had been labor mobility.

What exactly is a geographical shock? I interpret Lant's notion of a negative geographic shock to mean an event that reduces the value of the geography input in the production function. These geography inputs might include features such as the existence or nonexistence of coasts and ports or, for example, the climate—is it hot, temperate, or cold? The terrain—does it have mountains, deserts, swamps, or none of these? Is the country compact or is it extended? And then, of course, there is the critical question of resources—does the country have oil, gas, gold, water, or another exploitable resource?

What would be a shock to such geography inputs? In the idealized laboratory experiment, one might reach down and do something like take away the country's coast or remove a large river or throw up a mountain range between two major cities. One might raise or lower the average temperature of the country a couple of degrees. But can anything like that possibly happen in the real world? It might seem that geographical features do not change, that they are God-given. But there are in fact ways that geography, or at least the value of geography, can change. Lant lists a number of such events or circumstances. The most familiar of them is one in which a nonrenewable resource is exhausted or in which the price of a resource drops and makes that resource less valuable. This makes for an easily understandable situation. The reason people moved to the location was to exploit the resource. But, writes Lant, "when the extraction of the resource loses value, people want to leave."

It struck me on reading Lant's paper that with only minor modifications, his framework of ghosts and zombies can be usefully applied to an area I study, namely post-Soviet Russia. Let me explain the connection by citing a casual reference Lant makes to Antarctica. He writes that "labor mobility is not important for Antarctica because no substantial populations ever moved there—its attractiveness for human populations has not changed." In other words, no one wants to move *away from* Antarctica because no one ever wanted to move *to* Antarctica in the first place.

But what if there are "Antarcticas" in the world where people do live? That is, what if there are places whose geographical features make them highly unattractive, where people do not want to live, but where they were forced to live? The result would be an actual population in excess of the desired population. This is the definition of a zombie. I suggest that such a "zombie Antarctica" does exist. It is called "Siberia." (Or, more accurately, it is Siberia, the Russian Far East, and other remote northern and eastern locations in Russia.) In the Russian Federation tens of millions of people live in places they would not be living in if they had been able to choose. They (or their parents or grandparents) were forced to move there decades ago and then prevented from moving out.

The idea of forced mobility is one of the things that distinguishes the Russian case from the ones Lant discusses. In his paper mobility is a good thing, because it is assumed to be voluntary. Voluntary mobility lets people move where they want to go. Another kind of mobility is involuntary mobility. Involuntary mobility moves people where they do not want to go. Lant models barriers to (voluntary) mobility as a virtual tax. The tax represents the price equivalent of the constraint on people moving away from a place where they do not want to be. In the extreme case, when "borders are enforced using the compulsion of police and military power, the virtual tax could be large enough to prevent all movement." Involuntary mobility could be modeled as a virtual tax on refusal to move to where the authorities (the state) decide people should move. ("If you don't move, you will be penalized.") The extreme case—compulsory mobility—would be a large enough virtual tax to force one to move.

In the Soviet era millions of citizens were compelled to move to places where they did not want to be. The degree of compulsion (and thus the size of the tax) varied over time. In the Stalin years people were forcibly deported, or imprisoned in the Gulag. Later the compulsion was in the form of denial of alternatives. Imagine what would happen if this involuntary mobility were abolished and voluntary mobility were allowed. First, people would no longer have to move to undesirable locations. Second, they would move to where they wanted. If enough people left a region, it would become a ghost.

When Russia abandoned communism in the early 1990s, involuntary mobility was eliminated. People were much freer to live where they wanted, and many did in fact move—especially out of the most remote towns of Siberia. But numerous obstacles to free mobility remained. One of the important issues of Russia's transition has been to what extent the country has been able to correct the spatial misallocation of its Soviet past. Lant Pritchett's paper offers a new conceptual framework to examine that question. It allows us to pose the question as follows: "Has mobility been great enough to rid Russia of the zom-

Figure 8. Twentieth Century Population Growth, Duluth and Perm'.

Population

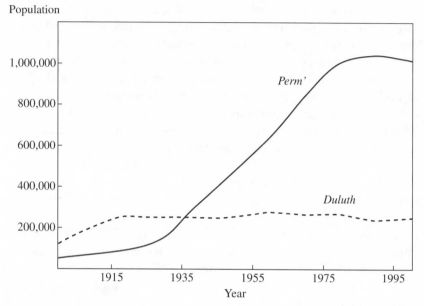

Year

Source: Hill and Gaddy (2003), figure 3-7.

bies it inherited from the Soviet Union?" To answer the question, it is necessary to do precisely as Lant did and somehow estimate the counterfactual "desired" population of cities and regions. How does it compare to the actual population?

It turns out that, without knowing it, this was precisely the exercise in which some colleagues and I were engaged in a pair of projects at Brookings over the past few years. The initial project was called "The Cost of the Cold." Follow-up research resulted in the book *The Siberian Curse.*[1] In that work we used three approaches to calculate desired populations. First, we examined the histories of individual Russian cities and compared them with similar cities in free economies. Second, we looked at the set of Russia's largest cities, using the country's own pre-Soviet history, and projected the evolution of those cities forward on the basis of certain regularities of city-size distributions in the rest of the world. Third, we modeled a counterfactual evolution of population distribution in the entire country using Canada as a benchmark.

Figure 8 illustrates a single case study of two cities we compared: Duluth, Minnesota, and Perm', Russia. These two cities are very similar in terms of cli-

1. Research on "The Cost of the Cold" was conducted jointly with Barry W. Ickes of Pennsylvania State University.

mate and location (distance from markets). They began the twentieth century roughly the same size, with the same sort of goals and aspirations of becoming major manufacturing centers. Between 1900 and 1910, Duluth was one of America's fastest-growing cities, as its population rose from 119,000 to 211,000. When the United States Steel Corporation announced it would build a huge steel plant there, there were predictions that Duluth would become a new Pittsburgh, Detroit, or even Chicago. As it turned out, Duluth's extremely cold climate and its distance from major iron and steel markets squelched the dreams of greatness. It stopped growing. Its current population of 300,000 is about the same as it was in about 1920.

A few decades later than Duluth's rise in population, the Russian city of Perm' underwent similar explosive growth. Objectively, it faced the same competitive disadvantages of cold and remoteness as Duluth did. But Perm' kept growing. The difference was that Perm's growth prospects remained entirely in the hands of central planners, while Duluth's were ultimately constrained by the market. As the figure shows, Perm's population did begin to slow and then plateau in the late 1970s, owing to a sheer lack of physical resources (including people) that could be moved there. Since the late 1980s, it has even declined slightly. But it remains larger than Duluth (in fact, larger than the entire Duluth–Superior, Wisconsin, metropolitan area) by a factor of four. Perm', it would seem, might be at least a partial zombie.

In the second approach, we imagined what the sizes of Russia's largest cities would have been if the urban population had been distributed relatively as it was before the Bolshevik Revolution of 1917. At that time Russia's population was concentrated in the European part of the country. Soviet policy moved people from European Russia to the Urals and Siberian regions of the country. (In our simulation of a counterfactual "virtual" history, the Siberian and Urals cities were not prohibited from growing. It was merely assumed that they would continue to grow at the same pace as they had before the advent of communist planning.) Table 7 shows the results for a few large cities. According to this calculation, these cities' current populations are two to four times larger than their desired populations. It is interesting to note how consistent this picture is with what Lant Pritchett finds for the United States (see the section on ghost regions in the United States). He labels as "legitimate ghosts" hundreds of counties or groups of contiguous counties whose populations shrank substantially between 1930 and 1990. If these ghosts had been constrained to grow at the rate of natural increase without free outmigration, they too, like the Russian cities, would have ended up about three times bigger than their "unconstrained, desired level."

Table 7. Selected Large Russian Cities in the Urals and Siberian Regions: Actual versus Desired Population
Thousands

City	Actual (1997)	"Desired"
Novosibirsk	1,397	?a
Yekaterinburg	1,321	406
Omsk	1,181	351
Ufa	1,088	520
Chelyabinsk	1,110	< 250
Perm'	1,035	433
Krasnoyarsk	874	271

Source: *Naselenie Rossii za 100 let (1897–1997)* [Population of Russia: 1897–1997]. Moscow: State Committee of the Russian Federation on Statistics (1998).

a. Because Novosibirsk, in contrast to the other cities in the table, had not yet emerged as a city before the Russian Revolution, it had no historical trajectory on which to base an estimate of desired population.

The third approach was to simulate a desired population distribution for the country as a whole. To create this benchmark, we used a comparison with Canada, a country also big in territory and endowed with natural resources. The idea was to take Canada as a proxy for a market economy and apply the Canadian dynamics to Russian regional characteristics and initial (1910) conditions. That is, we drew an economic map of a hypothetical Russia with Canadian-style development instead of central planning—asking, in effect, what would have happened if Russians had behaved like Canadians?

The simulation showed that Siberia and the far eastern regions of Russia have excess populations of from 10 million to 15 million people. Again, this suggests that there are towns, cities, and entire regions in Russia that are, if not potential ghosts, at least potential dwarfs relative to their historical size. They should be considerably smaller than they are.

Are they then zombies? Perhaps not, and here is where we may need to extend Lant Pritchett's terminology. Remember that zombies are the living dead, with low wages and incomes. At least some of the Russian cities illustrate another case, in which cities that by all rights ought to be zombies are kept alive by artificial means. Especially in the recent period, Russia has been awash in oil and gas rents that have allowed extensive subsidization of much economic activity that otherwise would not be justified. Large parts of the populations of the cities I have discussed survive by that activity. In sum, the Russian case is an illustration of what can happen when, on the one hand, policies prevent cities from becoming ghosts, while, on the other hand, society can afford costly policies that also prevent them from developing into full-fledged zombies. The infusions of value from the outside through overt and hidden subsidies prevent the cities from degenerating entirely into a zombie state. The potential zombies are being given blood transfusions. The infusions give the zombies more of a rosy color. They do not, however, give them true life.

Simon Johnson: Lant Pritchett has consistently produced thought-provoking papers that break new ground and prompt a great deal of further investigation. My own current favorite is "Where Has All the Education Gone?" a paper from the mid-1990s with first-order implications for both the recent push towards greater aid for developing countries and the current debate on the relative importance of human capital for growth.[1] But any list of high-impact papers in development and growth economics must include his "Divergence, Big Time" and "Growth Accelerations" and should also mention his work on growth patterns, health, volatility, and much more.[2]

Lant's work is characterized by big thoughts that are carefully documented and laid out clearly and provocatively. "Boom Towns and Ghost Countries" is no exception. The paper does nothing less than prompt readers to rethink how the modern era of economic development differs from the past and what this may imply for the future.

Thinking along the lines proposed by Lant, the movement of people around the world over the past 10 millennia or longer can be thought of as a kind of musical chairs—for most of this time, people moved in pursuit of new opportunities, in the form of either newly available resources or a more productively organized society. They moved in when there was a boom and out when local prospects faded (or it got too crowded). They did not, of course, always move quickly, and many of the moves were not without conflict, but there was a great deal of movement (in the modern era this was within Europe, to the New World and other "settler colonies," and in many other directions; in ancient times recall, for example, the large movements of peoples around the Mediterranean basin; there were many big migrations in between).[3] To some extent technology and ideas moved across countries, but people also moved across borders in large numbers.

In contrast, since 1945 or so, as Lant points out, people can no longer move to the same degree. Certainly there continue to be migrations, into some European countries and into the United States, for example. But these movements are on a much-reduced scale compared with the past, and they are also asymmetric—it is much easier to move into boom areas than it is to move out

---

1. Pritchett (2001).

2. Pritchett (1997); Hausmann, Pritchett, and Rodrik (2005).

3. I am referring here only to voluntary migrations, although there was often an element of "push" to these migrations from people or places that became hostile. There have also been significant forced migrations, often involving some form of slavery; it is hoped that these will never recur.

of bust areas.[4] And, perhaps most important, migrations out of small and poor countries are now quite difficult.

Lant's analogy to ghost towns, taken to its logical but not unreasonable extreme, leads in the following direction. If a single mining town was a separate country and attracted a great deal of labor while the mining resource was viable, then when the mine becomes unviable, there is a big problem. Either wages have to decline or there will be a great deal of unemployment, or both. This is a provocative but productive way to think about some of the problems in relatively poor countries today, from Haiti (whose economy was previously based on sugar) to parts of West Africa (where commodity booms come and go.)

Of course, if people cannot migrate out, there may be a couple of other outcomes (other than indefinite economic depression). First, the inhabitants of the area may find something else to do, unrelated to mining. Perhaps they have skills that are useful for other activities, or perhaps they can attract other kinds of investment. Second, if the organization of this mining society is a problem for new investment (for example, only a few people have all the accumulated wealth), the inhabitants can change the rules or even the allocation of resources in such a way as to favor faster growth.

The major risk hinted at by Lant but not perhaps fully explored is that the economic depression leads not to a rational pro-growth response but rather to deadlock and conflict. Perhaps the people with coercive power (the former mine owners) continue to live quite well from their rentier incomes and can block any redistribution. The former mine workers may either remain quiescent (and poor), or they may rebel. If they rebel, this could lead to a long-term conflict or to a situation in which the old oligarchy is replaced by a new oligarchy that also does not favor pro-growth rules.

Unfortunately, it is often the case that institutions (that is, the rules) do not adapt quickly to what would be a more efficient arrangement when resources or opportunities in a society shift. The consistent failure of many former sugar colonies to adapt, even over a century, to much lower real sugar prices offers many sobering experiences.

Or, perhaps to think more positively, we should ask questions such as, Why has Barbados managed to achieve a much higher level of income than Guyana, despite the fact that both have a strong heritage of sugar, slavery and other forms of forced labor, and deep ethnic divisions?[5]

4. In contrast, consider the emigrations from Europe in the nineteenth century. Lant rightly emphasizes the migration out of Ireland; there were also major migrations from other regions that were not doing well, including parts of Scandinavia and Italy.

5. In an IMF working paper, Michael Da Costa (2006, forthcoming) provides an interesting discussion of exactly this divergence within the Caribbean.

Lant is surely right that the scale and types of permissible migration have changed over the past 100 years, mostly in ways that do not help poor people in poor countries. But this does not necessarily mean that declines in commodity prices bring dire consequences. Almost all the great successes of the past fifty years (that is, rapid sustained growth, starting with weak or very weak institutions) were not based on commodity price booms but rather on figuring out how to better integrate into global manufacturing production chains.[6] Low wages are obviously not enough, but low wages are also not necessarily an obstacle to initiating a sustained growth process. If only we knew exactly how.

Discussion: The paper was applauded as extremely thought-provoking by many of the participants. Ralph Bryant began by suggesting a way to push the analysis further in a direction that complemented points made by the two discussants. He stressed that to build the type of general equilibrium, multiregional model that Pritchett suggested was necessary; the notion of geographic shocks—or more specifically, regional shocks—to labor demand would need to be more precise. He offered three examples to illustrate. There could be a worldwide shock to the relative price of a commodity which is important to the output of a region, such as copper in Zambia. There could be a harvest failure in a country where agricultural goods are very important. Finally, there could be a demographic shock, such as a sharp drop in life expectancy due to AIDS. He suggested that the effects of these shocks could be very different, including the effect on labor demand. Bryant noted that a general equilibrium model could get at these differences, but it would be important to distinguish between types of goods and to specify which kind of shock applied to each. He also pointed out that the elasticities of substitution between the different types of goods could have major effects on the results.

Lael Brainard noted that she was also seeking notions of equilibrium. She wondered whether the paper relied on a notion of equilibrium that was resource based or agglomeration based. The answer would influence whether one would ever expect to see the nonzero equilibrium that the paper was predicting. Her second question focused on opportunities related to moving across borders. Although it is easy to move across borders in sub-Saharan Africa, for example, there is little incentive to do so. The situation for China is quite different. The larger the disparities across borders, Brainard noted, the larger the migration flows. Finally, she asked whether out-migration caused changes in fertility trends in the sending countries.

6. Johnson, Subramanian, and Ostry (2006) find 12 to 13 such sustained accelerations, applying a method based on Hausmann, Pritchett, and Rodrik (2005); almost all of these were in East and Southeast Asia, and only one did not involve a significant increase in manufactured exports (Chile).

Carol Graham began by asking Lant if he had read the Dr. Seuss classic, *The Lorax*. His description of ghost towns is exactly like the story therein, where some greedy individuals come in, build a "sneed" factory, manufacture at a furious pace until all of the resources are depleted, and leave a ghost town that is empty and polluted. While a sad story for children, it provides a wonderful analogy for the paper.

Graham's comment was on differentials in labor mobility across regions and within countries. This is highlighted in table 2 of the paper, which shows much lower labor mobility within Europe than in the United States. Graham noted that Americans and Europeans have very different norms about moving, which might explain at least some of the differences. In terms of population dispersion across U.S. cities, she noted that the trends may be driven by factors other than jobs. For example, research by Richard Florida on the creative class finds that certain cities become very attractive to live in after they attract a critical mass of people, because of other features, such as arts and entertainment.

Robert Blecker queried the nature of the shocks in the paper. Although they were characterized as shocks to labor demand, the discussion made them sound more like shocks to demand for output, whether region specific or commodity specific. It is not just labor in North Dakota that has less demand but also land in North Dakota, and that is why capital does not move in—even though capital is clearly mobile in the United States.

A second, bigger question is whether these shocks are simply random, or are they systemic that affect individual countries differently. For example, could the greater openness to trade and capital flows over the past few decades of "globalization" be a source of such shocks to many countries? Countries that are better disposed are the lucky ones that get agglomeration effects and increasing returns, such as East Asian countries. Others, such as Bolivia or Malawi, end up as zombies. One way to test this would be to break the long historical period (1930–90) into shorter time periods, such as the post–war boom, which was a time of relatively closed economies after World War II and then the period of more open markets, trading systems, and capital markets since the 1970s. Are the magnitudes of the shocks different across these time periods?

Andrew Warner asked Pritchett if there was an analogy with agricultural transitions. The major migration in economic development in all countries occurs as they transition from agriculture to industry. Migration also typically plays a big part in raising incomes in rural areas. He provided the example of Mongolia, where there is a great deal of herding. But given the parameters of herding, there is no more than $70 million of GDP to be earned in the countryside. Average income in Mongolia will always be that number divided by the number of people, unless a lot of people move out of agriculture. In Taiwan, rural incomes quadrupled during a span of 50 years, but primarily because people left rice farming, not because rice farming became more efficient.

Zsolt Nyiri offered a perspective from the viewpoint of Hungary and the Central European University. He noted that people might leave their country just to work in western Europe, where the economic situation was better, but they still prefer their home geographic area. They send money back there and plan to return. He asked whether they are keeping zombie areas alive or whether this case is in a different category.

Carmen Pagés noted that it is easier for people in countries that speak English to migrate to the United States than it is for those in non-English-speaking countries. This is particularly relevant for jobs in sectors such as health care. Thus she suggested that the research might look across sectors within countries.

Susan Collins pointed out that Pritchett's data implied that with more cross-country migration we would see less variation in living standards. Presumably that would be more desirable from a broader perspective on living standards. If the paper is really attempting to look at variance in living standards across countries, she suggested that it may be more informative to focus on levels of per capita income or wages instead of on growth rates. In this context, she referred to her work with Barry Bosworth, in which they have used growth accounting to examine performances of 84 economies from 1960 to 2004. They found that only about 30 percent of the variation in 2004 income levels was associated with the variation in the growth rates since 1960. Much more of the variation had to do with differences in initial levels. If what you really care about is current living standards, then focusing on growth may be misleading. To illustrate her point, she noted that many of the countries with rapid growth in Lant Pritchett's time period were in East Asia. But in the 1950s, countries like Korea were basket cases. It is not necessarily the case that lots of migration into those countries, and in turn possibly slowing their growth rates, would have been a good thing. Thus a greater focus on income levels rather than on rates would be valuable in this context.

Gary Burtless suggested that the residents of the Heartland, Texaklahoma, and the Great Plains North (the Dakotas) are lucky in terms of their per capita incomes by virtue of the fact that their neighbors can migrate out of the region. He noted, however, that the interesting question for policy in rich countries was whether residents in the rest of the United States were made worse off because they allowed free migration off the prairies.

References

Acemoglu, Daron, Simon Johnson, and James A. Robinson. 2001. "The Colonial Origins of Comparative Development: An Empirical Investigation." *American Economic Review* 91, no. 5: 1369–401.

Alesina, Alberto, and Enrico Spolaore. 2003. *The Size of Nations.* MIT Press.

Alesina, Alberto, Enrico Spolaore, and Romain Warcziag. 2005. "Trade, Growth and the Size of Countries." In the *Handbook of Economic Growth*, vol. 1B, edited by Philippe Aghion and Steven N. Durlauf, chapter 23, pp. 1499–1542. Amsterdam: North Holland.

Auty, Richard M., ed. 2001. *Resource Abundance and Economic Development.* Oxford University Press.

Barro, Robert J., and Xavier Sala-i-Martin. 1997. "Technological Diffusion, Convergence, and Growth." *Journal of Economic Growth* 2, no. 1: 1–26.

Blanchard, Olivier J., and Lawrence Katz. 1992. "Regional Evolutions." *Brookings Papers on Economic Activity* 1: 1–61.

Braun, Matías, Ricardo Hausmann, and Lant Pritchett. 2002. "*Dis*integration and the Proliferation of Sovereigns: Are There Lessons for Integration?" Working Paper. Harvard University Center for International Development. Also, in *Integrating the Americas: FTAA and Beyond,* edited by Antoni Estevadeordal, Dani Rodrik, Alan M. Taylor, and Andrés Velasco, chapter 4 as "Proliferation of Sovereigns: Are There Lessons for Integration?" Harvard University Press (2004).

Da Costa, Michael. 2006 (forthcoming). "Colonial Origins, Institutions, and Economic Performance in the Caribbean: The Case of Barbados and Guyana." IMF staff working paper. Washington: International Monetary Fund.

Easterly, William, and Ross Levine. 2001. "It's Not Factor Accumulation: Stylized Facts and Growth Models." *World Bank Economic Review* 15, no. 2: 177–219.

Fujita, Masahisa; Paul Krugman, and Anthony Venables. 1999. *The Spatial Economy: Cities, Regions, and International Trade.* MIT Press.

Glaeser, Edward L., and Janet E. Kohlhase. 2003. "Cities, Regions, and the Decline of Transport Costs." NBER Working Paper w9886. Cambridge, Mass: National Bureau of Economic Research.

Glaeser, Edward L., and Joseph Gyourko. 2005. "Urban Decline and Durable Housing." *Journal of Political Economy* 113, no. 2: 345–75

Glaeser, Edward L., Rafael La Porta, Florencion Lopez-de-Silano, Andrei Shliefer. 2004. "Do Institutions Cause Growth?" NBER Working Paper 10568. Cambridge, Mass.: National Bureau of Economic Research.

Hatton, Timothy J., and Jeffrey G. Williamson. 1998. *The Age of Mass Migration— Causes and Economic Impact.* Oxford University Press.

———. 2006. *Global Migration and the World Economy.* MIT Press.

Hausmann, Ricardo, Lant Pritchett, and Dani Rodrik. 2005. "Growth Accelerations." *Journal of Economic Growth* 10, no. 4 (December): 303–29.

Helpman, Elhanan, and Paul Krugman. 1987. *Market Structure and Foreign Trade: Increasing Returns, Imperfect Competition, and the International Economy.* MIT Press.

Heston, Alan, Robert Summers, and Bettina Aten. 2002. Penn World Table version 6.0. Center for International Comparisons at the University of Pennsylvania (CICUP) (October).

Hill, Fiona, and Clifford G. Gaddy. 2003. *The Siberian Curse.* Brookings.

Isham, Jonathan, Lant Pritchett, Michael Woolcock, and Gwen Busby. 2003. "The Varieties of the Resource Experience: How Natural Resource Export Structures Affect the Political Economy of Economic Growth." Middlebury College Working Paper Series 0308. Middlebury, Vt: Middlebury College, Department of Economics.

Johnson, Simon, Arvind Subramanian, and Jonathan Ostry. 2006. "The Prospects for Sustained Growth in Africa: Benchmarking the Constraints." Working Paper. Washington: International Monetary Fund; and Boston: MIT, paper prepared for the NBER Africa meeting, April 2006.

Jones, Charles I. 2005. "Growth and Ideas." In the *Handbook of Economic Growth*, vol. 1B, edited by Phillippe Aghion and Steven N. Durlauf, chapter 16, pp. 1063–111. Amsterdam: North Holland.

Krugman, Paul. 1991a. *Geography and Trade.* MIT Press.

———. 1991b. "Increasing Returns and Economic Geography." *Journal of Political Economy* 99, no. 3: 483–99.

———. 1998. "The Role of Geography in Development." Paper prepared for the Annual World Bank Conference on Development Economics, Washington, D.C., April 20–21.

Krugman, Paul, and Anthony J. Venables. 1995. "The Seamless World: A Spatial Model of International Specialization." NBER Working Paper 5220. Cambridge, Mass: National Bureau of Economic Research.

Mellinger, Andrew D., Jeffrey D. Sachs, and John L. Gallup. 1999. "Climate, Water Navigability, and Economic Development." CID Working Paper 24. Harvard University Center for International Development (September).

Neary, J. Peter, and Kevin W. S. Roberts. 1980. "The Theory of Household Behaviour under Rationing." *European Economic Review* 13, no. 1: 25–42.

O'Rourke, Kevin H., and Jeffrey G. Williamson. 2001. *Globalization and History: The Evolution of a Nineteenth-Century Atlantic Economy.* MIT Press.

Pritchett, Lant. 1997. "Divergence, Big Time." *Journal of Economic Perspectives* 11, no. 3 (Summer): 3–17.

———. 2001. "Where Has All the Education Gone?" *World Bank Economic Review* 15, no. 3: 367–91.

———. 2006. *Let Their People Come: Breaking the Gridlock on International Labor Mobility.* Washington: Center for Global Development.

Rodrik, Dani, Arvind Subramanian, and Francesco Trebbi. 2002. "Institutions Rule: The Primacy of Institutions over Geography and Integration in Economic Development." CEPR Discussion Paper 3643. London: Centre for Economic Policy Research (November).

Romer, Paul M. 1986. "Increasing Returns and Long-Run Growth." *Journal of Political Economy* 94, no.5: 1002–37.

Sachs, Jeffrey D., and Andrew M. Warner. 2001. "The Curse of Natural Resources." *European Economic Review* 45, nos. 4–6: 827–38.

Sala-i-Martin, Xavier. 2002. "The Disturbing 'Rise' of World Income Inequality." NBER Working Paper 8904. Cambridge, Mass: National Bureau of Economic Research.

Sokoloff, Kenneth, and Stanley L Engerman. 1994. "Factor Endowments: Institutions and Differential Paths of Growth among New World Economies: A View from Economic Historians of the United States." NBER Working Paper h0066. Cambridge, Mass: National Bureau of Economic Research.

———. 2002. "Factor Endowments, Inequality, and Paths of Development among New World Economics." NBER Working Paper w9259. Cambridge, Mass: National Bureau of Economic Research.

———. 2003. "Institutional and Non-Institutional Explanations of Economic Differences." NBER Working Paper w9989. Cambridge, Mass: National Bureau of Economic Research.

World Bank. 2005. *Economic Growth in 1990s: Lessons from a Decade of Reforms.* Washington.

———. 2006. *World Development Indicators.* Washington.

MARK R. ROSENZWEIG
Yale University

Global Wage Differences and International Student Flows

There has been a long-standing interest in the flows of persons across countries and in particular the international flow of skilled migrants. There are two major components in the literature on international migration, each of which is concerned with the skill composition of international migrants. One strand of literature focuses on the impact of immigration on the receiving-country economy. Because the impact of immigration depends on the skill composition of immigrants, understanding the determinants of the skills of new immigrants is an important element of this research program. Most of the analyses of the determinants of the magnitudes and skill composition of U.S. immigrants use data on the foreign born from the U.S. Census Bureau.[1] However, this literature has two major shortcomings. First, Census data do not provide information on entry visas. The U.S. immigration system selects immigrants according to a wide variety of criteria, including mainly family relationships to U.S. citizens. And some foreign born are temporary migrants or migrants without a legal basis for staying or working in the United States. This heterogeneity in selection criteria and the constraints on immigration associated with ceilings on country and visa categories are not typically taken into account in the analyses, and thus little is known about immigrants who are selected by skill. Recently available survey-based data on legal immigrants, moreover, indicate that there are substantial educational differences across immigrants chosen by different criteria.[2]

The second shortcoming of the literature focusing on U.S. immigration is that the analytical framework used is based on a model originally designed to

Support for this work was in part provided by NICHD grant HD33843. I am grateful to Sarah Cattan for able research assistance.

1. Borjas' study (1987) was the first major systematic study of the determinants of immigration to the United States, and his methodology has been followed by many others, including, for example, Cobb-Clark (1993).

2. Jasso and others (2000).

Figure 1. Annual Number of Foreign Student Visas Issued, by Receiving Country, 2003 and 2004

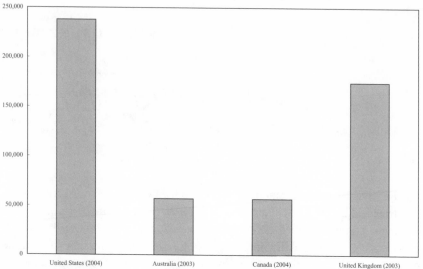

Sources: United States: *Report of the Visa Office 2004*, Table XVII (Part I) Nonimmigrant Visas Issued Fiscal Year 2004 (Washington: U.S. Department of State, Bureau of Consular Affairs, Visa Office); Australia: *Australian Student Visa Statistics—An Analysis: January–December 2003*, Sydney: IDP Education Australia; Canada: *Facts and Figures: Immigration Overview, Permanent and Temporary Residents 2004* (Ottawa, Ontario: Citizenship and Immigration Canada); United Kingdom: *International Migration: Migrants Entering or Leaving the United Kingdom and England and Wales, 2004* (London: Office for National Statistics, Migration Statistics Unit).

analyze the choice of occupations by workers of different skill levels in a domestic economy in which there are no differences in the rewards to skill.[3] The framework is thus not well suited for studying international migration in a world in which there are large differences in earnings for workers of the same skill. In addition, given the importance of family connections, job networks, and constraints on the number of immigrant visas, standard economic models of self-selection have not been wholly successful in providing empirical evidence on worker migration based on data on immigrant flows or the U.S. stocks of foreign born.[4]

A second strand of literature is concerned about the impact of skilled migration from the perspective of sending countries. Many of the earlier contributions to this literature, focusing on the outflow of workers and using the rubric "brain drain," were mostly theoretical.[5] However, in recent studies global information on the stocks of foreign born by education in developed countries has been

3. The model is that of Roy (1951).
4. Even illegal immigrants make use of informal job networks (Munshi 2003), which are not captured in the principal models used to study U.S. immigration.
5. For example, Bhagwati and Hamada (1974).

assembled to quantify the magnitude of the outflow of skilled migrants.[6] And the recent analytical literature has taken a somewhat more nuanced view of the phenomenon.[7] This newer literature, however, has underappreciated how much of the training of individuals born in poor countries occurs in rich countries. Just four receiving countries of international students—the United States, Australia, Canada, and Britain—are currently admitting more than 525,000 students a year. And, as indicated in figure 1, the United States accounts for close to half of this flow.[8]

The flow of foreign students admitted to the United States is considerably larger than the two other skill-based flows of immigrants and nonimmigrants to the United States. In contrast to the more than 240,000 foreign born who were admitted to the United States in 2004 as formal students coming to augment their skills, only 73,212 permanent immigrants who qualified for an employment visa on the basis of their skills were admitted.[9] And only 65,000 foreign workers were admitted as temporary migrants in 2004 on the basis of their skill qualifications within the H1B category.[10] Even if half of the students from abroad remain in the United States (and the fraction is considerably less), it is clear that the U.S. immigration system on net *seeks* to attract fewer skilled immigrants than the number of international skilled workers it trains.

Another long-standing literature has also been concerned with the low level of skills in low-income countries. This literature suggests that the level of education is low in such countries because of the lack of access to schools and points to high within-country estimates of "rates of return" in such countries as indicating underinvestment. Recent studies by World Bank economists provide these estimates for many countries of the world, suggesting that in countries such as Botswana the return to an investment in college education is as high as

---

6. Docquier and Marfouk (2006).

7. For example, Commander, Kangasniemi, and Winters (2004).

8. The U.S. annual visa count understates the flow of foreign students to the United States because citizens of Canada who study in the United States are not required to obtain a visa. This understatement is nontrivial, since in 2006 almost 9 percent of the stock of 635,443 U.S. foreign-born students are from Canada (SEVIS). Of course, there are many other countries that train large numbers of foreign students, including France and Germany.

9. This is the number of principal applicants in the third-, fourth-, and fifth-preference categories, of which 82,118 persons were admitted because they were the spouse or children of the immigrants screened for a skill. These family members were not themselves subject to employment criteria. Office of Immigration Statistics (2006).

10. H1B nonimmigrants, who in general must have a college degree, are admitted for a three-year period to work for a specific employer in a specialty occupation. The visa may be renewed for a subsequent three years, after which the worker must leave the United States for at least one year. This category also includes a small number of fashion models.

38 percent.[11] Although this literature ignores the outflow of skilled workers and students, the large flows of persons seeking to acquire schooling in developed countries could be interpreted as evidence supporting the idea that a shortage of training opportunities exists within low-income countries—the lack of schooling capacity in low-income countries induces the demand for training abroad.

Whether students come to high-income countries to acquire skills they could not otherwise acquire at home or come because high-skill employment is under-rewarded at home is not obvious, however. There has been little analysis of the determinants of the flows of international students. Borjas's recent polemic about the U.S. system of admitting students, while informative about the basic facts, does not contain any analysis of the demand for U.S. student visas.[12] Bratsberg examines the determinants of the "return" rates of foreign students to their home country.[13] However, that analysis uses the same analytical framework employed by Borjas and others to study the determinants of immigration and, moreover, uses data on cross-border flows (admittances) of persons with visas reported by the Immigration and Naturalization Service (now titled U.S. Citizenship and Immigration Services [USCIS]) rather than the appropriate information on student visas issued by the Department of State.[14] The former records border crossings by students, the latter counts students. The differences in these numbers in a given year are enormous—in 2004 there were 620,210 foreign born admitted with student visas, although only 237,791 students were given visas by the State Department in that year.[15] Because the discrepancy in the two numbers reflects the decisions by the students to visit their home, which may differ substantially across countries, the estimates in Bratsberg's study do not identify the determinants of the permanent return rates of students.

As noted, the literature examining the flows of immigrants has not developed self-selection models that take into account the legal constraints on immigrants. However, there are neither country-specific nor total ceilings pertaining to the admission of nonimmigrant students to the United States. There are just two main criteria—ability to pay and admission to a certified educational program, of which there are thousands. And although admission to a college of choice may be difficult, admission to some U.S. institutions of higher education, for those with money, is not difficult. Little or no screening is con-

11. See Psacharopoulos (1994); Psacharopoulos and Patrinos (2002).
12. Borjas (2002).
13. Bratsberg (1995).
14. Borjas (1987).
15. Office of Immigration Statistics (2006), table 23; Bureau of Consular Affairs (2004), table XVII.

ducted by the Department of Homeland Security (DHS) or the State Department (other than for criminal records or membership in terrorist organizations), and it is not necessary to have family ties to the United States to obtain a U.S. student visa. International student flows thus are substantially more likely than are immigrant flows to be accounted for by behavioral models emphasizing economic costs and returns.

In this paper I exploit administrative records and new data from the New Immigrant Survey (NIS) to examine empirically the determinants of the flow of students to the United States, the stock of U.S. foreign-born students, and the number of U.S. foreign-born students who become U.S. permanent immigrants (*student stayers*). In particular, I test competing models that might underlie the observed migration of students seeking training in high-income countries—a model of high schooling costs (schooling shortages) in low-income countries and a model of migration by workers seeking higher-paying skill jobs. Application of both models requires knowledge of how skills are rewarded in countries. I show that the two models have opposite predictions with respect to how the domestic price of a skill affects the outflow of students, as do investments in home-based university facilities. Information on the per capita GDP of potential sending countries, used in prior studies of the determinants of immigration, is thus insufficient, although not irrelevant, to the application of the models.[16] Therefore, a significant part of the paper is concerned with the estimation of worldwide, country-specific "skill prices." To carry out this analysis two data sources are used: information on the home-country wages of immigrants to the United States, from the NIS Pilot, and information on wages within occupations and industries across countries, from the Occupational Wages around the World (OWW) database.

Section one of the paper sets out the two models of student outflows. The *constrained domestic schooling model* implies that foreign students will predominantly come from countries with high rewards for skills (high skill prices) and low opportunities to acquire schooling domestically, so that investment in schools in sending countries will reduce the number of students studying in high-income countries. In contrast, the *migration model of international student flows* implies that students will acquire schooling abroad when skill prices at home are low and that increasing capacity for domestic schooling in such countries will increase student outflows. Both models imply, however, that for given skill prices increases in per capita GDP increase outflows. In section two, the methods for estimating country-specific skill prices are described and the determinants of the skill-price estimates from the two data sources, which

16. See Borjas (1987); Jasso and Rosenzweig (1990).

appear to be similar, are presented and compared. Section three presents the estimates of the determinants of the demand for U.S. visas, the stock of U.S. foreign students, and the number of students who stay on as permanent immigrants using the NIS- and OWW-based skill-price estimates.

The econometric results for all three measures of U.S. foreign students and for both measures of skill prices clearly reject the worldwide school shortage model. The numbers of students who come to the United States and who stay are higher when home-country rewards for skill are low, and as a result of increased university capacity in such countries, student out-migration rises. Moreover, consistent with the migration model in which students seek to acquire skills in high-skill-price countries to obtain higher-paying jobs in those countries, the effect of increasing the number of home-country universities on the outflow of students is attenuated the higher the domestic skill price is. The results thus suggest that from a global perspective the domestic rate of return estimates by country are misleading indicators of where schooling investments have high payoffs. The estimates suggest, for example, that investment in university capacity in Botswana, which evidently has a high rate of return domestically, would have a substantially lower domestic payoff than would such investment in Gabon. The patterns of the international flows of students reflect not underinvestment in school capacity in low-income countries but low payoffs to skill. Nevertheless, it would appear that, on net, high-income countries attracting large numbers of foreign students make a net contribution to the human capital stock of the sending countries, given the high fraction of students who do return and the total number of permanent, skilled immigrants admitted, some of whom also return.[17]

Modeling International Student Outflows

In this section two simple models are presented that are aimed at highlighting the important factors affecting the flow of students from low- to high-income countries and that can exploit available data. I assume a world economy in which there is a continuum of skills and in which workers acquire different levels of skills. Most important, rewards to skills (skill prices) differ across countries, because of country-specific conditions and imperfect factor mobility. Initially skills may also be imperfectly transferable across countries.

In each country j a worker i who has acquired x_i skill units earns a wage given by the following equation:

17. Jasso and Rosenzweig (1990).

Figure 2. Constrained Domestic School Supply Model

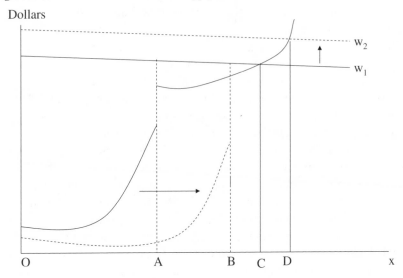

(1)
$$W_{ij} = \omega_j x_i,$$

where ω_j is the skill price in country j. Thus, variation in the average wages of workers across countries is due to intercountry differences in average skill levels and differences in the value of skills—given by skill prices ω_j. How many skill units a worker acquires depends on the skill price, the costs of acquiring the skill, and the worker's available resources to finance skill acquisition.

Constrained Domestic Schooling Model

I first assume that workers are always employed in their home country but may acquire schooling anywhere. The relevant skill price is thus the home-country skill price ω_j. Figure 2 illustrates a simple model in which the total amount of skill units in the economy X is determined at the point at which the marginal cost of adding one more skill unit just equals the marginal cost of doing so. The two solid curved lines represent the marginal cost of adding skill units: the leftward curve represents the cost curve for schooling at home, the top curve (next over) for schooling abroad. So I have assumed that adding skill units domestically at the extensive margin costs more than schooling abroad. The solid horizontal line labeled W_1 is the home-country skill price (which can diminish as aggregate skill increases in the domestic economy). In this case, some workers obtain their schooling abroad—the home-country skill price is high enough to justify expensive schooling, which cannot be satisfied at lower cost at home. In particular, O–A units are produced at home and A–C skill units are obtained abroad.

In this model an increase in the supply (reduction in the cost) of domestic schooling, given by the rightward shift in the domestic schooling cost curve, with no change in the skill price, always reduces the number of skill units produced outside the country: O–B units are now produced at home and B–C units go abroad, with A–C > B–C. Domestic schooling and foreign schooling are substitutes. Note that as long as the marginal cost of schooling domestically is less than that of skill acquisition abroad (the home-country schooling supply increase is inframarginal) for a sufficiently high domestic skill price, the total number of skill units does not increase when domestic school costs are lowered. However, a rise in the domestic skill price given the initial schooling cost functions increases the total number of skill units acquired, all of which occurs outside the country—the number of skill units obtained abroad rises from the initial A–C to A–D and total skill units from O–C to O–D. Thus increases in the domestic supply of schools lower the amount of schooling acquired abroad, while increases in the marginal value of skills in the home country increase foreign schooling.

Migration Model

We now examine a framework in which schooling acquired outside the home country reflects the demand for jobs in higher skill price environments. The expected initial earnings that worker i could earn in destination country u is given by the equation

$$(2) \qquad pW_{iu} = \omega_u x_i^{\delta iu},$$

where ω_u is the destination-country skill price and δ_{iu} $(0 \le \delta_{iu} \le 1)$ reflects the initial degree of transferability of worker i's skills to the destination country's labor market, and p is the probability of obtaining a permanent destination-country job. A worker of given skill earns a different wage in his or her origin country and initially in the destination country for two reasons: the skill price differs across the two countries, and the worker's own skill may not be fully transferable. A worker's skills may be incompletely transferable upon arrival in the destination country, because of a lack of job contacts, lack of familiarity with the job market or work practices, or poor English skills. With full transferability $(\delta_{iu} = 1)$, the migrant can initially make use of all of his or her skill in the destination country. If the skill is initially completely nontransferable across the origin and destination countries ($\delta_{iu} = 0$), the migrant enters the destination labor market as if he or she had the lowest skill level ($x = 1$). Both the probability of obtaining a destination-country job and the level of skill transferability are in part the outcomes of worker investments.

Given direct costs C_j and time costs $(1 + \pi_j)W_{ij}$ of migrating from j to u, the economic gain from migrating from j to u, G_{ij}, for worker i is

$$(3) \qquad G_{ij} = x_i[p\omega_u x_i^{\delta i \, u - 1 - [\mathbf{w}]}(1 + \pi_j)] - C_j.$$

Equation (3) shows that for any level of direct migration costs C_j the gains from immigrating, given a positive expected destination-origin skill price differential net of migration time costs $[\omega_u > \omega_j(1 + \pi_j)]$, are always higher for more-skilled workers and for workers for whom skill transferability is high.[18] Moreover, the gain from migrating associated with an additional unit of skill is lower the higher the home-country skill price is.

Workers choose the number of skill units and can also invest in the transferability of their skill and in augmenting the probability of obtaining a job abroad. If it is assumed that skill units are acquired at home, then in this framework lowering the costs of acquiring skill units in the home country and thus increasing x_{ij} raises the return to out-migration from j. Moreover, if augmenting skill transferability is less costly in the destination country than it is in the home country and obtaining training in the destination country increases the probability of obtaining a permanent job there, then workers with higher numbers of skill units will more likely migrate to the destination country, where they will invest in skill transferability and in facilitating a permanent job offer.[19] In this framework, in contrast to the constrained domestic schooling model, schooling taken abroad is for the purpose of acquiring a higher skill price for a skill (by migrating). And in contrast to that model, in which schooling abroad contributes to the home-country human capital stock, lowering the costs of domestic schooling increases the amount of schooling (additionally) acquired abroad—domestic schooling and foreign schooling are complements; increases in the home-country skill price reduce the number of workers acquiring schooling outside the country; and the number who leave the country as domestic schooling is increased is lower the higher the skill price of the country is.

---

18. Chiswick (2000) shows that, if higher skill also lowers direct migration costs, immigration will be more skill-intensive.

19. In the U.S. context, the ability to obtain a permanent place in the U.S. job market also depends on the ability to find a U.S. citizen spouse. This may also be facilitated by acquiring U.S. schooling.

Estimating World Skill Prices

The preceding framework implies that to assess the determinants of the movements of students and thus whether such movements reflect home-country school scarcity or international labor arbitrage requires information on schools by country as well as country-specific skill prices. However, country-specific skill prices are not directly observed.

Data

In prior studies of the determinants of immigration flows and student return rates based on the Roy model, the ratio of income accruing to the top 10 percent and bottom 20 percent of the population is used as a proxy for the skill price.[20] This ratio, however, also reflects skill differences and so confounds differences in rewards to skills across countries and skill distributions. Similarly, skill prices cannot be inferred from information on GDP per worker without concomitant information on the distribution of skills. To estimate the set of world skill prices that potentially affect the magnitude and composition of foreign student (immigrant) flows requires comparable information on wages across countries for workers of the same skill. Data from two sources are used. The first is the predecessor survey to the NIS, the New Immigrant Survey Pilot (NIS-P), which provides the home-country earnings for a sample of new U.S. legal immigrants. The sampling frame for the NIS-P consists of the 148,987 persons who were admitted to legal permanent residence during the months of July and August of 1996. The sample of immigrants was drawn from the administrative records of the Immigration and Naturalization Service (now USCIS), which provided information on the immigrant's age, type of visa, and country of origin, as well as the address provided by each immigrant to which his or her green card (the paper evidence of legal immigration status) was to be sent. This stratified random sample drawn from the USCIS records also oversampled migrants with employment visas and undersampled children and numbers 1,984 persons, of whom 1,839 were adult immigrants. Sample size for adult immigrants who provided complete information in the survey is 1,032.[21]

Of the sampled immigrants, 332 had worked in a foreign country in the ten years before the survey and provided earnings data for their last job in that country. These respondents provided information on worker earnings for fifty-four countries. Earnings in the last job abroad, provided by the immigrants in native currency units, were converted to dollar amounts using estimates of the country-specific purchasing power of the currencies from databases of the Cen-

20. See Borjas (1987); Cobb-Clark (1993); Bratsberg (1995).
21. Details on the survey are given in Jasso and others (2000).

ter for International Comparisons at the University of Pennsylvania (CICUP).[22] These conversion factors are explicitly designed to take into account differences in the cost of living across countries and to avoid the distortions associated with exchange rate regimes, thereby facilitating cross-country comparisons. The estimates of purchasing power parity (PPP) thus permit comparisons of origin-country earnings across U.S. immigrants who have worked in many different countries, and these origin-country earnings are comparable with their U.S. earnings, all of which are denominated in dollars of purchasing power. Using information on work time and pay periods to adjust for labor supply differences across workers, I converted all pay data to full-time earnings. The advantage of this data source is that earnings were elicited in a common survey frame and information was available on the number of years of schooling of the worker and on the gender and age of the worker. The disadvantage is that the immigrants are not a random sample of workers in the home country. Indeed, the migration model implies that the sampled workers will be positively selected with respect to unobservables. I will take this into account below.

The second source of information that can be used to estimate skill prices is the Occupational Wages around the World (OWW) database, compiled by Freeman and Oostendorp. This database provides monthly wage data for men for 161 occupations in more than 150 countries from 1983 to 2003 derived from the International Labor Organization (ILO) October Inquiry database. Presumably, within countries the data are representative of all workers, but not all countries are represented in all years, and fewer countries appear to have participated in more recent years. I selected 1995, which is a year with a peak number of countries and close in time to the NIS-P information on wages. In that year there are 4,924 observations representing 67 countries. I use monthly earnings from the series expressed in U.S. dollars based on exchange rates, as estimated by Freeman and Oostendorp.[23] Disadvantages of this data set are that the information across countries may not be comparable and information is not available on the schooling or age of workers. Table 1 presents descriptive statistics for both international samples of workers.

Identification and Prediction of Skill Prices

To use the NIS-P data to estimate country-specific skill prices we assume that a worker's level of skill depends on unobservable and observable components, μ and S (schooling), respectively, such that

22. Described in Summers and Heston (1991).
23. Freeman and Oostendorp (2005). Specifically, I use the wages computed by using exchange rate information and country-specific calibration with lexicographic imputation.

Table 1. Characteristics of Global Earnings Data Sets

Variable	NIS-P[a]	OWW[b]
Mean annual earnings in U.S. dollars	14,719[c]	10,208[d]
of respondents	(2,602)[e]	(13,289)
Mean age of respondents	34.6	n.a.
	(8.53)	
Mean years of schooling of respondents	14.4	n.a.
	(4.5)	
Number of industries	n.a.	49
Number of occupations	n.a.	161
Number of countries	54	67
Number of workers	332	4,924

Source: The New Immigrant Survey Pilot (NIS-P), predecessor survey to the NIS; the Occupational Wages around the World (OWW) database, compiled by Freeman and Oostendorp.
n.a. Not available.
a. Consists of persons admitted to legal permanent residence during the months of July and August of 1996. (See text for details.)
b. Monthly wage data for men for from 1983 to 2003; 1995 selected, which is a year with a peak number of countries and close in time to the NIS-P information on wages.
c. Adjusted for purchasing power parity (PPP).
d. Exchange-rate adjusted, country-specific calibration with lexicographic imputation.
e. Standard deviations in parentheses.

(4) $x_{ij} = \mu_{ij}\exp(\beta S_{ij})$.

Then the log of worker i's wage in country j, from equation 1, can be written as

(5) $\ln(W_{ij}) = \ln\omega_j + \beta S_{ij} + \ln\mu_{ij}$.

The intercepts, which are allowed to differ across countries, then provide the log of the skill price for the fifty-four countries in the data.

For the OWW data set, it is assumed that skill units are a nonparametric function of industry and occupation; that is,

(6) $x_{ij} = \mu_{ij}\exp(\mathbf{I}_{ijk}\gamma)$, so that

(7) $\ln(W_{ij}) = \ln\omega_j + \mathbf{I}_{ijk}\gamma_k + \ln\mu_{ij}$

where $\mathbf{I}_{ijk}$ is a vector of occupation and industry dummies for worker i in country j and γ_k is a vector of coefficients. Again, the country-specific set of intercepts provides the set of skill prices for sixty-seven countries.

Both of the data sets at most provide comparable information on skill prices for only sixty-seven countries. To predict skill prices for more countries, we can use information on aggregate country characteristics that are available for a large number of countries to estimate the proximate determinants of skill prices from the comparable wage microdata countries. One can then use those estimates to predict skill prices for countries without sampled workers. It is assumed that the skill price is the marginal value product of skill and that aggregate output Y_j in country j is produced according to Cobb-Douglas technology

(8) $$Y_j = AL_j^\alpha \Pi K_{nj}^{\gamma_k}$$

where K_{nj} is country j's stock of nonlabor resources (for example, land, capital, minerals) and L_j is the country's aggregate stock of labor in skill, given by

(9) $$L_j = N_j[a(x_{ij})],$$

where N_j is the total number of workers in j and $a()$ is an inverse function yielding the average skill units per worker in country j in terms of observables.

The skill price ω_j is the marginal product of an efficiency unit of labor, given by

(10) $$\omega_j = \alpha Y_j / N_j[a(x_{ij})]$$

so that

(11) $$\ln(\omega_j) = \ln\alpha + \ln(Y_j/N_j) - \ln(a(x_{ij}))$$

or, for individual worker data on wages,

(12) $$\ln(W_{ij}) = \ln\alpha + \ln(Y_j/N_j) - \ln(a(x_{ij})) + \beta S_{ij} + \ln\mu_{ij}.$$

Thus, the log of the skill price for any country j is just the log of the labor output coefficient (in skill units), plus the log of the output per worker in country j (with a coefficient of 1.0), minus the log of country j's average skill per worker. Equations 11 and 12 imply that among workers residing in countries with the same output per worker, those workers residing in countries in which workers have higher average skill levels are paid lower skill prices, while among workers in countries with the same average worker skill levels, those in countries with higher output per worker receive higher skill prices.

Estimating equations 11 or 12 to predict country skill prices requires economic information at the country level. However, although there is information on comparable measures of output per worker for all countries, the transform function $a(x_{ij})$ converting measured variables like schooling into aggregate skill units for the economy is not known and needs to be estimated. For the NIS-P sample of world workers I appended information on the characteristics of the immigrant's origin country using information on the last country of residence; for the OWW sample I used the worker's country of employment. To estimate skill prices in accordance with the model, I used the real (PPP-converted) GDP *per worker* estimates from the Penn World Table (PWT Mark 5.6) supplemented with updated 1995 estimates from the CICUP Penn World Table database.[24] I assume that in the transform function, $a()$, aggregate worker skills depend on

24. Summers and Heston (1991).

schooling years and schooling quality, and thus I assembled estimates of the average schooling levels of the population aged 25 and older and student-teacher ratios for primary and secondary schools.[25] Average schooling estimates are available for a large but not complete subset of countries for which there are PPP-GDP estimates. For those countries for which no information exists on estimates of schooling characteristics, I constructed a variable indicating that schooling was missing and set the schooling variable to zero.

In using the NIS-P sample of workers, one needs to take into account that immigrants are not randomly selected (rather they are self-selected) from the population of a country's workers. In particular, selection will be made on the unobservable component of skill, μ, such that among workers with the same schooling those workers from high-skill-price countries will have higher levels of unmeasured skills (positive selectivity on unobservables). The error term in equation 12 containing the unobservable component of worker earnings, μ, will be correlated with the determinants of the country skill price, leading to biased estimates. For example, it can be shown that because of immigrant selectivity the coefficient on GDP per worker will be greater than 1, that is, biased upwards. To obtain consistent estimates of equation 12 using the NIS-P sample requires that this selectivity be taken into account.

One remedy is to use the standard selection-correction model.[26] This requires obtaining estimates of the probability that a worker is observed in the sample, which in this case is the probability that a worker in a sending country migrates to the receiving country, then computing the relevant Mills ratio, λ, for each immigrant, and including it among the regressors in equation 12. In the second immigration-based model of student flows, the probability of sample inclusion (immigration) depends on the determinants of the home-country skill price and on factors affecting the costs of migration and the degree of cross-country skill transferability from equations 4 and 5. The latter two sets of variables do not directly affect the home-country skill price, and thus the selection model is identified.

To carry out the selection-correction procedure for the NIS-P sample, country-specific information related to the costs of immigration and transferability were appended to the NIS-P data on workers. To characterize direct migration costs, the surface distance is obtained of every potential origin country's capital to the closest major entry city in the United States. Also information is obtained from the PWT 6.1 on GDP *per adult equivalent* to construct a proxy for the resources available to finance migration.[27] Finally, information on the

25. Barro and Lee (1993).
26. Heckman (1979).
27. Heston, Summers, and Aten (2002).

population of the origin countries in 1990 is appended, which represents the potential pool of immigrants.[28] The number of countries for which information is available on all of these variables is 125. Jasso and Rosenzweig estimated and reported a blocked probit regression incorporating all of the country-specific variables to estimate the determinants of the probability of migrating to the United States, using the population of the sending country as the population at risk of migration and the number of U.S. immigrants in the NIS-P sample as the dependent variable.[29] These estimates of the determinants of migration were used to correct biases in the skill-price estimates due to immigrant self-selection that are reported below.

Skill-Price Estimates

The columns one and two (left and center) of table 2 report the estimates of the skill-price determinants based on the home-country wages of the sample of U.S. immigrants from equation 12. The first specification omits the Mills ratio, λ, from the probit selection (immigration) estimates, which were not reported, while the second includes it as a regressor. The sets of country and individual worker characteristics explain 35 percent of the total variation in home-country wages among the immigrants, and all coefficients but that for the gender variable (gender coefficient not reported in table 2) are statistically significant. The sign patterns for per worker GDP and for schooling, moreover, conform to the model—wages are higher for workers of given education and age in countries with greater output per worker and given average country skill levels, and worker wages are lower among countries with the same output per worker but with higher average schooling levels. The point estimate in column one for per worker GDP is above 1, consistent with positive selectivity. And, indeed, the coefficient on the Mills ratio coefficient based on the probit selection equation λ in column two is positive. Inclusion of the Mills ratio moreover lowers the coefficient on per worker GDP such that the hypothesis that the coefficient is 1 as indicated by equation 11 cannot be rejected.

One can assess how well the estimates from the NIS-P sample do in predicting skill prices using the "out-of-sample" skill prices obtained from the OWW sample of workers estimated from equation 11. First, one can use the estimates from column 2 (middle column) of table 2 to predict skill prices for all countries with the requisite (and more available) aggregate data and then examine the association between the predicted skill prices and the skill prices

28. A more refined analysis would use the population of persons in the age group 25–59, corresponding to the age group of the migrants. This would require accurate information on the population age structure for all countries.

29. Jasso and Rosenzweig (2004).

Table 2. Estimates of the Determinants of the Country Log Skill Price

Sample Variable	U.S. immigrant home-country wages GLS	GLS with selection correction	OWW wages GLS
Country characteristics			
Log GDP per worker	1.41	1.35	1.10
	(5.01)[a]*	(5.21)*	(10.4)*
Log mean schooling	−1.77	−1.97	−0.330
	(3.18)*	(3.23)*	(1.47)
Log of students per teacher,	−1.90	−2.17	−0.509
primary schools	(3.68)*	(3.80)*	(1.83)
Log of students per teacher,	1.44	1.36	0.457
secondary schools	(2.51)*	(2.56)*	(1.60)
Immigrant skill characteristics			
Schooling	0.0683	0.0745	. . .
	(3.50)*	(3.79)*	
Age	0.0428	0.0436	. . .
	(4.32)*	(4.50)*	
Summary statistic	. . .	0.800	. . .
λ	(1.46)		
Constant	−1.02	0.713	−3.75
(2.10)*	(2.04)*	(2.60)*	
Number of countries	54	54	67
Number of immigrants	332	332	4, 924
F (d.f.,d.f.)	17.02 (10,53)	25.33 (11,53)	46.0 (7,51)
R^2	0.35	0.36	0.82

Source: Author's calculations.
. . . Not applicable.
*Coefficient statistically significant at least at the 5 percent level.
GLS = generalized least-squares regression.
a. Absolute value of t statistics corrected for clustering at the country level are in parentheses.

obtained for the common set of sixty-seven countries represented in the OWW worker data. The country-specific determinants of skill prices obtained from the OWW sample can also be estimated, using equation 7, and then those estimates can be compared with those obtained for the NIS-P worker sample.

Figure 3 displays the scatterplot between the NIS-P–based predicted skill prices and the OWW skill prices estimated from equation 7 from the sample of OWW wages for the sixty-seven OWW countries; the correlation between the predicted NIS-P–based estimates and those skill prices obtained (not predicted) from the OWW is 0.78. The third (far right) column of table 2 reports estimates of the country-specific determinants of the OWW skill prices, which are to be used to predict the OWW skill prices for all countries, based on equation 11. The set of regressors explains 82 percent of the variation in skill prices across the sixty-seven countries. The coefficient on the log of per worker GDP is closer to 1 than that estimated from the immigrant sample, and one cannot reject the hypothesis that the coefficient is 1. The sign patterns are the same for

Figure 3. Relationship between Skill Price Estimates

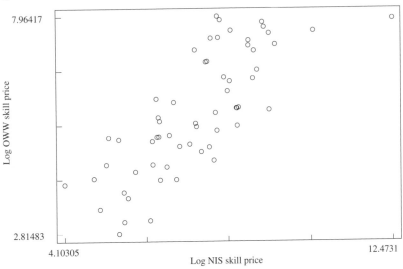

the OWW and the NIS-P data sets. In sum, these independently collected world-wide worker data appear to yield similar estimates of worldwide skill prices.

One advantage of the NIS-P sample of worldwide workers is that one gets an estimate of the average within-country return on schooling, β, which is evidently around 7 percent (columns one and two in table 2). The estimates of β and the country-specific skill prices can be used to illustrate that even if the within-country return to schooling is the same for all countries, the large inter-country differences in skill prices make the contribution of investments in schooling across countries highly unequal.[30] That is, investment in building schools in low-skill-price countries, while increasing earnings there, adds substantially less to global output than does investing in schooling in high-skill-price countries.

Figure 4 displays the annual PPP full-time earnings of high school and college graduates for seven selected countries—Nigeria, India, Indonesia, Mexico, Korea, and the United States. These figures are based on an identical 7 percent within-country return to schooling and the estimated country-specific skill prices based on the estimates from column 2 of table 2 for all but the United States.[31] For the United States, the 1990 Census Public Use sample is used to

---

30. The restriction that the contribution of schooling to skill units is the same across countries is necessitated by the limitations of the data. With enough observations within each country, it is possible to estimate country-specific schooling returns, but not with 332 workers across 54 countries. The OWW data have no information on schooling.

31. The formula is the following: $W_j = \exp(\ln\omega_j + 0.07S_i)$, where $S_i = 12$ or 16.

Figure 4. Estimated Earnings of High School and College Graduates across Selected Countries[a]

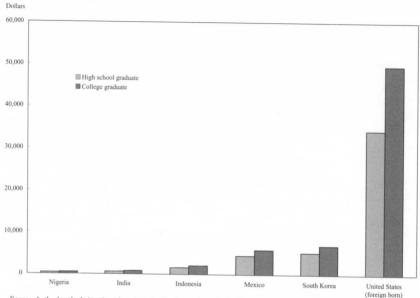

Dollars

Source: Author's calculations based on the estimates from column 2 of table 1.
a. Earnings are in 1996 dollars adjusted for purchasing power parity.

obtain the mean earnings of the foreign-born full-time workers. As can be seen, within each schooling level, earnings differences across countries are substantial—the estimated PPP earnings of high school graduates in Nigeria is $400 compared with $4,500 for Mexican high school graduates, which is in turn $30,000 lower than the earnings of U.S. foreign-born high school graduates. Relatedly, college graduates in Nigeria earn $121 more than high school graduates, while Mexican workers with a college education earn $1,392 more than Mexican high school graduates; in Indonesia, the difference is $490. Average schooling differences are clearly swamped by differences in the country-specific valuation of skills, in accounting for worldwide inequality, and in the gains from investing in schooling.

Estimating the Determinants of the Flows and Stocks of U.S. International Students

Data

With the (two) estimates of skill prices for 125 countries, one can examine how cross-country variation in skill prices and the quantity and quality of domestic schools influence the transnational flow of students to assess whether such flows reflect a shortage of schools in poor countries or skill-price arbitrage. There are now a number of different data sources describing the flows of foreign students to and stocks of foreign students in the United States. The State Department provides annually the number of new student (F-1) visas issued by country to those persons who are neither U.S. citizens nor permanent resident aliens. The average number of F-1 visas issued by country for 2003 and 2004 are used. One deficiency of these data is that Canadian citizens are not required to obtain a visa for study in the United States, so they are excluded from the visa counts. The citizens of all other countries are required to obtain some kind of student visa.[32]

A second source of information on U.S. foreign students is the Student and Exchange Visitor Information System (SEVIS), which provides information by country on the stocks of current foreign-born students. All foreign-born students with F-1 and other nonimmigrant visas and all Canadian citizens studying in the United States are required to register in the system. The current stocks (for 2006) of students in the United States by country are used from this data source. Relative to the visa flow data, students who have stayed in the United States longer are more heavily weighted in these data, and family members of students are not included.[33]

A third variable constructed is the annual flow of students who become permanent resident aliens (and thus can enter the U.S. labor market permanently), which is based on information from the New Immigrant Survey. The adult portion of the NIS sampled 4.3 percent of the 289,478 persons 18 and older who were admitted as permanent resident aliens, including principal applicants and accompanying spouses, in the seven-month period May through November 2003. The survey oversampled principal-applicant employment and diversity immigrants, and sampling weights need to be used to obtain representative statistics from the survey. The data provide a large array of information on these "new" immigrants, including a complete history of their prior trips to the United States and the documentation they had for each trip. From these histories it is possible to identify those new permanent resident aliens who had once held

32. Some students obtain an exchange visitor (J) visa. They are a small proportion of all U.S. foreign students. Some F-1 visas holders are immediate family members of foreign students. This number is also a small portion of F-1 visas.

33. Another source of data on the stocks of students is from the Institute of International Education (IIE). The research department of IIE surveys each spring and fall all accredited institutions of higher education in the United States (that number 2,700) on enrolled foreign students. Statistics from the survey are presented in the annual *Open Doors* report. The IIE claims that the response rate for the survey is "approximately 90 percent." In principle, all students are registered in SEVIS.

F-1 visas and thus were formerly U.S. foreign students. The weighted number of these former student immigrants is computed for all of the home countries of the immigrants. This variable, the number of permanent immigrants who were former students, effectively weights foreign students by their permanence.

The NIS data indicate that about 5 percent of permanent resident aliens were once foreign students in the United States. Assuming that the rate of adjustment is in a steady state, the NIS and nonimmigrant visa data from the State Department can also be used to obtain a rough estimate of the fraction of all foreign students who become permanent resident aliens, which is the ratio of the (survey-estimated) number of permanent resident aliens who once held F-1 visas to the total number of F-1 visas issued in a year. Taking the visa flows for 2003 reported by the State Department (and excluding Canada), I estimate that about 10 percent of foreign students become legal immigrants. This figure is surely an underestimate of the nonreturn rate—the appropriate construct is the cumulative number of persons from a given cohort of students who become permanent resident aliens. Information for one cohort of permanent resident aliens only is available. The estimate from the NIS is similar to the estimate of Bratsberg, 12.5 percent, who did cumulate the number of permanent immigrants who were once students by the year they obtained their student visa across many cohorts of new immigrants.[34] However, as noted, that estimate is based on the inflated USCIS (INS) visa admittance data and only counts those who immediately adjusted their status from student to immigrant, so it is likely to be too small, perhaps one-third the true number. Even these lower-bound estimates are substantially higher than the probability of winning a U.S. immigrant visa through the diversity lottery system, an alternative route to U.S. immigration for those without family connections in the United States. In fiscal year 2005, 6.3 million applications were received in response to the diversity immigrant visa program, from which 90,000 winners were chosen (1.4 percent).[35]

The NIS also provides, from the USCIS immigrant records, the immigrant visa of the respondents, which indicates by what route immigrants gained permanent resident status. Figure 5 reports the fraction of former students and nonstudents who became permanent immigrants by marrying a U.S. citizen, by getting a job (employment visa), by obtaining a visa through the diversity lottery, and by sponsorship by other family members. Not surprisingly, former

34. Bratsberg (1995).
35. The student adjustment rate is also higher than having a paper accepted in the *American Economic Review* or getting into Yale. Both institutions receive large numbers of submissions or applications.

Figure 5. Visa Categories of Admission to Permanent Residence Status for Prior U.S. Students and Nonstudents

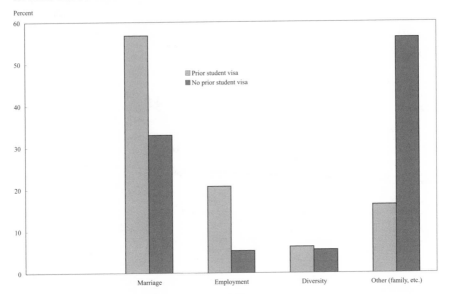

Sources: New Immigrant Survey; author's calculations.

U.S. foreign students were substantially more likely than were other immigrants to obtain a visa by getting a job offer or by marrying a U.S. citizen. While only 4 percent of those who never attended a U.S. institution of higher learning received an employment visa, more than 20 percent of former student immigrants did so. With respect to the marriage market, 32 percent of those who were never U.S. students (in the higher-education system) married a U.S. citizen, while 56 percent of former students obtained a green card through marriage.

Of course, students are of marriageable age and are thus likely to be married around the time and in the place they are students. To put this in additional perspective, however, one can compare the probability of marrying a U.S. citizen, and thus obtaining a green card, for a person who remains in his or her home country with that of a student from that country who attends an institution of higher learning in the United States. I will use India as an example. In 1999 an estimated 212,984,000 persons aged 15 to 24 resided in India.[36] In 2003 the State Department issued 20,300 student visas to persons from India.[37] The NIS data indicated that 321 persons from India married a U.S. citizen and

36. Office of the Registrar General, (1997).
37. Bureau of Consular Affairs (2003), table XVII.

Table 3. Top Ten Sending Countries of U.S. Foreign Students, by Measure[a]

Student visas issued, 2003–04[b]		Number of foreign students, 2006[c]		Number of student stayers, 2003–04[d]	
Country	Number	Country	Number	Country	Number
South Korea	34,697	South Korea	86,626	China	1,328
Japan	25,962	India	77,220	India	1,151
India	20,230	China	59,343	South Korea	893
China	19,251	Japan	54,816	Japan	697
Taiwan	12,071	Taiwan	36,091	Taiwan	682
Mexico	9,077	Canada	32,153	Mexico	534
Brazil	7,625	Mexico	14,863	Kenya	516
Turkey	5,592	Turkey	12,795	Canada	459
Germany	5,376	Thailand	10,940	Turkey	419
United Kingdom	5,076	Indonesia	8,610	Indonesia	353

Source: Department of State; Student and Exchange Visitor Information System (SEVIS); and New Immigrant Survey (NIS).
a. Measures of the stocks and flows of foreign students.
b. The State Department provides annually the number of new student (F-1) visas issued by country to persons who are neither U.S. citizens nor permanent resident aliens. Canadian citizens who become U.S. students are not required to obtain a U.S. visa. The average number of F-1 visas issued by country for 2003 and 2004 are used.
c. SEVIS provides information by country on the stocks of current foreign-born students. All foreign-born students with F-1 and other nonimmigrant visas and all Canadian citizens studying in the United States are required to register in the system.
d. NIS sampled persons 18 and older admitted as permanent resident aliens, including principal applicants and accompanying spouses, in the seven-month period May through November 2003.

received a green card in 2003, of whom 6 were former students.[38] This suggests that the probability of an Indian student in the United States marrying a U.S. citizen is almost 200 times that of a resident of India.[39] Clearly, being a U.S. student provides an advantage in the U.S. marriage and labor markets.

Table 3 reports the top ten sending countries of U.S. foreign students for each measure of the stocks and flows of foreign students. Interestingly, for all three measures of student outflows, the top five countries are all located in Asia. Moreover, they are countries with high growth rates, although not necessarily high skill prices (that is, China and India). They are also countries far from the United States, within which at least one university is ranked in the top 200. It is thus difficult to assess from these limited data the patterns underlying the determinants of the flows of international students. Thus I look at how cross-country variation in skill prices, domestic schooling costs, and migration costs jointly affect student migration using data for 125 countries.

In addition to obtaining information on U.S. foreign student flows and stocks by country, I obtained information characterizing the cost (supply) of domestic schooling and the determinants of the cost, C, of migrating. In particular, I added to the database the number of universities in each country and a variable

38. India has a substantially smaller fraction of immigrants who obtain a visa via marriage compared with other groups.
39. The rates are 0.000295 (6/20,320) and 0.00000148 [(321 − 6)/212,984,000].

indicating whether any of the country's universities were ranked in the top 200 of all universities in the world.[40] I assume that countries with more universities (per capita), with higher quality universities, and with smaller numbers of pupils per teacher deliver skill units at lower marginal cost. Thus all of these home-country variables will be negatively associated with the outflow of students to the United States if students are domestically oriented and will be positively associated if students are seeking to maximize earnings by exploiting international skill-price gaps.

Finally, I included two variables reflecting the direct costs of migration. The first is the surface distance from the capital of each country to the nearest port of entry for immigrants into the United States, which I assume to be positively correlated with migration costs. Distance also affects the cost of returning home, and so it may be a determinant of the number of students who stay. Bratsberg indeed found that distance to the home country affected positively his measure of the fraction of students who stay.[41] But because he used the number of admittances rather than the number of students in the denominator of his dependent variable, some of the variation across countries in permanent return rates reflects variation in the propensity of students to visit their homeland while students. Indeed, in the data, the ratio of the number of students crossing the U.S. border (admittances) to the number of students (persons) issued student visas in 2004 in that year is negatively and statistically significantly related to distance, indicating that migration costs affect temporary visits and not necessarily long-term commitments as interpreted by Bratsberg.

Financing education abroad is also costly. I added the sending country's GDP per adult equivalent to the database, which I assume is positively related to the average ability of individuals to finance migration. Thus, for given skill prices, a country with a higher GDP per adult equivalent would be expected to send more migrants. Thus, economic growth can increase out-migration, if it is not accompanied by sufficient increases in skill prices. This contrasts with prior analyses, which inadequately control for skill prices, and thus per capita GDP partly serves as a proxy for wages. Table 4 reports descriptive statistics for the 125 countries for which data on U.S. foreign students, skill price estimates, and school information are available.

Estimates

Tables 5 through 7 report the estimates for the three dependent variables measuring U.S. international student flows and stocks—demand for U.S. stu-

40. Data are from the *The Times Higher World University Rankings 2005*.
41. Bratsberg (1995).

Table 4. Characteristics of Cross-Country Data Set of 125 countries

Variable	Mean	Standard deviation
Number of U.S. student visas (F-1) issued in 2003–04, excluding Canada	1,687	4,668
Number of foreign-born students registered in SEVIS, 2006	4,562	1,2685
Number of prior students (F-1 visa holders) who became permanent resident aliens in 2003–04	168.6	349.1
Estimated country skill price based on NIS-P (annual PPP earnings, 1996 dollars)	2,799	4,027
Estimated country skill price based on OWW (annual earnings, 1995 dollars)	4,866.2	234
GDP per adult equivalent (PPP, 2000 dollars)	2,798.8	4,026.7
Total number of universities	40.4	73.8
Any universities ranked in the top 200 world universities	0.224	0.419
Students per teacher, primary schools	25.0	17.1
Students per teacher, secondary schools	14.9	10.5
Surface distance to nearest U.S. city of entry (miles)	4,964	2,197
Population in 2000 (000s)	40,076	138,847

Source: Author's calculations.

dent visas, stock of U.S. foreign students, and foreign students becoming permanent resident aliens, respectively—for two specifications, using alternatively the NIS-P–based skill-price estimates and the OWW skill prices. All variables are in logs. The first specification is linear in logs; the second specification adds an interaction term for the log skill price and the log number of universities to permit an assessment of whether the impact of increasing the domestic supply of schools on student out-migration is attenuated when the home-country skill price is high, as suggested by the schooling migration model.

The set of skill price and university stock coefficients in the noninteractive specification (columns I) are estimated with precision—five of the six skill price and five of the six university stock coefficients are statistically significant at the 5 percent level at least. Most important, for all three measures of the flows of foreign students, the sign patterns are consistent with the model of student migration for employment rather than with the model of schooling supply constraints in sending countries. In particular, the number of U.S. visas issued annually to students, the stock of U.S. foreign-born students, and the number of students who remain as U.S. permanent immigrants are higher for countries with low skill prices and for countries that have a larger number of universities per capita. The coefficients for the crude university quality measure are also all positive, consistent with the migration model, but none are statistically

Table 5. Determinants of the Demand for Log U.S. Student Visas, 2003–04[a]

	NIS-P skill-price estimates		OWW skill prices	
Country characteristics	I	II	I	II
Log of country skill price	–0.361	–0.234	–0.947	–0.883
	(2.42)[b]*	(1.32)	(2.41)*	(2.23)*
Log of GDP per adult equivalent	0.682	0.692	1.35	1.35
	(2.95)*	(3.00)*	(2.95)*	(2.96)*
Log of number of universities	0.218	0.768	0.266	0.435
	(1.90)	(2.28)*	(2.26)*	(1.60)
Log of number of universities x	. . .	–0.0796	. . .	–0.0328
log of country skill price		(1.86)		(0.67)
Any ranked universities	0.467	0.630	0.312	0.381
(top 200 worldwide)	(1.72)	(2.20)*	(1.10)	(1.36)
Log of students per teacher,	–0.377	–0.418	–0.240	–0.246
primary schools	(1.17)	(1.31)	(0.77)	(0.79)
Log of students per teacher,	0.783	0.770	0.659	0.628
secondary schools	(2.09)*	(2.03)*	(1.86)	(1.75)
Log of population	0.476	0.492	0.487	0.491
	(3.57)*	(3.60)*	(3.47)*	(3.44)*
Log of distance to nearest	–0.293	–0.289	–0.313	–0.315
U.S. city of entry	(1.98)*	(1.92)	(1.95)*	(1.94)
Constant	–0.801	–1.73	–4.04	–4.19
	(0.30)	(0.66)	(1.30)	(1.34)
Number of countries	125	125	125	124
R^2	0.733	0.741	0.729	0.730

Source: Author's calculations.
. . . Not applicable.
*Coefficient statistically significant at least at the 5 percent level.
(NIS-P) = New Immigrant Survey Pilot; Occupational Wages around the World (OWW) database.
a. The first specification is linear in logs; the second specification adds an interaction term for the log skill price and the log number of universities to permit an assessment of whether the impact of increasing the domestic supply of schools on student out-migration is attenuated when the home-country skill price is high, as suggested by the schooling migration model.
b. Absolute values of robust *t* ratios in parentheses.

significant in the noninteractive specifications.[42] Migration costs also evidently influence student flows and stocks—countries farther from the United States, for given skill price, per capita GDP, and schooling stocks, send significantly fewer students, while for given distance and the domestic price of skill, countries with higher per capita incomes send more students. All six distance coefficients and five of the six per capita GDP coefficients are statistically significant at the 5 percent level.

The point estimates (elasticities) for the skill price are large in absolute value, particularly for the estimates based on the OWW data. They suggest that on the one hand a doubling of the skill price (for example, raising India's skill price to that of Indonesia's) would lower the number of student visas by 36 percent using the NIS-P–based estimates (by 95 percent using the OWW skill

42. Two of the six coefficients are statistically significant in the interactive set.

Table 6. Determinants of the Log Stock of U.S. Foreign Students, 2006[a]

Country characteristics	NIS-P skill-price estimates		OWW skill prices	
	I	II	I	II
Log of country skill price	−0.342	−0.156	−0.829	−0.666
	(2.45)[b]*	(0.95)	(2.17)*	(1.72)
Log of GDP per adult equivalent	0.603	0.618	1.17	1.16
	(2.64)*	(2.72)*	(2.65)*	(2.69)*
Log of number of universities	0.308	1.12	0.354	0.808
	(2.46)*	(3.64)*	(2.75)*	(3.02)*
Log of number of universities x	...	−0.117	...	−0.0885
log of country skill price		(2.92)*		(1.76)
Any ranked universities	0.281	0.522	0.150	0.333
(top 200 worldwide)	(0.95)	(1.79)	(0.48)	(1.11)
Log of students per teacher,	−0.355	−0.426	−0.195	−0.222
primary schools	(1.04)	(1.31)	(0.59)	(0.68)
Log of students per teacher,	0.954	0.940	0.813	0.737
secondary schools	(2.35)*	(2.37)*	(2.09)*	(1.90)
Log of population	0.404	0.429	0.410	0.424
	(3.03)*	(3.13)*	(2.97)*	(2.95)*
Log of distance to nearest	−0.205	−0.207	−0.215	−0.229
U.S. city of entry	(2.71)*	(2.64)*	(2.68)*	(2.72)*
Constant	−0.133	−1.42	−3.03	−3.41
	(0.05)	(0.53)	(1.00)	(1.12)
Number of countries	125	125	125	125
R^2	0.695	0.713	0.690	0.698

Source: Author's calculations.
... Not applicable.
*Coefficient statistically significant at least at the 5 percent level.
(NIS-P) = New Immigrant Survey Pilot; Occupational Wages around the World (OWW) database.
a. The first specification is linear in logs; the second specification adds an interaction term for the log skill price and the log number of universities to permit an assessment of whether the impact of increasing the domestic supply of schools on student out-migration is attenuated when the home-country skill price is high, as suggested by the schooling migration model.
b. Absolute values of robust t ratios in parentheses.

prices), the stock of foreign students by 34 and 83 percent, and the number of student stayers by 13 and 75 percent, respectively. On the other hand, doubling per adult equivalent GDP, without any change in the skill price, would increase student out-migration—by 68 percent (135 percent), 60 percent (117 percent), and 12 percent (79 percent), respectively, for the three student outflow measures. The estimates also suggest that doubling the number of universities in a country on average would also increase the number of students obtaining U.S. visas, the number of students from that country studying in the U.S., and the number of students from that country who become immigrants by 24 percent, 33 percent, and 18 percent, respectively.[43]

43. The university stock coefficients are similar whether the NIS-P estimates or OWW skill prices are used; the estimated percentages are based on averages of the university number coefficients across each of the two estimates for each dependent variable.

Table 7. Determinants of the Log Number of Prior Students Who Became Permanent Resident Aliens, 2003–04[a]

Country characteristics	NIS-P skill-price estimates		OWW skill prices	
	I	II	I	II
Log of country skill price	−0.133	−0.0392	−0.751	−0.588
	(1.48)[b]	(0.47)	(2.56)*	(2.03)*
Log of GDP per adult equivalent	0.121	0.135	0.792	0.782
	(0.91)	(1.07)	(2.58)*	(2.53)*
Log of number of universities	0.164	0.916	0.191	0.644
	(2.00)*	(4.56)*	(2.35)*	(3.14)*
Log of number of universities x	...	−0.109	...	−0.0884
log of country skill price		(3.85)*		(2.22)*
Any ranked universities	0.407	0.631	0.248	0.0556
(top 200 worldwide)	(1.54)	(2.45)*	(0.89)	(0.20)
Log of students per teacher,	0.179	0.113	0.0825	0.190
primary schools	(0.61)	(0.40)	(0.29)	(0.65)
Log of students per teacher,	0.190	0.178	0.265	0.628
secondary schools	(0.64)	(0.62)	(0.93)	(1.75)
Log of population	.182	.206	.194	.209
	(2.05)*	(2.54)*	(2.20)*	(2.41)*
Log of distance to nearest	−0.108	−0.111	−0.117	−0.131
U.S. city of entry	(2.59)*	(2.58)*	(3.04)*	(3.20)*
Constant	−1.96	−3.16	−4.52	−4.89
	(1.10)	(1.96)*	(2.43)*	(2.57)*
Number of countries	125	125	125	125
R^2	0.456	0.500	0.479	0.501

Source: Author's calculations.
. . . Not applicable.
*Coefficient statistically significant at least at the 5 percent level.
(NIS-P) = New Immigrant Survey Pilot; Occupational Wages around the World (OWW) database.
a. The first specification is linear in logs; the second specification adds an interaction term for the log skill price and the log number of universities to permit an assessment of whether the impact of increasing the domestic supply of schools on student out-migration is attenuated when the home-country skill price is high, as suggested by the schooling migration model.
b. Absolute values of robust *t* ratios in parentheses.

The interactive specification (columns II), consistent with the migration model, suggests that the effects of increasing the number of universities on student outflows is not the same across countries, however, with the out-migration of students declining as the magnitude of the skill price increases, particularly with respect to the number of students who stay in the United States. Three of the six interactive coefficients are statistically significant at the 5 percent level, two of those for the student stayer measure. Figure 6 displays the percentage increase in the number of U.S. student stayers when doubling the number of domestic universities for Nigeria, India, Indonesia, Mexico, and Korea based on the NIS-P and OWW estimates. As can be seen, the student brain drain from a country that results from investing in domestic university capacity depends importantly on how skills are valued domestically. Thus doubling university

Figure 6. Estimated Percentage Increase in the Number of U.S. Student Stayers when Doubling the Number of Home-Country Universities, by Selected Countries

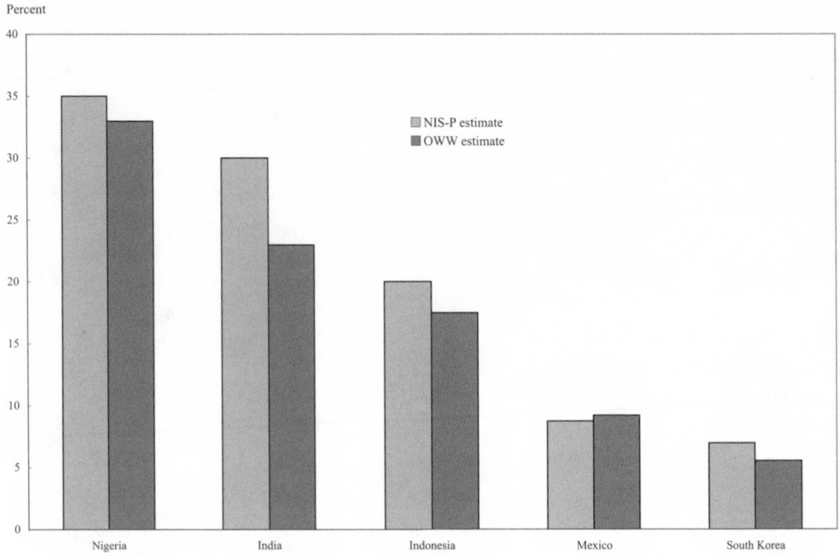

Percent

Source: Author's calculations based on the estimates from columns II of table 7.

capacity in Nigeria evidently would result in a 33 to 35 percent increase in the permanent outflow of students, while Korea, which has 13 (NIS-P) to 23 (OWW) times the skill price of Nigeria, would lose only from 5.5 to 6.9 percent more student stayers.

The interactive estimates also can be used to identify which (high-skill-price) countries would lose little human capital as a result of university expansion— for which there would be no net increase in student outflows from increasing the number of universities. The set of countries outside the OECD evidently consists of Malaysia, Tunisia, Gabon, Hong Kong, Kuwait, Singapore, Iran, Bahrain, Taiwan, Qatar, Oman, and Saudi Arabia. Relaxing the constraint to less than 5 percent brain drain adds Mauritius, Lebanon, Estonia, Latvia, Botswana, Turkey, Egypt, Greece, Belize, Algeria, and Uruguay to the list of countries in which, from a global perspective, investment in higher education would appear to have high payoffs that principally benefit the population of the country.

Conclusion

International migration by persons to acquire schooling appears to be the least regulated and restricted among migration flows and makes up a substantial fraction of the international movement of skilled persons. In this paper I have used a variety of recently available data sources to explore the relationship among the flow of foreign students to and the temporary and permanent stocks of foreign students in the United States and the global distribution of the prices of skill and the level and quality of schools. The patterns in the merged data appear to be consistent with a model in which students from low-wage countries seek schooling in high-wage countries as a means of augmenting their chances of obtaining a high-wage job in those countries, and they are inconsistent with the view that the large flows of international students reflect constraints on opportunities for schooling in low-wage countries. In particular, higher skill prices in home countries are negatively associated with student outflows, while given skill prices, greater domestic investment in skills is positively associated with greater student out-migration. Higher home-country income and smaller distances between high- and low-wage countries are also associated with more student outflows to high wage countries.

Although the interpretation of the relationship between domestic schooling and migration in the model is that increased schooling capacity at home augments the returns to migration, given skill-price gaps, it is not necessarily the case that the school stock–outflow association is causal. It is possible that the stock of schools in a country reflects demand factors. However, the fact that the positive association between student outflows and the domestic stocks of schooling is strongly attenuated the higher the home-country skill price is again not supportive of the view that there is too little domestic investment in schools. In any case, the key determinant of student migration is the gap in skill rewards across developed and underdeveloped countries. The results thus strongly suggest the need to understand better the fundamental determinants of global wage disparities to determine the optimal distribution of additional investments in schooling across countries given an increasingly global labor market. No doubt this means attention to trade policy, governance, traditional and historical institutions, legal structures, and geography, which have been the focus of development economists.

It is also clear that improved data on the wages of workers by skill group comparable across a large set of countries are needed to better understand even the proximate causes of student migration or any component of international migration. Relaxing the assumption of the model here, for example, that there is one homogeneous skill, would require more detailed and comparable information on schooling and other determinants of skill as well as on wages across workers of the world. Also, much better data are needed that delineate the quality of schooling across countries. It would also be interesting to assess the importance of networking in student flows, using information on prior stocks of students. Investigation of this factor, however, would require multiple years of information on country characteristics and student flows and attention to the fact that lagged student stocks are endogenous.

Finally, the finding that student migration principally reflects wage arbitrage in the face of massive world differentials in rewards to skills, and not schooling constraints, does not necessarily imply that the more open policy of high-wage countries to foreign students is to the detriment of the sending countries. The data suggest that only a small fraction of students become immigrants in the host country, although current estimates likely overstate the number who eventually leave the United States. An appropriate analysis of the determinants of return rates of students needs to be carried out.[44] This would require information across many cohorts of foreign students and immigrants, with information on the latter similar to that in the NIS. However, information on the number of students who adjust to permanent resident status is insufficient to gauge the impact of student migration on sending and receiving countries, as even permanent immigrants are not permanent. In the NIS data on new U.S. immigrants ("permanent" resident aliens), 17 percent of those who were formerly foreign students in the United States (the student stayers analyzed here) indicated that they were not going to stay in the United States "the rest of their life."[45] Those returnees will presumably contribute to the development of their home countries, though their contributions will be greater in those places in which the marginal product of skill is high.

---

44. Students who do not remain in the United States do not necessarily return to their home country.

45. This proportion is more than 50 percent higher than that for new immigrants who were not students.

Comments
and Discussion

Douglas A. Irwin: This paper focuses on an important and interesting issue: the flow of students from developing countries to the developed world. As the author notes, many highly educated workers in developing countries received their training in OECD countries. In addition, student migration is one of the largest and most unregulated categories of immigrant flows into the United States and other Western countries. Thus, there are a host of questions that can be raised about this migration and its impact.

The paper sets up a horse race between two competing models of student migration: the *school-constrained* model and the *migration* model. The school-constrained model suggests that foreign students come from countries with high returns to education but with few domestic opportunities to invest in human capital. In this case, students seek training in the United States and elsewhere with the ultimate goal of returning to their home country and reaping the rewards of the high return to education. The migration model suggests that students will acquire schooling abroad as means of entering and staying in the foreign country when the returns to education are low in their home country. In this case, students are simply escaping the low wages at home in search of higher incomes.

The main difference between the two models is the relationship between student migration and the domestic returns to education. If the returns to education increase in the student's home country, more students will seek education abroad in the school-constrained model, but fewer students will seek education abroad in the migration model.

The two models also have different implications for educational policy in the home country. In the school-constrained model, an increase in the quantity and quality of home education institutions will reduce the number of students who seek education abroad. In the migration model, an increase in schooling

87

opportunities will complement outward student flows, and may increase student outflows.

Looking at U.S. data, Rosenzweig finds strong evidence that students come to the United States and stay when the return to education is low in their home country. In other words, according to the author, there is overwhelming evidence for the migration model. Part of the reason, the author suggests, is that student migrants are motivated not by the return to education in their home country, but the huge gaps in wage levels (regardless of skill level) between OECD and developing countries. In contrast, even if the local returns to education are significant, the gross wage differentials between developed and developing countries are simply enormous.

The author should be commended for setting up a simple framework in which to think about and evaluate the question of student migration. But, at least to this outsider to the field of labor economics, there are some reasons for skepticism about drawing strong conclusions from the results.

First, the paper notes that the apparent stay rate of students (that is, the proportion of students who stay in the United States and do not return to their home country) is low, at about 10 percent, although the author suggests that this is an underestimate because of imperfect measures of visa adjustments, among other reasons. That is close to what was found by Bratsberg who focused exclusively on the stay rate of students and found it to be about 12 percent in the early 1970s.[1] He argued that this number was also improperly measured and was much too low, perhaps being just a third of the true figure. Granting the many difficulties of estimating the true stay rate, and even granting that the stay rate may be as high as 30 percent (something one would certainly like to know with greater certainty), the question remains: If students are largely motivated by the huge wage gaps between countries, as the paper contends, why do only a third stay in the United States? Furthermore, why would foreign students undertake the effort to get an education in the United States if, at a minimum, two-thirds of them will return to their home country? Is this high return rate (low stay rate) planned or unplanned? The stay rate seems relatively low if the migration model is really the most accurate depiction of what is going on.

Furthermore, Bratsberg found a great deal of variation across countries of origin in the propensity of students to remain in the United States. While a large percentage of Asian and African students who came to the United States to study in the early 1970s stayed in the country, very few students from the Americas did. Bratsberg reports that the overall visa adjustment rate of students differed widely across regions, ranging from 8 percent from Europe, 25 per-

1. Bratsberg (1995).

cent from Asia and Africa, and 3 percent from the Americas.[2] Even if the level of these figures is flawed in some way, this disparity is quite interesting.

Given that the economic characteristics of the country of origin, such as mean earnings and the return to education, are similar across many countries in these regions, perhaps some other omitted variables explain why the stay rate from the Americas was low and (relatively) high from Asia. At any rate, the question remains an interesting one: How much do the economic characteristics explain the return rates, or do specific country effects dominate them?

Second, the paper finds empirical support for the migration model through the cross section. I would speculate that time series evidence might give more support to the school-constrained model. For example, if one thinks about the demand from South Korea for schooling in the United States over time, the broad story seems inconsistent with the migration model. When the return to education was low in South Korea in the 1950s and 1960s, few Koreans came to the United States to receive higher education. In the 1970s and 1980s, when the return to skills was higher, more Koreans sought training in the United States. (In addition, higher incomes made this possible, so income effects on the demand for schooling may be important as well.) The rewards to having a higher degree in engineering in South Korea were much greater in the 1970s and 1980s than they were in previous decades. Hence, across time, the higher return to skills in South Korea was associated with a higher demand for foreign education, because domestic schooling opportunities were considered insufficient or inadequate.

For this reason, I would speculate that we may not be able to close the book on the school-constrained model just yet. In addition, I would caution against the implication of the student migration model that developing countries should not invest more in schooling just because it would promote a greater student outflow. The precise effect may depend upon whether investments are made in primary or secondary education. And even if greater schooling investment promoted greater student outflows, there are many other societal (as well as economic) reasons to promote education in developing countries.

Thus an agenda for future research would be to investigate these issues using a panel approach—combining the cross section with time series evidence. The ultimate goal of such an exercise would be to say something about a topic lurking behind the issues raised in the paper, namely, the brain drain and whether or not it poses a problem for developing countries.

2. Bratsberg (1995, table 1).

Jeffrey G. Williamson: This is an excellent paper, executed with the usual empirical care that we have come to expect from Mark Rosenzweig. Furthermore, it speaks to a very important policy issue: Is the flow of students from low-income to high-income countries significantly affected by low schooling capacity in the sending countries? If so, would not investment in Third World schooling lower brain drain? These are old questions, but only recently have economists started to offer persuasive answers to them. Rosenzweig's paper adds significantly to that literature.

The paper begins with two facts that are sometimes obscured in the debate about the brain drain. First, two to three times as many foreign students are admitted to the United States today than are those already-schooled foreign born who are admitted on the basis of their skills. It follows that the brain drain debate would be better served if researchers spent more time understanding the migration of foreign students. Second, it is much easier for potential immigrants to get permanent skilled jobs in the United States as students than in any other way, by a ratio of 5:1 to 7:1. It follows that U.S. immigration policy acts as if it favors training students from abroad rather than importing foreigners already skilled. These two facts also apply to those high-income OECD (Organization for Economic Cooperation and Development) countries competing with the United States for foreign students. However, the United States gets just less than half of the flow. It makes sense, therefore, to start the analysis with the United States.

The paper emerges with two very important findings. First, student migration is correlated with skill-wage gaps. That is, Third World economies with low skill wages compared with the U.S. economy send more of their young adults to get schooling in the United States, ceteris paribus. Real-income differentials between high- and low-wage economies have, of course, been key determinants of global migration since its inception two centuries ago.[1] But in this case, the elasticities are very large. Second, more and better schools at home are correlated with more student emigration, not less, ceteris paribus, where the ceteris paribus that matters most is low skill wages at home. This is a powerful finding, which might suggest that investment in the quantity and quality of educational institutions in poor countries will serve to push more students abroad, rather than to retain more at home. However, it is wise to stress that both findings speak to *correlations* only. As shall be shown below, Rosenzweig and others need to work harder at establishing *causation*.

I see three potential flaws in this paper that might influence these inferences, if not to offset the sign on impact, at least to reduce the magnitudes. I have

1. Hatton and Williamson (2005), chapters 4 and 11.

already suggested problems of causality, which I will return to below. In addition, I think there are serious problems of *selectivity* that Rosenzweig has not been able to deal with fully. Finally, Rosenzweig's migration analysis is much too parsimonious, and *omitted variables* may be driving some of his results. Let me take each of these in turn.

The author alerts us to selectivity problems throughout the paper, but I think he has missed the most important possibility. "Good" students go to "good" schools in host countries *and* at home. Although the author controls for average schooling quality at home, it is the quality and number of good schools that matter, not the average. Any academic reading these lines will know just how selective this process is. Third World students in our classes come from rich and middle-class families, not from poor families; and they come from the big cities, not from small towns and villages. Teacher-student ratios (especially when they are adjusted for teacher absentee rates) and teacher qualifications vary enormously across educational institutions in the Third World, and the rich families make sure that their children get to the good schools. My guess is that the students from rich and middle-class families in Third World countries with a shortfall in the number and quality of schools still have access to very good schools from which the best emigrants are selected. Somehow Rosenzweig must find a way to deal with this serious problem of selectivity before one can be confident about the correlations he presents.

Any discussant can always make the critical argument that bias exists in the empirical results because of an omitted variable, but I think the argument may be especially relevant in this case. Tables 5, 6, and 7 have most of the standard explanatory variables researchers have come to expect in any empirical analysis of global migration: the wage differential, distance between host and sending country, population size, GDP per adult in the sending country, and the measures of schooling in the sending country. Although population size is not the biggest problem with Rosenzweig's regression model, future work should try replacing this variable with the share of the university-aged population. The Third World has been undergoing a spectacular demographic transition that has profoundly influenced the size of the youth cohort.[2] This, in turn, has had an equally profound impact on the population at risk (the young adult share) and thus on emigration. If this share is bigger for late-comer countries, skill-wage differentials and GDP per adult may be doing the work of demography in Rosenzweig's regressions. But my more serious concern is about another omitted variable: where is the "famous friends and relatives" effect in the Rosenzweig regressions? As the author points out, long-distance migration is

2. Bloom and Williamson (1998).

an expensive affair, and ever since 1820, friends and family in the host country have been a key source of funds to help finance the move and to help with job search and assimilation. Are today's foreign students from such rich families that they have no need for this kind of help? Rosenzweig assumes as much, but future work needs to supply an explicit test of this hypothesis. Evidence exists documenting foreign-born (FB) stocks of previous immigrants in the United States, and these FB stocks vary inversely with distance and with source country poverty. (That is, while long-distance migration is constrained by the cost of the move, it is even more sharply constrained by poverty traps at home.) My guess is that the addition of FB stocks to the regressions will dramatically change the results in tables 5 to 7.

Finally, what about causality? Table 2 reports that more and better schools at home (except for teacher-pupil ratios at secondary schools) are correlated with low skill wages at home. Why? Is it because a supply glut of skilled workers lowers the skill wage at home? Or is it because an immigration option dominates (for example, skill-wage convergence)? Tables 5 to 7 report that more and better schools at home are associated with more students abroad. Is this because more and better schools lower the cost of migration, as Rosenzweig argues? Or does the emigration serve to encourage schooling demand by the next cohort? This latter possibility is now being explored in the brain drain–brain gain literature, and Rosenzweig could have made a greater effort to reconcile his results with that literature. As an economic historian, I also encourage Rosenzweig to read about a similar debate that took place at the turn of the last century during the age of free mass migration. Europe underwent a schooling revolution in the few decades before the United States passed the allegedly restrictive Literacy Act in 1917. Did the surge in overseas emigration contribute to the demand for primary education in Europe, or was it exogenous to that emigration? Some economic historians think it was endogenous.[3]

Rosenzweig only deals with the immediate present and thus misses four great opportunities to deal with the past and the future.

First, when did foreign students start arriving in big numbers at Australian, Canadian, British, and American universities? Was the surge driven by the sharply rising skill premium in the United States and the rest of the OECD countries after about 1970? Did the schooling revolution in the Third World add fuel to the fire? Did the surge in student migration ease off after the 1990s when the skill premia peaked in the OECD sphere? Recent historical time series would offer a way to confirm or deny Rosenzweig's conclusions based, as they are, only on contemporary cross sections.

3. Hatton and Williamson (2005), chapters 8 and 9.

Second, how will student migration flows play out over the next few decades? Will the spread of industrial revolutions abroad keep future potential skilled immigrants in schools at home? It did not have that impact on total emigrations in the past: a country's mass emigration has always obeyed a life cycle, rising from low levels as development takes place, then peaking, before falling to low levels again.[4] Is the emigrant life cycle irrelevant for the skilled?[5] Will the demographic transition create a skilled migration bust as the young-adult share falls in the Third World?[6]

Third, how do host countries compete for students, and what difference does it make for Rosenzweig's conclusions? Shouldn't his conclusions be influenced by who pays for schooling at home and in the host country?

Fourth and finally, if opportunities in OECD countries increase skilled immigration from poor countries, why does this paper not allow it to reduce the skilled wage gap? Why does it not allow the emigration to increase skill scarcity at home? This paper cannot speak to this point since it adopts a partial equilibrium approach and ignores labor market impact: skilled wages are determined exogenously, and the student migrations are not allowed to have an impact on the cost of skills at home. This was not true during the great mass migrations before 1913, when European emigration helped contribute to wage convergence in the Atlantic economy. Why would we expect things to be different in the twenty-first century?

Discussion: A number of participants stressed that they found this paper particularly interesting and informative. Given the lack of attention to cross-border flows of students, the work was seen as an important contribution to existing literature on migration. The paper generated a very active discussion.

Some participants wondered how well the empirical analysis was able to control for differences in educational quality. In particular, John McHale asked about the distinction between the roles of home-country education quantity and education quality. The paper assumes that limited school quantity will drive up the price of skill. But in his view, limited school quantity often goes hand in hand with limited school quality, which presumably would also lower the price of skill. Students may be migrating because of the low educational quality at home, rather than to gain access to higher skill prices in rich-country labor markets. Thus inability to fully control for school quality would lead to an

4. Hatton and Williamson (2005), chapter 4; Williamson (2006).
5. The reader should note the absence of such nonlinearities on the cost variables in tables 5, 6, and 7.
6. To repeat, there are no such demographic variables in tables 5, 6, and 7.

identification problem, making it difficult to distinguish between alternative theories.

Carol Graham asked whether the results might be driven by what happens for the larger, wealthier developing countries that are sending large numbers of student migrants to the United States. Her concern was that this group may behave differently from the much smaller group of students from small, relatively poor source countries. Also she did not find it surprising that those migrants who entered as students are more likely to get married than are other migrant groups. She saw this finding likely to be a reflection of the fact that student migrants are in a school setting and typically young and are thus more likely to find a mate.

Some participants agreed with Irwin that the estimate of only 10 percent of student migrants to the United States end up staying seems very low. Gary Burtless noted the much higher 50 percent figure in recent reports by the National Science Foundation (NSF). He also wondered whether data from the decennial censuses could be used to gather additional information since these contain information about country of origin, year of entry and school attainment. However, Rosenzweig pointed out that NSF data include a select group primarily of students who are unlikely to be representative of all student migrants, half of whom are undergraduates. He also stressed that there are a number of problems with census data that render it as a poor source for learning about immigration. The New Immigrant Survey data used in his analysis was designed for this purpose and is the gold standard for data on immigrants in the United States.

Susan Collins finished the discussion making two points. One was that it should not be assumed that those who do not stay in the United States necessarily return to their home countries. In fact, many of these nonstayers really settle in a third country. Anecdotally, she noted that it is not uncommon for Caribbean students to come to the United States for college or graduate school and end up settling in Canada. She also highlighted an additional reason for student migration. As mentioned in the paper, student migrants are more likely to obtain green cards and become citizens than are other types of migrants. One benefit of citizenship is that it gives an individual the option to return to live in the United States in the future. This is extremely valuable, particularly for people from countries subject to high political or economic instability. She hypothesized that the desire to increase the possibility of one's becoming a citizen is one factor motivating student migrants and that it is distinct from but complementary to the two determinants examined in the paper—lack of schooling opportunities at home and access to higher wage opportunities in the United States.

References

Barro, Robert J., and Jong Wha Lee. 1993. "International Comparisons of Educational Attainment." *Journal of Monetary Economics* 32, no.3: 363–94.

Bhagwati, Jagdish, and Koichi Hamada. 1974. "The Brain Drain, International Integration of Markets for Professionals and Unemployment: A Theoretical Analysis." *Journal of Development Economics* 1, no. 1: 19–42.

Bloom, David E., and Jeffrey G. Williamson. 1998. "Demographic Transitions and Economic Miracles in Emerging Asia." *World Bank Economic Review* 12, no. 3 (September): 419–55.

Borjas, George J. 1987. "Self-Selection and the Earnings of Immigrants." *American Economic Review* 77, no. 4: 531–53.

———. 2002. "An Evaluation of the Foreign Student Program." *Backgrounder*. Washington: Center for Immigration Studies (June).

Bratsberg, Bernt.1995. "The Incidence of Non-Return among Foreign Students in the United States." *Economics of Education Review* 14, no. 4: 373–84.

Bureau of Consular Affairs. 2003. *Report of the Visa Office, 2003*. Washington: U.S. Department of State (travel.state.gov/visa/frvi/statistics/statistics_2786.html).

———. 2004. *Report of the Visa Office, 2004*. Washington: U.S. Department of State (travel.state.gov/visa/frvi/statistics/statistics_2786.html).

Chiswick, Barry. 2000. "Are Immigrants Favorably Self-Selected? An Economic Analysis." Discussion Paper 131. Bonn: Institute for the Study of Labor (March).

Cobb-Clark, Deborah. 1993. "Immigrant Selectivity and Wages: The Evidence for Women." *American Economic Review* 83, no. 4: 986–93.

Commander, Simon, Mari Kangasniemi, and L. Alan Winters. 2004. "The Brain Drain: A Review of Theory and Facts." *Brussels Economic Review* 47, no. 1: 29–44.

Docquier, Frédéric, and Abdeslam Marfouk. 2006. "International Migration by Education Attainment, 1990–2000." In *International Migration, Remittances & the Brain Drain,* edited by Çağlar Özden and Maurice Schiff, pp. 151–99. Washington: World Bank, and New York: Palgrave and Macmillan.

Freeman, Richard B., and Remco H. Oostendorp. 2005. Occupational Wages around the World (OWW) Database. (September 13) (www.nber.org/oww).

Hatton, Timothy J., and Jeffrey G. Williamson. 2005. *Global Migration and the World Economy: Two Centuries of Policy and Performance*. MIT Press.

Heckman, James J. 1979. "Sample Selection Bias as a Specification Error." *Econometrica* 47, no. 1: 153–61.

Heston, Alan, Robert Summers, and Bettina Aten. 2002. Penn World Table Version 6.1. Center for International Comparisons at the University of Pennsylvania (CICUP). (October) (pwt.econ.upenn.edu).

Institute of International of Education. 2005. *Open Doors 2005, Report on International Educational Exchange*. New York: IIE.

Jasso, Guillermina, and Mark R. Rosenzweig. 1990. "Self Selection and the Earnings of Immigrants: Comment." *American Economic Review* 80, no. 1: 298–304.

————. 2004. "Selection Criteria and the Skill Composition of Immigrants: A Comparative Analysis of Australian and U.S. Employment Immigration." Paper presented at the conference "Skilled Migration Today: Prospects, Problems, and Policies," cosponsored by the Columbia University Program on Immigration Economics, the Russell Sage Foundation, and the Council on Foreign Relations, New York City, March.

Jasso, Guillermina, Doug Massey, Mark Rosenzweig, and James Smith. 2000. "The New Immigrant Survey Pilot: Overview and New Findings about Legal Immigrants at Admission." *Demography* 37, no. 1: 127–38.

Munshi, Kaivan. 2003. "Networks in the Modern Economy: Mexican Migrants in the U.S. Labor Market." *Quarterly Journal of Economics* 118, no. 2: 549–99.

Office of Immigration Statistics. 2006. *Yearbook of Immigration Statistics: 2004*. Washington: U.S. Department of Homeland Security.

Office of the Registrar General. 1997. *Census of India, 1991: Population projections for India and States, 1996–2016*. New Delhi: Office of the Registrar General, Ministry of Home Affairs.

Psacharopoulos, George. 1994. "Returns to Investment in Education: A Global Update." *World Development* 22, no. 9:1325–343.

Psacharopoulos, George, and Harry A. Patrinos. 2002. "Returns to Investment in Education: A Further Update." Policy Research Working Paper 2881. Washington: World Bank.

Roy, Andrew D. 1951. "Some Thoughts on the Distribution of Earnings." *Oxford Economic Papers* 3, no. 2: 135–46.

SEVIS, Student and Exchange Visitor Information System. 2006. U.S. Immigration and Customs Enforcement, Department of Homeland Security. (March 31) (www.ice.gov/sevis/numbers/student/country_of_citizenship.htm).

Summers, Robert, and Alan Heston. 1991. "The Penn World Table (Mark 5): An Expanded Set of International Comparisons, 1950–1988." *Quarterly Journal of Economics* 106, no. 2: 327–68.

The Times Higher World University Rankings 2005, edited by John O'Leary. London: TSL Education (www.thes.co.uk/worldrankings).

Williamson, Jeffrey G. 2006. "Global Migration." *Finance and Development* 43, no. 3 (September): 23–27.

ANDREW M. WARNER
Millennium Challenge Corporation

Wage Dynamics and Economic Development

The primary purpose of this paper is to introduce new data on wages by occupations across fifty-eight countries. The main distinguishing feature of the data is that they were collected with exactly the same methodology at the same time in many countries, thus permitting a high degree of comparability across countries. The data are from surveys of firms, which ask what the firm pays for broad occupational categories, such as office cleaners, secretaries, and managers.

The second purpose of the paper is to show empirical evidence from a number of sources on how wage levels correlate with GDP and to interpret this evidence. Various sources of wage data are compared through this lens, both across countries and across time within countries. The paper discusses conditions under which wage growth should keep pace with GDP growth and shows econometric evidence on the determinants of wage levels across countries.

This paper begins by showing figures of wages plotted against GDP per worker or GDP per person using a variety of wage data. GDP is used as a common denominator against which wages can be displayed for a variety of occupations across time and across countries. Such plots, however, inevitably provoke criticism: "Of course wages correlate with GDP, since wages are by definition part of GDP." The answer is yes, but not so fast. Among the variables that can break the link between wage levels and GDP are changing participation rates of the labor force, shifting employment between sectors with different wage levels, and changes in the share of labor income in GDP.

The paper shows that after these forces play themselves out, simple elasticities between log wage levels and log GDP per worker or log GDP per capita tend to lie in the range 0.6 to 1.0. Some of the wage data presented in this paper show a 1-for-1 elasticity, and some of the regression results show a partial 1-for-1 association after holding constant other variables.

97

The paper presents econometric evidence to shed light on the forces that drive wage levels around the world. These regressions deal with two methodological issues that need to be confronted by any empirical study of wages and GDP across countries: the bias toward 1 from the fact that wages are part of GDP and the simultaneous determination of wage levels and GDP levels. The paper deals with both issues by using the capital-labor ratio as the driving force behind the determination of wages and GDP. This variable is used both as an instrument for GDP and directly in the estimated wage equations.

Some of the important factors found to mediate the wage-GDP relationship are the extent of skill accumulation during growth; the degree of structural change during growth; and, when the wage data are for specific occupations or industries, special factors associated with those occupations or industries. The paper also shows evidence about the role of labor market policies, market competition, and global forces. The paper is organized as follows. The first section discusses the existing wage data. The second section describes the new fifty-eight-country occupational wage data. The third section reviews related studies on wages. The fourth section discusses the evidence on the association between wages and GDP using a variety of data. And the final two sections present and discuss regression evidence in a more formal setting.

Data on Wages

Until very recently, wage data from different countries were characterized by a low degree of comparability due to differences in the way occupations were classified and wages were measured (sources varied in terms of inclusion of bonuses, in-kind benefits, and pension and insurance contributions). Also data on wages outside of the manufacturing sector were lacking, which is a significant issue because manufacturing can make up a small share of GDP. Data from the 2006 edition of *World Development Indicators* show that for 1998 the median share of manufacturing in GDP ranged from 1 to 43 percent, with a median of just 15 percent, across the 183 countries for which data were available.[1] Relatively poorer countries tended to have few data for analysis. The lack of coverage for poorer countries hampered an examination of questions such as the association between wages and GDP growth that require high variation across income levels.

The availability of data is improving. Rama organized data from the United Nations Industrial Development Organization (UNIDO) on wages, salaries, and

1. World Bank (2006).

compensation in manufacturing.[2] These data were subsequently distributed as part of the World Bank Labor Market Data Base and later were used by Rodrik.[3] The data are available across time (1970–94) and across 138 countries but with many missing values. Some countries report "wages and salaries," which include regular wage payments plus bonuses, paid vacation, in-kind payments, and family allowances paid to the employee directly by the employer. Other countries report "compensation of employees," which is basically wages and salaries plus payments made by the firm on behalf of the employee to pension or insurance schemes. Rodrik made an effort to control for these differences in wage concept and argued that his results were robust to alternative measures of wages. These UNIDO data are not broken down by occupation, and therefore presumably they cover a range of occupations within manufacturing.

The distinguishing feature of the Rama-UNIDO data at the time they were made available was the large cross-country coverage. In previous studies, wages for much smaller samples of countries were used. The most widely used data for international comparisons were and continue to be those of the U.S. Bureau of Labor Statistics (BLS), which reports average hourly compensation costs for production workers in manufacturing. The BLS makes a substantial effort to standardize what is being measured in different countries. The BLS wage data include time and piece rates, overtime premiums, shift differentials, regular and irregular bonuses, cost-of-living adjustments, as well as all employer expenditures for insurance programs including life, accident, and occupational injury, and all other labor taxes that can be regarded as labor costs. The 2006 edition of the BLS data covers thirty-two OECD (Organization for Economic Cooperation and Development) and Asian emerging-market countries between 1975 and 2002.[4] Turner and Golub used the BLS data but extended the sample to include additional countries from national sources.[5]

Richard Freeman and Remco Oostendorp made a major advance by standardizing the data kept by the International Labor Organization (ILO).[6] Since 1924 the ILO has sent a questionnaire to national governments to collect data on pay by occupation and industry. The first "October Inquiry" surveys collected earnings data for males in 15 countries and 18 occupations; by the 1980s

---

2. UNIDO (1998); Rama (1996).

3. Rodrik (1999).

4. (www.bls.gov/fls/hcompsupptabtoc.htm).

5. Turner and Golub (1997). The 1997 edition of these data covered 21 countries: Australia, Austria, Belgium, Canada, Denmark, Finland, France, Germany (West), Greece, Ireland, Italy, Japan, Netherlands, New Zealand, Norway, Portugal, Spain, Sweden, Switzerland, the United Kingdom, and the United States. All the wage data were from the BLS, except for Italy and Sweden, where the data were taken from national sources.

6. Freeman and Oostendorp (2000).

the survey was expanded to include 156 countries and 161 occupations. As Freeman and Oostendorp noted, however, the main problem with the data is that countries have responded to the inquiry by drawing on existing sources that are sometimes not even comparable within a country over time, to say nothing about international comparability. In response to this, Freeman and Oostendorp estimated standardized wages and earnings by country occupation and time that cleaned the data of many of the inconsistencies.[7]

Description of the Cross-Country Occupational Wage Data

For the new occupational wage data, surveys were conducted in fifty-eight countries in January and February of 1999, by survey firms, business schools, or research institutes that collaborate with the World Economic Forum in conducting its Executive Opinion Survey. The question on wages, which asked for monthly pay of office cleaners, company drivers, secretaries, mid-managers, and top managers, was thus part of a larger survey. I worked with the Forum in suggesting the questions in the survey and guiding the partners on sampling methodology. In an effort to achieve comparable samples of firms across countries, the partner institutes were each given data on employment by economic sector in their country (manufacturing, construction, and so on). They were asked to choose samples in which the distribution of firms was proportional to the distribution of nonagricultural employment across economic sectors.[8]

The survey partners were also asked to conduct personal interviews with the CEO or top managers in each enterprise. It is reasonable nevertheless to expect that some top executives delegated this work to a lower-level executive or an assistant. There is no reason, however, to believe that this delegation introduced a bias in the responses.

The requested information was the typical monthly wage or salary for the year 1998 for the following occupations: office cleaner, driver, secretary with five-years experience, mid-level manager, and senior manager.[9] The survey requested full time equivalent wages or salaries in local currency. Firms were asked to report wages and salaries without contributions paid by the firm on

---

7. These are reported and updated in Freeman and Oostendorp (2000, 2005: see the technical documentation by Remco Oostendorp, "The Standardized ILO October Inquiry 1983–2003.").

8. The employment data used for this purpose were taken from the International Labor Office, _Yearbook of Labor Statistics 1998_; see p. 1287 or p. 1293 for examples.

9. "Office cleaner" is the term used in all the surveys. Hereafter, "janitor" is used interchangeably with "office cleaner" as a shorter synonym.

behalf of the worker. They were also asked not to deduct any subsequent income taxes paid personally by the worker.[10]

The choice of the five occupational categories was motivated by a desire to maintain a balance between simplicity to generate a high response rate and specificity about the occupations. Virtually all companies have office cleaners, secretaries, and managers. This is less true for the driver category, but it was thought to be important to obtain wages for an occupation between a janitor and a secretary. For example, it is very common in eastern Europe, parts of western Europe, and South America for companies to have drivers dedicated to running errands, but it is less common in the United States.

These monthly wages in local currency were then converted to annual rates by multiplying by 12 and to a uniform currency (U.S. dollars) by using the average annual exchange rate during 1998.

Table 1 provides details on the countries, number of respondents by country (to any part of the survey), and the number of respondents to the wage questions specifically. In total, 3,843 companies filled out some part of the survey. Of these returned surveys, 3,256 (or 84.7 percent) responded to at least one of the questions on wages. The final column shows that a majority of respondents completed the set of five questions on wages.

Even though the questions asked for typical monthly wages in local currency, 680 of the 15,420 wages reported nevertheless were listed in other currencies, and of these, 330 were in U.S. dollars. When the currency was clearly indicated, the data were retained. Some also reported annual rather than monthly wages. A small fraction of the replies, 241 out of 15,420, were eliminated because of grossly implausible values or apparent mistakes. Values were judged implausible after examining other reported wages for a given country.

Given that nonreporting (due to top coding that imposes an upper bound on reported income) or misreporting of high incomes is an issue in other data, when analyzing the characteristics of the nonresponding firms in greater detail, the question arose: Were respondents in fact reluctant to report the top salaries? The answer was no. It turns out that nonresponses were slightly more likely to be among the low-wage occupations. For example, 2,798 surveys responded to the question on janitor's wages, and 3,046 surveys responded to the question on mid-manager wages.

As a gauge of the extent to which the salaries reported for top managers in these data are those of top CEOs, the median annual wage of a senior manager in the United States is $132,000, which is below the typical base salary for a U.S.

---

10. Documentation for the data is available from the author on request.

Table 1. Sample Size and Response Rates

	Number of surveys returned (1)	Number that completed at least one wage question (2)	Percentage that completed at least one wage question (2)/(1)	Percentage that completed all five wage questions
Argentina	121	97	80	56
Australia	58	49	84	67
Austria	53	44	83	68
Belgium	30	21	70	67
Bolivia	101	95	94	50
Brazil	85	74	87	85
Bulgaria	83	62	75	65
Canada	85	70	82	59
Chile	150	138	92	71
China	121	108	89	83
Colombia	76	56	74	51
Costa Rica	100	93	93	42
Czech Republic	70	62	89	80
Denmark	31	26	84	81
Egypt	40	39	98	95
El Salvador	100	95	95	77
Finland	19	18	95	89
France	24	18	75	71
Germany	56	45	80	73
Greece	47	41	87	77
Hong Kong	54	47	87	78
Hungary	82	69	84	68
Iceland	39	33	85	67
India	98	86	88	84
Indonesia	33	30	91	88
Ireland	59	45	76	49
Israel	38	30	79	66
Italy	66	53	80	64
Japan	75	54	72	49
Jordan	51	49	96	96
Korea	41	36	88	76

CEO. Note that the data do not include in-kind benefits, bonuses, stock options, or other incentives that can be an important part of executive compensation.

There are two further issues that should be of concern to researchers using these data. One is the small sample size for some countries, and the other is the composition of the sample across sectors of the economy and across types of firms and whether this composition is sufficiently comparable across countries.

On the small sample size, cutting the sample further had little impact on average wages, casting doubt on whether increasing the sample would have

Table 1 (continued).

	Number of surveys returned (1)	Number that completed at least one wage question (2)	Percentage that completed at least one wage question (2)/(1)	Percentage that completed all five wage questions
Luxembourg	9	8	89	67
Malaysia	38	36	95	92
Mauritius	38	34	89	84
Mexico	29	23	79	76
Netherlands	36	30	83	72
New Zealand	88	80	91	52
Norway	50	42	84	68
Peru	76	64	84	71
Philippines	42	37	88	81
Poland	56	49	88	75
Portugal	123	92	75	69
Russian Federation	147	128	87	75
Singapore	67	62	93	73
Slovak Republic	17	14	82	65
South Africa	160	142	89	83
Spain	76	49	64	53
Sweden	26	23	88	77
Switzerland	54	40	74	57
Taiwan	50	43	86	78
Thailand	66	63	95	95
Turkey	36	31	86	83
Ukraine	67	39	58	54
United Kingdom	54	44	81	63
United States	132	109	83	56
Venezuela	117	94	80	64
Vietnam	62	59	95	87
Zimbabwe	41	38	93	88
All countries	3,843	3,256	85	70

Source: Author's calculations using raw data from the Executive Opinion Survey conducted by the World Economic Forum, 1999.

had a large impact. For each country, the sample was cut by dropping half of the observed wages (selected by the observation number, which was not correlated with the wage), and then mean wages were recomputed. Focusing first on wages for office cleaners, mean wages calculated with half the sample were on average 4.6 percent different in absolute value from mean wages computed with the whole sample. For top managers, the difference was 7.3 percent. Median wages were even more insensitive to 50 percent cuts in the sample sizes.

Overall these results suggest that larger samples would not result in markedly different average (or median) wages.

Regarding the composition of the sample, adjustments for observable differences in the samples of firms across countries produced mean wages similar to unadjusted mean wages. Warner estimated regressions of log wages by firm and country on separate country intercepts and a number of firm characteristics, including whether the firm's primary ownership was international or domestic, whether the firm had significant government ownership, firm size, and economic sector.[11] Wages were positively associated with multinational status and negatively associated with public-sector status. Wages were also positively associated with firm size and are significantly different in sectors such as textiles (low wages) and finance (high wages). Country-specific intercepts from these regressions provided estimates of wage levels, controlling for the composition of the sample of firms. These adjusted wages were then compared with the simple median wages to gauge the importance of the sample composition on wage levels.

The main finding was that although the characteristics of firms were significantly correlated with wages, the magnitudes of the impacts were small enough that adjusted (median) wages were close to unadjusted (median) wages. Regressions of adjusted on unadjusted wages had an R squared of at least 99 percent in all five cases. As measured by the absolute value of the residuals, the average difference between adjusted and unadjusted wages for office cleaners was 7.3 percent, and for top managers, 10.7 percent. This variation, however, was small when compared with the variation in median wages across countries, which differ by much more than 100 percent. Hence, when explaining international variation in median wages, the choice between adjusted or unadjusted wages is not very consequential.

Previous Studies

There appear to be few previous studies directly on the subject of this paper, but there are several related studies. Freeman and Oostendorp found that skill *premia* (ratio of wages of skilled to less-skilled labor) tended to be smaller in countries with higher per capita incomes.[12] They also found that wage dispersion was smaller in communist countries (their data predates 1989) and that countries with higher levels of unionization had lower wage dispersion.

11. Warner (2003).
12. Freeman and Oostendorp (2000).

Rama reviewed the relationship between openness and wages using, in part, the Freeman and Oostendorp data.[13] He concluded that the data suggested that wage growth was faster in more open economies (measured by the ratio of trade to GDP). However, the impact he discussed may be conceived as the full effect of openness on wages (namely the impact of openness on GDP plus the impact of openness on wages conditional on GDP). Hence his result should not be directly compared with studies (including the present study) that examine wage determination after conditioning on GDP.

The impact of trade liberalization on wages in low-income countries has been studied by Robbins; Robbins and Gindling; and Beyer, Rojas, and Vergara, using data for specific countries rather than cross-country data.[14] These studies tended to find that growth in the supply of skills lowered the skill premium or wage dispersion but that, when controlling for skills, trade liberalization has led to an increase in the skill premium. Although trade theory suggests that a shift from autarky to free trade by poorer, labor-abundant countries should lower the skill premium since it makes skills in those countries relatively less scarce, these studies did not confirm this expectation. However, if protectionism is not uniform but rather protects low-income workers specifically, then of course the lifting of protection can lower wages at the bottom end. This kind of result was found by Currie and Harrison to describe Morocco and by Hansen and Harrison for Mexico.[15]

There are relatively few studies that attempt to explain empirically the variation in wage levels across a large number of countries, and several that do have other primary objectives. Trefler in a study about trade found that a large fraction of the variation in wage rates can be explained by variation in aggregate productivity measures.[16] Freeman showed that indirect measures of productivity (average years of education, urbanization, and share of trade in GDP) help explain national wage differentials.[17] Krajnyák and Zettelmeyer examined exchange rate misalignment in eastern Europe using dollar wages as the key variable.[18] To explain wages levels empirically, they used several GDP variables (GDP per person, GDP per worker), several educational attainment variables (primarily the fraction of persons in the relevant age cohort enrolled in secondary education), the share of agriculture in GDP, and an OECD dummy variable. All of these were justified as proxies for labor productivity in explain-

13. Rama (2003).
14. Robbins (1997); Robbins and Gindling (1999); Beyer, Rojas and Vergara (1999).
15. Morocco: Currie and Harrison (1997) and Mexico: Hansen and Harrison (1999).
16. Trefler (1993).
17. Freeman (1994).
18. Krajnyák and Zettelmeyer (1998).

ing wages. Rodrik argued that greater political liberties and civil rights helped explain higher wages in manufacturing.[19] He controlled for productivity proxies such as value added per worker in manufacturing, GDP per worker, the local price level (a control for cost of living), and the variables used by Freeman.[20]

Association between Wages and GDP

This section shows the empirical association between wage levels and GDP per worker using the occupational wage data from the fifty-eight-country sample. It then shows the same kind of evidence for other wage data and discusses possible explanations for varying patterns. Finally, it shows similar evidence over time within countries using data on wages in manufacturing.

The common denominator of previous studies on wage determination across countries has been the use of GDP per capita or GDP per worker as a basic proxy for differences in labor productivity. This section follows that practice, plotting the wage data across countries and across time against GDP per worker. The use of GDP is convenient because it is widely available across time and across countries, permitting comparisons of disparate wage data in a common framework.

There is of course no iron law that dictates a fixed pattern in the relation between wages and GDP, since both are endogenous variables. To assist the interpretation of wage-GDP plots, consider the following simplified national income identity. This states that payments to labor and profits must sum to the nation's economic output. It is shown below for the case of two occupations, letting Y stand for GDP.

(1)
$$\frac{Y}{N} \equiv \frac{\left(L_1 w_1 + L_2 w_2 + \pi\right)}{N}.$$

The term L stands for employment, N for population, w_i for wages, and π for profits. The equation may be rearranged to highlight the roles of the ratio of employment to population (L/N), shares of employment (s), average wages, and the ratio of profits (or all nonwage income) to employment:

(2)
$$\frac{Y}{N} \equiv \frac{L}{N}\left[s_1 w_1 + (1 - s_1) w_2 + \frac{\pi}{L} \right].$$

19. Rodrik (1999).
20. Freeman (1994).

It is important to clarify that presentation of such an equation is not a claim about causality. This equation would normally be one in a larger system in which the variables were simultaneously determined by exogenous factors. The purpose of the equation is rather to set the bounds for what is theoretically possible.

The equation serves to remind us that growth in GDP per capita on the left-hand side must be matched by growth of any or all of the variables on the right-hand side. A *benchmark case* is where the labor force participation rate is constant and the shares of labor in each occupation are also constant. In this case, if all wages and profits grow at the same rate, they must grow at the same rate as GDP per person.

To focus specifically on wage growth and GDP growth, the following is a list of events that could account for wages in a particular occupation growing more slowly than GDP:

—rising labor force participation

—faster growth in other wages or profits

—migration of labor toward higher-wage occupations or sectors

Each of these may be adduced as explanations for any discrepancy between wage growth and GDP growth. Of course, where growth is measured by GDP per worker, rising labor force participation would not apply.

Figures 1a to 1e show plots of median wages by occupation against GDP per worker for 1998. The wage data are from the fifty-eight-country occupational wage data described in this paper. Both log wages and log GDP are in U.S. dollars, converted with the average annual exchange rate in 1998. To facilitate visual comparison of wage levels with economy-wide productivity (which is approximated by GDP per worker), each figure also presents the 45-degree line representing equality between annual wages and per worker GDP. The other line in each figure is the OLS (ordinary least squares) regression line. Median wages for office cleaners in figure 1a tend to be below the 45-degree line, while executive wages in figures 1d and 1e tend to be above this line.

Two basic facts are immediately apparent from the figures. There is a strong simple association between wages and GDP for office cleaners, but the strength of the relationship diminishes for higher-paying occupations. For the higher-paying occupations (figures 1d and 1e), there appears to be greater dispersion across countries at lower levels of GDP. It is not clear whether the facts are best described as greater dispersion at low income levels or simply that countries appear to sort themselves into two groups, with Ukraine, Vietnam, and Russia in the group with low executive wages for their levels of income and Indonesia, India, and Zimbabwe with high wages for their levels of income.

Figure 1a. Wages versus GDP per worker, by occupation: Office Cleaners[a]

log of annual income of office cleaners

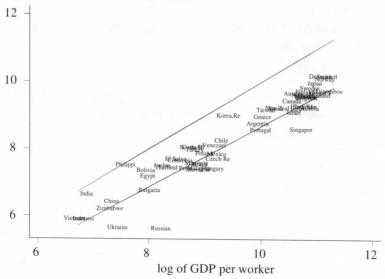

log of GDP per worker

Source: Author's calculations using raw data from the Executive Opinion Survey conducted by the World Economic Forum, 1999.
a. Wages are monthly wages multiplied by 12 and converted to U.S. dollars with 1998 average exchange rate.

Figure 1b. Drivers

log of annual income of drivers

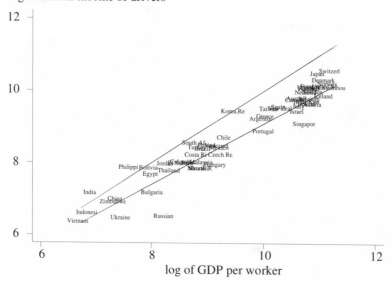

log of GDP per worker

Figure 1c. Secretaries

log of annual income of secretaries

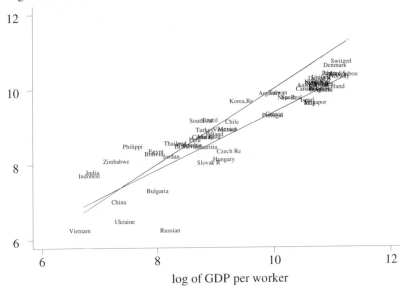

log of GDP per worker

Figure 1d. Mid-Managers

log of annual income of mid-level managers

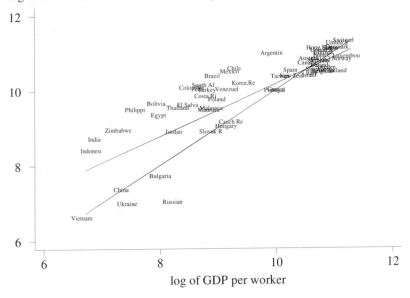

log of GDP per worker

Figure 1e. Top Managers

log of annual income of top managers

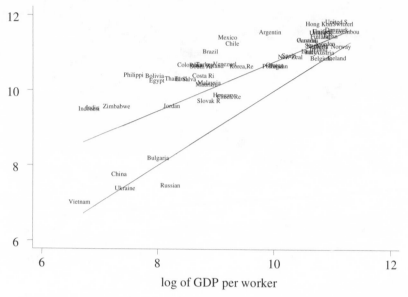

log of GDP per worker

Later sections of this paper will consider a number of explanations for this pattern.

Several scenarios are now discussed that could account for different patterns in these wage-GDP plots. First, different driving forces behind GDP growth will give rise to distinct patterns. Skill accumulation during growth should be associated with a reduction in the skill premium and thus flatter wage-GDP profiles for higher-skilled activities as one looks across countries or over time for a given country. This could be one of the explanations for the flatter wage-GDP profiles of wages of managers than those of office cleaners. Similarly, capital accumulation during growth would raise the relative returns to different kinds of labor depending on the degree of substitutability with the labor in question. Other things constant, theory suggests that demand would grow faster and wage growth would be faster the more that capital is complementary to labor. Labor supply growth across occupations is also relevant for changes in the wage structure as economies grow.

Growth that is driven by structural change may result in low wage growth for given levels of GDP growth. To take an extreme example to establish the point, if GDP growth consisted in laborers moving to higher-paying occupations as the economy shifted to new industries, it would be possible to observe zero wage growth for a specific occupation even with positive overall growth. In this extreme case wage-GDP profiles for specific occupations would be flat. Trade models would also predict flat wage-GDP relationships, at least over some range of capital accumulation. In the Heckscher-Ohlin case, factor prices will be equalized as long as endowments are in a special set known as the *cone of diversification*. Nevertheless, across time periods where capital accumulation shifted the economy to new patterns of product specialization in different cones of diversification, there would be a positive relation between real wages and real GDP per capita.[21]

A separate issue is whether wage determination is different in industries dominated by multinational firms that are internationally mobile, such as textiles or electronics. Some argue that the option of such firms of moving to China serves to drive down wages for textile and electronics workers in countries with incomes higher than China's. To the extent that workers in such industries always have the option of working in other industries in their own country, the going wage for labor of a particular skill level in the country would be the determining factor for wages, rather than the options open to multinational firms. Mobile multinational firms can leave the country if unit labor costs were too high in comparison with such costs in China, but it is not clear that they can impose a lower-than-equilibrium wage in a particular country. Nevertheless, if companies could impose lower-than-equilibrium wages in countries with higher incomes than China's, one would observe flat wage-GDP profiles for industries (textiles and electronics) in which such firms dominate. Data on wages and GDP for textile workers are used below to shed light on this issue.

Finally, it was noted above that if skills are in more scarce supply in poorer countries than in rich countries, the market will bid up wages for skilled workers, and wage differentials for skilled labor will be higher in poorer countries. There is an additional impetus to wages for skilled labor in poorer countries if immigration rules in richer countries are more liberal for skilled labor. In this case the reservation wage for some of the skilled labor can be the skilled wage in a richer country, and if this is higher than the equilibrium domestic skilled wage, this can further bid up skilled wages in the poorer country. Both kinds of effects are examined in the regressions at the end of this paper.

We now turn to data from previous studies to plot wages against GDP.

Consider first the standardized October Inquiry data from Freeman and Oostendorp for the year 1998.[22] These data contain a large number of occupations;

---

21. For trade models with capital accumulation, see Smith (1984).
22. Freeman and Oostendorp (2000, 2005: see technical documentation, "The Standardized ILO October Inquiry 1983–2003.").

Figure 2a. Wages for Field Crop Farm Worker versus GDP per worker[a]

log monthly wages

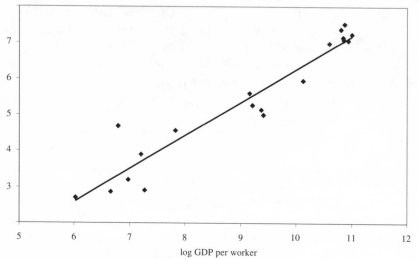

log GDP per worker

Source: Freeman and Oostendorp (2005).
a. Log hourly wages and log GDP per worker are in U.S. dollars.
$y = 0.0175x - 2.9221$; $R^2 = 0.9149$.

however, few of these match closely the classifications of office cleaners, drivers, secretaries, and managers. Wage-GDP plots are presented for three distinct occupations: "field crop farm workers," "room attendant or chambermaid," and "motor bus driver."

Figures 2a to 2c show that the wage-GDP elasticities when using these data range between 0.7 and 0.92. These associations are lower than the unit elasticity estimated between office cleaner wages and GDP per worker in figure 1a. One possible explanation is that demand for this kind of labor grows more slowly as economies develop than does demand for office cleaners. Another is that hotels in poorer countries generally are owned by foreign nationals who may pay chambermaids a wage premium over their reservation wage, which declines as GDP rises.

Another general explanation for less-than-unit elasticities between wages and GDP would be a decline in the labor share as GDP rises. Gollin showed evidence and argued that this is in fact not the case.[23] This nevertheless appears to be the case with some official data because informal jobs and the income of the self-employed are poorly measured in low-income economies. Poor measurement raises another possible reason for low responsiveness of measured

23. Gollin (2002).

Figure 2b. Wages of Room Attendant or Chambermaid versus GDP per Worker[a]

log monthly wages

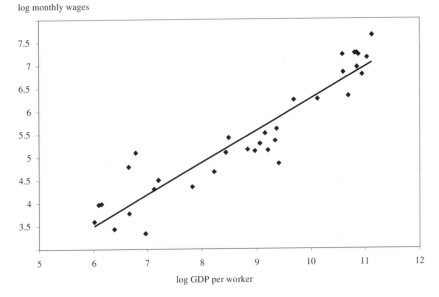

a. Log hourly wages and log GDP per worker are in U.S. dollars.
$y = 0.6927x - 0.6673$; $R^2 = 0.873$.

Figure 2c. Wages for Motor Bus Driver versus GDP per Worker[a]

log monthly wages

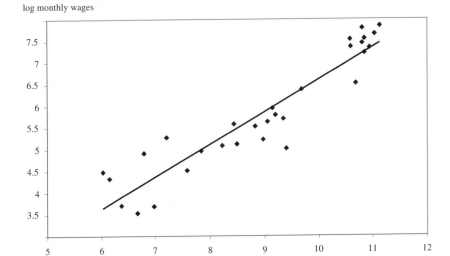

a. Log hourly wages and log GDP per worker are in U.S. dollars.
$y = 0.7461x - 0.8591$; $R^2 = 0.8702$.

Figure 3. Hourly Wages at McDonald's Franchises versus GDP per Worker[a]

log hourly wages

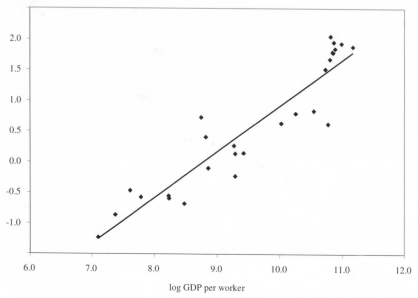

log GDP per worker

Source: Ashenfelter and Jurajda (2001).
a. Log hourly wages and log GDP per worker are in 1998 U.S. dollars.
$y = 0.7483x - 6.5701; R^2 = 0.8669$.

wages to GDP across countries. To the extent that wages for low-wage jobs are better measured with increasing income, the average wage would be pulled down as GDP per worker increased, possibly explaining the slope of less than unity.

Ashenfelter and Jurajda have compiled wages of McDonald's workers in different countries.[24] They argued that such data are better for international comparisons because McDonald's workers in every country perform similar tasks, with very similar equipment, and sell a highly standardized product. Figure 3 shows that these wages correlate strongly with GDP per worker. The estimated simple regression coefficient is 0.75.

As Ashenfelter and Jurajda recognized, similarity in tasks does not imply that wages should be similar across countries. The product is perishable, so it is not possible for a McDonald's in a low-wage country to sell and undercut the higher prices in a high-wage country. And immigration barriers are sufficiently high to prevent immigrant labor from establishing a single wage for McDonald's workers. A simple explanation for the positive association with GDP per worker is that the reservation wage for a McDonald's worker in the

24. Ashenfelter and Jurajda (2001).

United States is simply much higher than the reservation wage for a McDonald's worker in China. So it is supply and demand and productivity conditions in the rest of the economy that influences wages rather than the specific tasks performed at McDonald's.

To the extent that McDonald's workers are substitutes for the office cleaners, a discrepancy worth noting is that wages of office cleaners (figure 1a) correlate with GDP per worker with an elasticity of 1, while wages of McDonald's workers correlate with an elasticity of 0.75. Several explanations that could be adduced to account for the low wage-GDP association for McDonald's wages, such as a shift to higher-skilled occupations as GDP rises, should apply equally well for office cleaner wages.

Figures 4a and 4b show hourly wage rates in U.S. dollars for textile and apparel workers derived from the office of the U.S. Trade Representative.[25] The simple associations with GDP per worker are positive, contradicting simple predictions of factor price equalization for footloose industries. Moreover, the elasticities of approximately 0.7, although on the low side, are not clearly out of line with the other evidence in this paper.

To examine wage-GDP associations over time, the data that provide the most comparable information for a large number of countries are the BLS manufacturing wage data.[26] Table 2 shows regressions summarizing the linear associations between (log) hourly wages in manufacturing and (log) GDP per capita.[27] In most countries, wages in manufacturing have grown 1-for-1 with GDP per capita. In a few countries (Ireland, Portugal, Mexico, and the United States), however, wages in manufacturing have grown more slowly than GDP.[28]

In twenty-five of the twenty-nine countries shown in table 2, the 1-for-1 association in which growth in wages equals growth in GDP per person is a good summary of the data. In four countries, however (Ireland, Spain, Taiwan, and the United States), growth in wages in manufacturing has slowed in recent years, falling behind growth in GDP. This deceleration in wage growth was established by the fact that for these four countries there is a negative and significant estimated coefficient on GDP squared in regressions of log wages on log GDP and GDP squared. Such deceleration of wage growth in manufacturing is consistent with a decline in the derived demand for labor in manufacturing in these countries, an increase in structural change as manufacturing labor migrates to

---

25. U.S. International Trade Commission (2004).

26. The data are hourly compensation costs in U.S. dollars for production workers in manufacturing from the website of the Bureau of Labor Statistics.

27. Brazil is excluded because of insufficient wage data.

28. We do not focus on the low estimated coefficient for Mexico because the underlying wage data are very erratic.

Figure 4a. Hourly Wages in Textiles versus GDP per Person, 2002[a]

log wages per hour

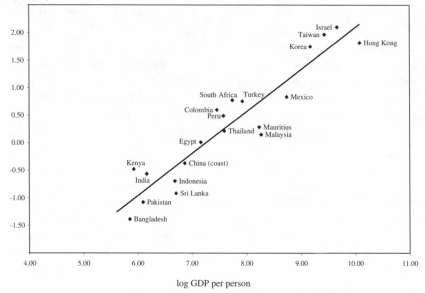

log GDP per person

Source: Authors calculations using data from the U.S. International Trade Commission (2004).
a. Log hourly wages in textiles and log GDP per person are in 2002 U.S. dollars.
$\ln (W) = 0.7641 \ln(Y) - 5.5471; R^2 = 0.8847.$

Figure 4b. Hourly Wages in Apparel versus GDP per Person, 2002[a]

log wages per hour

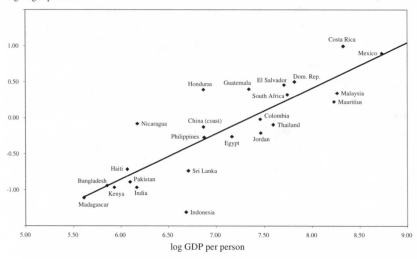

log GDP per person

a. Log hourly wages in apparel and log GDP per person are in 2002 U.S. dollars.
$y = 0.6319x - 4.6446; R^2 = 0.7295.$

Table 2. Regressions of Manufacturing Wages on GDP per capita[a]

	Estimate of a1	Standard error of a1	t ratio
Australia	0.928	0.028	33.14
Austria	0.984	0.012	82.00
Belgium	0.935	0.027	34.63
Canada	0.873	0.041	21.29
Denmark	0.961	0.039	24.64
Finland	1.100	0.043	25.58
France	1.020	0.034	30.00
Germany	1.010	0.049	20.61
Greece	1.130	0.123	9.19
Hong Kong	0.863	0.021	41.10
Ireland	0.650	0.056	11.61
Israel	1.000	0.049	20.41
Italy	0.733	0.040	18.33
Japan	0.954	0.031	30.77
Korea	1.170	0.048	24.38
Luxembourg	0.623	0.059	10.56
Netherlands	0.892	0.026	34.31
Mexico	0.392	0.108	3.63
New Zealand	0.853	0.036	23.69
Norway	0.863	0.051	16.92
Portugal	0.693	0.035	19.80
Singapore	0.999	0.033	30.27
Sri Lanka	0.670	0.042	15.95
Spain	0.883	0.059	14.97
Sweden	0.956	0.015	63.73
Switzerland	0.968	0.020	48.40
Taiwan	1.050	0.018	58.33
United Kingdom	0.883	0.013	67.92
United States	0.732	0.022	33.27

Source: Author's calculations using raw data from the Bureau of Labor Statistics (1998), "International Comparisons of Hourly Compensation Costs for Production Workers in Manufacturing, Supplementary Tables (1975–96)."
a. Estimated equation: $\ln(\text{wage}) = a0 + (a1)\ln(\text{GDP}) + e$.

other sectors, or faster wage growth in other sectors that boosts GDP without boosting manufacturing wages.

East Asian countries, alleged to be restricting wage growth to boost economic growth, do not exhibit lower wage growth relative to GDP growth. Real wage growth in manufacturing has been almost exactly equal to GDP growth in Singapore and slightly above GDP growth in Taiwan and Korea. Only in Hong Kong is manufacturing wage growth slower than GDP growth among East Asian economies.

In summary, for a number of countries, especially relatively rich countries, the norm is a unitary elasticity between broad wage categories such as manufacturing and GDP per capita. Notable exceptions to this in recent years include the United States.

I turn now to the relation between the dispersion of wages and GDP levels. The full dispersion of wages across countries can be decomposed into between-country dispersion and within-country dispersion. The between-country dispersion is covered implicitly by the wage-GDP plots in figures 1a to 1e. Since wages of managers rise less rapidly with GDP than do wages of office cleaners, it follows that wage dispersion between countries tends to fall with higher GDP, consistent with Freeman and Oostendorp.[29] Therefore, the cross-country data suggest that the gap between high- and low-paying occupations declines as GDP rises.

What about wage dispersion within occupational groups? Here one finds that the dispersion of wages of office cleaners does not change with higher levels of GDP, nor does the dispersion of wages of drivers. However, wages of secretaries and managers do show declining dispersion with GDP. Within countries, managers' salaries tend to be more concentrated at higher income levels.

Regression Evidence

So far we have not offered any testing of hypotheses about the variables that explain wage and GDP dynamics. This section shows some preliminary results using the new occupational wage data.

Variation across countries in the quantity and sophistication of capital is the most basic explanation for variation in labor productivity and GDP across countries. In a wide variety of frameworks, the marginal productivity of labor and GDP itself would depend positively on the capital-labor ratio. Consequently, this section uses estimates of the capital-labor ratio directly or as instruments for GDP per worker in wage equations.

Previous studies, notably by Rodrik and Krajnyák and Zettelmeyer, have used GDP per worker, GDP per person, or value added per worker in manufacturing as proxies for labor productivity, and they estimated OLS regressions using them as independent variables.[30] An example is presented below where such an approach can be motivated as an estimation of first-order conditions from a Cobb-Douglas technology. This framework would suggest that controls should be introduced for the relative supply of skill labor or the share of the labor force in certain occupations.

---

29. Freeman and Oostendorp (2000).
30. Rodrik (1999); Krajnyák and Zettelmeyer (1998).

Consider the case of two occupations, one of which is more demanding of skills. Production requires both kinds of labor. L stands for raw labor hours, H is a skills index that augments labor hours of skilled labor, K is capital, and Y is output. The human capital index, or skills index, is normalized to equal 1 for the low-skilled or low-education intensive occupation.

$$(3) \qquad Y = AK^\phi L_u^\alpha (L_s H)^\beta$$

Maximizing with respect to the human capital variables and setting wages equal to the value marginal products yields wage equations in which wages are a function of aggregate output per worker (Y / L), the human capital index, H, and the shares of labor in the two occupations, skilled and unskilled.

$$(4) \qquad w_u = \frac{dY}{dL_u} = \frac{\alpha Y}{s_u L}$$

$$(5) \qquad w_s = \frac{dY}{dLs} = \frac{\beta Y}{s_s LH}$$

$$(6) \qquad \ln(w_s) = \ln(\beta) + \ln(Y / L) - \ln(H) - \ln(s_s)$$

$$(7) \qquad \ln(w_u) = \ln(\alpha) + \ln(Y / L) - \ln(1 - s_s)$$

In tables 3 to 6, estimates guided by these last two equations are presented. It is important to clarify that data are not available to measure skills or employment share variables that are specific to each of the five occupations. In some cases it would be hard to define, in others hard to measure, skills or employment data that are specific to secretaries rather than to drivers or to mid-managers as opposed to top managers. Our data for skills and employment shares discriminate in a binary fashion between high- and low-skill human capital and employment.

To measure skills, an index is used that weighs raw years of education in each country by estimates of the rate of return. In addition, the index includes an adjustment for quality of education.[31] This index is called "skills" in the regression tables.

Data from ILO on the labor force by occupation in 1998 is used to measure the share of the labor force in skilled occupations.[32] The occupational cate-

31. The survey questions are available from the author by request.
32. ILO (1998).

Table 3. Regressions of Median Wages (First Specification)[a]

	Janitor	Driver	Secretary	Mid-manager	Top manager
Ln(GDP/L)	0.99	0.94	0.95	0.96	0.93
	(11.41)**	(13.12)**	(10.64)**	(9.28)**	(7.96)**
Skills	0.03	–0.01	–0.11	–0.36	–0.36
	(0.19)	(0.10)	(0.82)	(2.23)**	(1.93)
ln(1 – s1)	1.33	1.07	1.92		
	(1.25)	(1.23)	(1.77)		
ln(s1)				–0.52	–0.62
				(2.25)*	(2.37)*
Constant	–1.02	–0.08	0.31	–0.25	0.50
	(1.25)	(0.12)	(0.36)	(0.22)	(0.40)
Observations	45	45	45	45	45
R-squared	0.87	0.90	0.83	0.74	0.68

Source: Author's calculations using raw data from the Executive Opinion Survey conducted by the World Economic Forum, 1999.
s1 = share of employment in manager-like occupations. See text for further details.
* Significant at the 5 percent level.
** Significant at the 1 percent level.
a. The capital-labor ratio is used as an instrument for GDP per worker. Absolute value of t statistic is in parentheses.

gories "senior official and managers" and "professionals" are assigned to the skilled labor category. Although the term "skill" is used for convenience, the variable measures the proportion of the labor force in manager-like positions. This share is called "$s1$" in the regression tables.

Table 3 reports instrumental variable regressions where log wages for each of the five occupations are regressed on three kinds of variables. The first is GDP per worker, instrumented by the capital-labor ratio. The second, the employment share variable, is denoted by "$s1$" to correspond to "s" in the equations. For the wages of the three nonmanager occupations, this variable is the fraction of nonmanager jobs in the economy (denoted by "$1 - s1$" in the regression tables). For the two manager wages, this is the fraction of manager jobs in the economy. The third variable is the skills index, measured as a quality-adjusted education attainment variable. This is designed to measure the stock of skills relevant to higher-skilled occupations such as managers.

These regressions are undoubtedly a crude simplification of a more complex reality. The matching between the overall national skills index and the skills relevant for managerial jobs may be especially problematic. Nevertheless, the regressions serve to point out that a framework that takes into account cross-country differences in physical capital accumulation and skills acquisition can account for a substantial fraction of the observed variability in wage

Table 4. OLS Regressions of Median Wages (First Specification)[a]

	Janitor	Driver	Secretary	Mid-manager	Top manager
Ln(capital-labor ratio)	0.92	0.87	0.88	0.89	0.87
	(10.47)**	(12.05)**	(9.85)**	(8.56)**	(7.51)**
Skills	0.07	0.03	−0.07	−0.31	−0.31
	(0.50)	(0.28)	(0.47)	(1.80)	(1.60)
Ln(1 − s1)	0.94	0.70	1.55		
	(0.82)	(0.75)	(1.33)		
Ln(s1)				−0.48	−0.58
				(1.91)	(2.09)*
Constant	−1.42	−0.45	−0.07	−0.51	0.24
	(1.53)	(0.59)	(0.08)	(0.41)	(0.18)
Observations	45	45	45	45	45
R-squared	0.85	0.88	0.80	0.70	0.63

Author's calculations using raw data from the Executive Opinion Survey conducted by the World Economic Forum, 1999.
s1 = share of employment in manager-like occupations. See text for further details.
* Significant at the 5 percent level.
** Significant at the 1 percent level.
a. Absolute value of t statistic is in parentheses.

and salary levels. After controlling for the skills variable and the employment share variable, the association between wages and GDP is very close to 1 for all occupations.

Table 4 shows similar regressions that use the capital-labor ratio directly as a regressor rather than as an instrument for GDP per worker. The estimated elasticities of wages with respect to the capital-labor ratio are slightly smaller than those for GDP per worker in table 3, but since GDP per worker is highly correlated with the capital-labor ratio, the estimated equations are otherwise quite similar.

In table 3 and table 4, the skills index and the employment share variables have the anticipated signs and are close to statistical significance for the two manager wages. They also turn out to be collinear because each increases strongly with national GDP per worker. For this reason, it was decided to reestimate the regressions with only one of these variables, and the skills index was chosen because data were available for fifty-six rather than forty-five countries. These reestimated regressions are shown in tables 5 and 6. At face value, these regressions suggest that higher stocks of skilled labor in higher-income countries are a factor accounting for lower wages to managers at given income levels.

Table 5. Regressions of Median Wages (Second Specification)[a]

	Janitor	Driver	Secretary	Mid-manager	Top manager
Ln(GDP/L)	0.94	0.89	0.91	1.03	1.02
	(13.01)**	(14.76)**	(11.21)**	(10.80)**	(9.29)**
Skills	−0.05	−0.08	−0.27	−0.63	−0.68
	(0.42)	(0.80)	(2.12)*	(4.22)**	(3.95)**
Constant	−0.66	0.21	0.44	0.13	0.84
	(0.99)	(0.37)	(0.59)	(0.14)	(0.82)
Observations	56	56	56	56	56
R-squared	0.90	0.92	0.84	0.78	0.71

Source: Author's calculations using raw data from the Executive Opinion Survey conducted by the World Economic Forum, 1999.
* Significant at the 5 percent level.
** Significant at the 1 percent level.
a. The capital-labor ratio is used as an instrument for GDP per worker. Absolute value of *t* statistic is in parentheses.

Further Factors Affecting Wage Determination

This section discusses additional empirical results that are based in part on previous results in Warner, where they are discussed in more detail.[33] In addition to the variables included in the regressions presented so far, results with the following variables are reported.

Minimum wage is a subjective rating of whether minimum wage legislation is binding (rated on a scale of 1 to 7, where a higher value means binding). A positive sign would mean that wages are higher in countries where minimum wage rules are binding.

Competition is a subjective rating of the intensity of competition in local product markets (rated on a scale of 1 to 7, where a higher value means more intense competition). A positive sign would mean that wages are higher in countries with more product-market competition.

Foreign language for non-English-speaking countries is the subjective rating of the extent to which managers in the country speak a foreign language, either English or another. This is rated on a 1 to 7 scale, where the higher value indicates maximum language attainment. For English-speaking counties, since the managers already speak the *lingua franca*, this is set at 6.

Foreign language times GDP per worker is an interaction variable between log GDP per worker and the foreign language attainment variable. It is designed to test whether the extent of foreign language attainment explains the differing relationships between wages and GDP for the salaries of managers. The reasoning is that managers with foreign language skills have different reser-

33. Warner (2003).

Table 6. OLS Regressions of Median Wages (Second Specification)[a]

	Janitor	Driver	Secretary	Mid-manager	Top manager
Ln(capital-labor ratio)	0.85	0.81	0.82	0.93	0.93
	(11.99)**	(13.57)**	(10.53)**	(10.22)**	(9.02)**
Skills	0.05	0.01	−0.18	−0.52	−0.58
	(0.40)	(0.14)	(1.39)	(3.52)**	(3.44)**
Constant	−0.77	0.10	0.33	0.00	0.71
	(1.05)	(0.16)	(0.41)	(0.00)	(0.67)
Observations	56	56	56	56	56
R-squared	0.88	0.90	0.82	0.75	0.69

Source: Author's calculations using raw data from the Executive Opinion Survey conducted by the World Economic Forum, 1999.
** Significant at the 1 percent level.
a. Absolute value of t statistic is in parentheses.

vation wages from those that do not. Poor countries with higher fractions of such managers would have average salaries that are pulled up to global pay standards.

The regressions with these additional variables are presented in table 7. I note that the results seen in the previous regressions on the impact on log wages of log GDP per worker instrumented by the capital-labor variable and the negative impact on managers' wages of the skills variable also hold in these extended regressions. Therefore those results will not be discussed again here.

Focusing first on the minimum wage variable, the estimates suggest that countries with binding minimum wage rules are estimated to have 15 percent higher wages for the lowest-income occupation (janitors), holding constant other variables. The pattern of estimates across occupations is as expected: minimum wage regulations impact only wages in the lower-paying occupations.

Much of the cross-country variance for estimating such an effect comes from the comparison of European countries, with relatively strong minimum wage laws, and East Asian countries, with little or no minimum wage laws. Of all the European countries in our sample, France is perceived to have the strictest and most binding regulations.

The results suggest that competition in product markets also has some influence on wage levels. The competition variable is measured on a scale of 1 to 7, and the estimates imply that a unit change in this rating (more competition) raises wage levels by approximately 30 percent, all else constant. The estimated coefficients are on the margin of significance. The fact that the magnitude of this effect is similar across the five occupations lends support to the idea that competition squeezes profits and thus raises the wage bill. The estimated effect is just below significance for top managers, however.

Table 7. Regressions of Median Wages with Additional Variables[a]

	Janitor	Driver	Secretary	Mid-manager	Top manager
Ln(GDP/L)	1.03	1.08	1.15	1.54	1.70
	(4.39)**	(5.52)**	(4.96)**	(5.55)**	(5.31)**
Minimum wage	0.15	0.11	0.09	0.05	0.04
	(2.38)*	(2.02)*	(1.39)	(0.73)	(0.42)
Competition	0.34	0.36	0.31	0.33	0.34
	(2.58)*	(3.26)**	(2.41)*	(2.13)*	(1.88)
Foreign language (FL)	0.68	0.75	1.18	1.72	2.13
	(1.74)	(2.29)*	(3.06)**	(3.72)**	(4.00)**
ln(GDP/L) × FL	–0.06	–0.07	–0.10	–0.16	–0.20
	(1.34)	(2.00)	(2.32) *	(3.06)**	(3.33)**
Skills	0.08	0.05	–0.10	–0.41	–0.42
	(0.82)	(0.63)	(1.04)	(3.51)**	(3.14)**
Constant	–4.24	–3.97	–4.83	–7.65	–8.65
	(2.08)*	(2.33)*	(2.41)*	(3.17)**	(3.12)**
Observations	56	56	56	56	56
R-squared	0.94	0.95	0.92	0.88	0.85

Source: Author's calculations using raw data from the Executive Opinion Survey conducted by the World Economic Forum, 1999.
* Significant at the 5 percent level.
** Significant at the 1 percent level.
a. The capital-labor ratio is used as an instrument for GDP per worker. Absolute value of t statistic is in parentheses.

Another variable considered in table 7 is the foreign language variable, inter-acted with GDP per worker. The motivation for constructing this variable is the reasoning that managers with foreign language skills in poorer countries may have higher reservation wages than those who do not have this skill, because of greater outside job offers. Their language skills make them close substitutes in their own country for expatriate foreign managers, and this tends to bid up their wages in the domestic market. Even though such managers may only constitute a fraction of the managerial pool in their own country, their presence raises the average wages for all managers, resulting in the pattern observed back in figures 1d and 1e: higher median wage levels for managers for some of the poorer countries.

The measurement of this variable is based on the response from a survey on whether managers in each country tended to speak foreign languages. Countries that scored high on this variable were considered to have managers with language skills that rendered them highly substitutable for managers in other locations around the globe. This variable was coded as 6 in cases where the native language in the country was already English (a relatively high value given that the survey range was from 1 to 7).

The estimates in table 7 are consistent with the hypothesis that poor countries with higher fractions of such managers have average salaries that are pulled up to global pay standards. In terms of the plots in figures 1a to 1e, the regression results argue that wage-GDP relationships are much flatter (indicating greater wage equalization) in countries in which managers tend to speak foreign languages or in which the domestic language already is an international language (for example, English in India or Zimbabwe).

Note that when the language variable is interacted with log GDP per worker it produces a strong negative coefficient for manager wages but not for office cleaner wages. This is to be expected since language skills of managers are relevant for managers and not for janitors. The negative coefficient means that the manager salary–GDP slope is *low* in countries where managers have high levels of foreign language attainment and *high* in countries where managers have low levels of foreign language skills. The latter category of countries tends to include postsocialist countries where professionals were isolated from the outside world for long periods (for example, Russia and Vietnam).

This evidence is consistent with the view that managers in certain poor countries face pay scales that are influenced by global pay standards. This also implies that through this channel global forces serve to increase skilled-unskilled wage gaps in such countries.

Conclusions

This paper began by showing graphically how wage levels correlate with GDP per worker, using a variety of data on wage levels by occupation, including new data introduced here. The data show that a 1 percent change in GDP per worker is associated with a 0.6 to 1.0 percent change in wages, both across countries and across time. The fact that there is a positive correlation is not surprising, but the magnitude and the variation across kinds of occupations is potentially interesting, as is an analysis of the underlying forces that influence wage levels as GDP changes.

Although some may regard a 1-for-1 association between wages and GDP as being a normative benchmark, this paper argues that this is not necessarily correct. GDP per capita can rise without wages changing, if workers move to higher-paying occupations or if overall labor force participation rises. What would have implications for inequality would be slow wage growth due to a decline in the overall share of labor in national income. However, the data in this paper suggest that the overall labor share is not in fact significantly correlated with GDP per capita.

Inequality of wages by occupation across countries can be divided into dispersion of average wages across countries and dispersion of wages for a particular occupation within a country. The data show that dispersion of average wages across countries *declines* as GDP rises. The data also show that dispersion of wages within occupations declines as GDP rises, but only for wages and salaries of secretaries and managers.

On the determinants of wages, differences in capital accumulation and thus the stock of capital around the world, coupled with still significant barriers to mobility of labor, capital, and goods and services, are the major reasons for vastly different wage levels for similar work or similar occupations around the world. The econometric evidence supports the view that variation in the capital-labor ratio, either alone or as an instrument for GDP per worker, accounts for a large fraction of the variation in wage levels around the world. Quite simply, workers work with vastly different levels of capital, they do not have the option to migrate, and many of the goods and services they produce are not traded in the international market.

The question of what determines wage levels can be divided into two questions: What determines GDP levels? What determines wage levels conditional on GDP? This paper, along with almost all previous studies of wage determination across countries, implicitly focuses on the second question, conditioning in some way on GDP per capita or GDP per worker as a proxy for the general level of productivity. Which additional factors account for cross-country variation in wage levels over and above the contribution of broadly defined differences in productivity (GDP per worker)? The econometric evidence in this paper is consistent with the view that growth in the supply of skills has exceeded growth in demand for skills as economies have developed, so that richer countries have reached equilibria with higher supplies of skills relative to poorer countries and also with lower wage premiums for skills. There is also disagreement in the literature, not settled in this paper, about the relative roles of labor market institutions, openness to trade, and democratic institutions in the determination of wages. This paper presents some evidence of the impact that minimum wage rules and competition in product markets have on wages.

On the reasons why the gap between the wages of managers and office cleaners tends to decline as GDP increases, the paper offers two explanations. One is the previously mentioned increases in the relative supply of skills as GDP grows, which serves to drive down the skilled wage premium. The other is econometric evidence that pay for managers in poorer countries may be pulled up to global pay standards to the extent that managers in such countries acquire skills, such as foreign languages, that make them substitutable with rich-country managers. A by-product of this phenomenon is that there would be less scope for manager wages to grow with GDP compared with office cleaner wages, and thus a narrowing of the wage gap as GDP grows would be observed.

Comments
and Discussion

Harry J. Holzer: Andrew Warner has written a very interesting paper on patterns in wages and wage growth across developed and developing countries around the world. Indeed, he addresses one of the most important questions concerning global labor markets—namely, the extent to which different groups of workers in different countries share in the economic growth associated with international trade and are compensated for the higher risks and growing inequality that trade often generates.

Warner's results are based, to a large extent, on data that he has gathered in his own large-scale survey of companies around the world to make his case. This survey effort has been very ambitious and likely yields data that are more comparable across countries than has usually been true for other such studies (as the data are based on very specific occupations and wage definitions as well as on consistent timing).

There are essentially three sets of results in Warner's paper. The first set is from the simple regressions across countries of wages against per capita GDP that are highlighted in figures 1a to 1e. The findings that wages in less-skilled occupations tend to rise proportionately with real GDP, but that managerial wages rise less than proportionately, is quite interesting. The results also imply declining wage dispersion with rising GDP, both between and within countries.

The second set of results appears in tables 3 to 6, from regressions based on a Cobb-Douglas production function. These results show strong effects of capital-labor ratios on wages, as well as negative effects of average levels of skill accumulation on wages in highly-skilled occupations across countries. The third set of results then appears in table 7, where a variety of additional market and institutional characteristics—such as minimum wages, product market competition, and foreign language proficiency among managers—appear to have effects on wages as well, in ways that are broadly consistent with our expectations.

Before getting to the particular empirical findings, one might quibble a bit with the quality of the survey data that Warner has generated. For one thing, the data cover over 50 countries, and the wage measure for each country is based on only about 50 to 60 employers in each case. Warner argues fairly convincingly that his average wage measures are not heavily affected by sample size and are not too sensitive to observable characteristics of the firms in the survey. But there is little information here on how the samples of firms themselves were generated, how response rates varied with firm characteristics (both observable and unobservable), and therefore how representative the data really are within countries and across them.

Regarding the three sets of empirical results, the first set of simple regressions presents clean and straightforward evidence on how average wages and their dispersion varies with real GDP across countries. The tendency of wages to rise strongly with real GDP in each occupation considered cannot be disputed. But the fact that responsiveness to real GDP declines with the rise in skill level of the job is somewhat contradicted by the other studies that Warner cites (Freeman and Oostendorp as well as Ashenfelter and Jurajda), and it is unclear why his results differ from theirs and which are more plausible.

The second set of results, based on production function estimates, clearly indicates the importance of capital-labor ratios in explaining wages across countries within each occupation. It would have been nice to see a bit more about the partial contribution of this variable to the results and about the relationship between this instrument variable and real GDP. More important, there are some questions about the two variables, skill and employment share, that Warner has constructed from other data sources. The descriptions in the appendix of their construction lead me to believe they might be measured with some error, which should lead to downward biases in their coefficients (if the measurement error is "classical," that is, uncorrelated with other variables in the model). This, in turn, might lead the estimated coefficients on capital-labor ratios to be upward biased. Furthermore, whether the skill measures really account for the tendency of managerial wages to rise less than proportionately with real GDP here is not clear, since we do not see any equations in which these variables are omitted (and since the above-mentioned studies found that result in more- and less-skilled occupations).

The regressions in table 7 are interesting, but major questions can also be raised about the variables added to these models. For instance, the variable measuring the respondent's perception of the intensity of competition does not specify any kind of reference point; it is not clear how to interpret cross-country responses to these questions. Even the notion that product market competition should raise real wages because it reduces profits is not clear in theory, since product market competition should also make labor demand more elastic. Also, the variable measuring foreign language skills arbitrarily assigns a value of 6 on a scale of 7 to countries where the use of English is widespread. And, aside from the measurement issues, it seems as though such a measure could be a proxy for many different characteristics of countries in the regressions that are estimated.

By the end of the paper, the exact value added by the results in this paper relative to the rest of the literature remains somewhat in doubt. But I personally am more convinced than before that wages across the skill spectrum do rise heavily, if not always proportionately, with real GDP and that capital and average skill levels across countries have positive and negative effects on wages, respectively, across the spectrum as well.

The more specific criticisms above do not detract from the fact that Warner has addressed some of the most important questions in international labor markets, generated a potentially important new set of data, and produced some descriptive findings that are very useful. One hopes that these findings will stimulate other researchers to explore these questions more fully.

Nina Pavcnik: Andrew Warner's piece examines a very important question of how workers fare during the process of economic growth. This is a very broad and ambitious topic, so I confine my comments to the role of globalization in shaping this relationship.

Warner's analysis relies on new cross-sectional data on occupational wages that he collected in a survey of firms conducted in fifty-eight countries. One of the main objectives of the paper is to provide a detailed description of the data and highlight its strengths and shortcomings relative to the existing databases with similar information. Warner's discussion is quite useful for researchers interested in examining the patterns of wages across countries. The data have some nice features. For example, the data overcome some of the problems of data comparability that usually plague data used in cross-country studies. The data also cover wage information on a large set of developing and developed countries that could be easily linked to the usual measures of globalization available in the Penn World Tables or the World Development Indicators databases. These data also contain some information about the characteristics of firms (including their exposure to foreign direct investment [FDI] and export markets). Although this aspect of the data is not employed in the current study, it could be useful for future work. Unfortunately, the data do not have a panel dimension, so one cannot examine differential changes in wages across countries with differential changes in exposure to globalization, a standard practice in recent cross-country studies on related topics. In addition, some caution is warranted in using the data. For example, it is unclear how countries and firms within a country were selected for inclusion in the survey. Consequently, questions remain about whether the data are nationally representative.

Warner subsequently uses these data to examine the relationship between occupational wages and economic growth by looking at simple correlations between average (occupational) wages and GDP per capita across countries. It is reassuring that average occupational wages have a strong positive correlation with GDP per capita for all occupations. Also, it is interesting that this positive correlation is somewhat smaller in magnitude (but not significantly different statistically) for higher-paying occupational groups such as managers. The final part of the paper (table 7) examines the determinants of wage levels across countries by relating average occupational wages to variation across countries in capital per worker, skill abundance, labor market institutions, product market competition, and exposure to globalization. Globalization is measured with a subjective variable (on a 1 to 7 scale) of the extent to which managers in a country speak a foreign language. The author finds that the positive association between average wages of managers and GDP per capita is weaker in countries with a higher share of managers who are proficient in English language.

A reoccurring theme in this empirical work is the extent to which the weaker correlation between occupational wages and GDP per capita observed for managers (especially in countries with high foreign language proficiency) reflects that the labor market for managers is more influenced by global factors than is the labor market for lower-skill occupations such as janitors and drivers. Unfortunately, these results are difficult to interpret given that some occupations do not map transparently to industries or skills whose demand is differentially affected by changes in trade costs within trade models. In addition, the use of a variable for foreign language as a measure of globalization is somewhat questionable, as it likely reflects country characteristics such as the country's colonial ties and the quality of domestic institutions.

In general, the empirical section of the paper would benefit by focusing the discussion on a particular aspect of globalization. Globalization is an all-encompassing term that includes phenomena ranging from trade in final products to technology diffusion to footloose capital and immigration. A more focused analysis would help pinpoint the channels through which an aspect of globalization might affect wages. The implicit assumption underlying the paper's argument on globalization is that globalization should make average wages less dependent on local economic conditions. However, even if we simply confine ourselves to trade in final goods, theory does not necessarily predict that wages should equalize across countries in response to trade liberalization. If trade is driven by differences in relative factor abundance across countries, wages could equalize if the countries produce the same goods (that is, they are in the same cone of diversification) and produce goods with the same technology. In a model in which trade is driven by relative productivity differences across countries, real wage differences might persist even in the case of free trade.

I should emphasize that establishing the link between globalization and aggregated wages (or other aggregated outcomes, such as growth) has been very difficult in the cross-country studies. More recent work in international trade has moved beyond looking at cross-country averages and instead uses microlevel surveys of workers and firms to emphasize the importance of heterogeneity in the impact of globalization within a country (see Goldberg and Pavcnik for a survey).[1] These recent studies show that trade due to changes in industry tariffs affects individuals with similar observable characteristics differentially depending on their industry affiliation. Others have documented heterogeneity in wages between foreign-owned and domestic firms (FDI premium) and between exporters and those firms that only serve the domestic market (export premium).

Admittedly, the above studies based on microdata within a country ask a narrower question than the ambitious question posed in the current paper. They also provide case studies about the experiences with globalization within a country that might not necessarily generalize to other contexts. By exploiting the differential effects of trade reform across industries, or regions, or firms, these types of studies also cannot capture the overall effects of globalization on wages or other measures of well-being. But perhaps these more narrow questions are the only ones we can answer, at least without imposing strong modeling assumptions on the data.

Warner has collected on the level of the firm a unique data set of occupational wages and firm characteristics for a large set of developing and developed countries. I imagine that future work will make additional use of these more detailed data to further our understanding of determinants of wages in a globalized world.

Discussion: During the general discussion, a number of participants focused on how best to interpret the foreign language indicator used in the regression analysis. Carol Graham introduced the issue by wondering why the ability of managers

1. Goldberg and Pavcnik (2004).

to speak a foreign language should matter for janitors' wages. She thought it more likely that the indicator was actually picking up omitted country characteristics. In this context, Jeffrey Williamson suggested that the foreign language indicator might be a proxy for such things as colonialism and institutional development that the recent growth literature highlights as important determinants of productivity. He also noted that it would be interesting to explore other dimensions of the impact of language in global labor markets. What is the timing of language convergence versus wage convergence, and how do the two interact?

Carmen Pagés raised the concern of reverse causality associated with the foreign language indicator. Her view was that in Latin American countries (and perhaps elsewhere as well) it is members of the wealthy, elite groups who are most likely to learn English. Members of these groups are also more likely to become managers—but not because of their language skills per se. She also asked how representative the sample is in terms of firm size, noting that larger companies and affiliates of multinationals may have quite different wage levels and structures than other firms in developing economies.

Susan Collins commented that it would be interesting to distinguish wage developments within countries over time (as their GDP increases) from wage differences among countries at points in time. She noted that variations in cross-country data compared with time series data can be very different and that it can be quite misleading to attempt to draw conclusions about the latter from the former. However, pinning this down would require panel data.

There was also considerable discussion of alternative ways to interpret the wage regressions presented at the end of the paper, with suggestions for other possible ways to specify the empirical equation. Lant Pritchett suggested controlling for physical capital per worker, which has been incorporated in the revised version of the paper. Mark Rosenzweig suggested exploring the role of differences in educational attainment across countries, which Warner agreed would be an interesting direction for future analysis.

References

Ashenfelter, Orley, and Stapán Jurajda. 2001. "Cross-Country Comparisons of Wage Rates: The Big Mac Index." Princeton University and CERGE-EI/Charles University (October).

Beyer, Harald, Patricio Rojas, and Rodrigo Vergara. 1999. "Trade Liberalization and Wage Inequality." *Journal of Development Economics* 59, no. 1 (June): 103–23.

[BLS] Bureau of Labor Statistics. 1998. "International Comparisons of Hourly Compensation Costs for Production Workers in Manufacturing, Supplementary Tables (1975–96)." Washington: U.S. Department of Labor, BLS (February 9) (www.bls.gov/fls/hcommsupptabtoc.htm).

Currie, Janet, and Ann Harrison. 1997. "Sharing the Costs: The Impact of Trade Reform on Capital and Labor in Morocco." *Journal of Labor Economics* 15, no. 3, pt. 2 (July): S44–S71.

Freeman, Richard B. 1994. "A Global Labor Market? Differences in Wages among Countries in the 1980s." Paper prepared for Labor Markets Workshop. Washington: World Bank, July 6–8.

Freeman, Richard B., and Remco H. Oostendorp. 2000. "Wages around the World: Pay across Occupations and Countries." Working Paper 8058. Cambridge, Mass.: National Bureau of Economic Research (December).

———. 2005. Occupational Wages around the World (OWW) Database (September 13) (www.nber.org/oww/).

Goldberg, Pinelopi, and Nina Pavcnik. 2004. "Trade, Inequality, and Poverty: What Do We Know? Evidence from Recent Trade Liberalization Episodes in Developing Countries." In *Brookings Trade Forum 2004*, edited by Susan Collins and Carol Graham, Brookings, pp. 223–69.

Gollin, Douglas. 2002. "Getting Income Shares Right." *Journal of Political Economy* 110, no. 2 (April): 458–74.

Hansen, Gordon H., and Ann Harrison. 1999. "Trade Liberalization and Wage Inequality in Mexico." *Industrial and Labor Relations Review* 52, no.2 (January): 271–88.

[ILO] International Labour Office. 1998. *Yearbook of Labour Statistics 1998*. 57th ed. Geneva.

Krajnyák, Kornélia, and Jeromin Zettelmeyer. 1998. "Competitiveness in Transition Economies: What Scope for Real Appreciation?" *IMF Staff Papers* 45, no. 2 (June): 309–62. International Monetary Fund.

Rama, Martín, 1996. "A Labor Market Cross-Country Database." Washington: World Bank [accessed in 2002].

———. 2003. "Globalization and Workers in Developing Countries." Policy Research Working Paper 2958. Washington: World Bank.

Robbins, Donald. 1997. "Trade and Wages in Colombia." *Estudios de Economia* 24, no.1: 47–83.

Robbins, Donald, and Thomas H. Gindling. 1999. "Trade Liberalization and the Relative Wages for More-Skilled Workers in Costa Rica." *Review of Development Economics* 3, no. 2 (June): 140–54.

Rodrik, Dani. "Democracies Pay Higher Wages." 1999. *Quarterly Journal of Economics* 114, no. 3 (August): 707–38.

Smith, Alasdair. 1984. "Capital Theory and Trade Theory." In *Handbook of International Economics*, vol.1, edited by Ronald W. Jones and Peter B. Kenen, pp. 289–324 (ch. 6). Amsterdam: North Holland.

Trefler, Daniel. 1993. "International Factor Price Differences: Leontief Was Right!" *Journal of Political Economy* 101, no. 6 (December): 961–87.

Turner, Anthony G., and Stephen S. Golub. 1997. "Towards a System of Multilateral Unit Labor Cost-Based Competitiveness Indicators for Advanced, Developing and Transition Countries." Working Paper of the International Monetary Fund WP/97/151. Washington: IMF (November) (www.imf.org/external/pubs/ft/wp/wp97151.pdf).

[UNIDO] United Nations Industrial Development Organization. 1998. *International Yearbook of Industrial Statistics 1998*. New York.

U.S. International Trade Commission. 2004. "Comparative Assessment of the Textile and Apparel Sector in Selected Countries." In *Textiles and Apparel: Assessment of the Competitiveness of Certain Foreign Suppliers to the U.S. Market*. Investigation no. 332-448, sent to the U.S. Trade Representative in June 2003. Publication 3671. Washington: U.S. International Trade Commission, chapter 3 (http://63.173.254.11/pub3671/chap3.pdf).

Warner, Andrew M. 2003. "Wage Determination in 58 Countries." Working Paper. Washington: Center for Global Development (October).

World Bank. 2006. *World Development Indicators*. Washington.

DEVESH KAPUR
University of Pennsylvania

JOHN MCHALE
Queen's School of Business, Kingston

What Is Wrong with Plan B? International Migration as an Alternative to Development Assistance

The enormous differences in living standards across the world have, over the past half century, prompted, on the one hand, a large analytical effort to understand the key underlying causes of these differences and, on the other, efforts to address them.[1] In recent years analytical efforts have increasingly focused on differences in institutional quality as the most important determinant of these disparities in living standards.[2] However, these efforts have been more insightful with regard to how institutions matter than they have concerning the practical implications, that is, how to put institutions into place.[3]

Efforts at alleviating the vast differences in living standards have been a key driver behind foreign aid. While some believe that a large scaling up of investments in poor countries would help them break out of poverty traps, others are skeptical.[4] For decades the international community has striven to improve foreign aid as well as find additional mechanisms (such as greater trade access) to further the development prospects of the poor. A recent ambitious attempt to improve the lives of the world's poorest people is the Millennium Development Goals (MDGs), but if the past is any guide, the targets are unlikely to be

We thank the participants at the Brooking Trade Forum 2006 and especially Susan Collins, Carol Graham, and Gary Burtless for extremely valuable feedback.

1. For example, according to the *Human Development Report 2005*, Sierra Leone's GDP per capita (adjusted for purchasing power parity) in 2003 was just 1.5 percent of the United States' level (UNDP 2005).
2. Hall and Jones (1999); Rodrik, Subramanian, and Trebbi (2004); Acemoglu, Johnson, and Robinson (2005).
3. Fukuyama (2004); Rodrik (2006).
4. For a discussion of scaling up of investments, see, notably, Sachs (2005); for skepticism, see, notably, Easterly (2006).

met.[5] Those concerned with the well-being of the world's poor clearly need more arrows in their quiver, and it is in this spirit that Lant Pritchett has proposed a provocative Plan B: "My plan B is that we begin today to develop mechanisms for enhanced labor mobility so that, when in 2015 MDGs are not achieved (and in many countries there is no progress) . . . these can be scaled up and integrated into an international system that is truly globalized."[6] Accepting that "no one would embrace entirely free labor flows," he suggests as a starting point a more politically realistic plan with industry-specific quotas and explicitly temporary visas.[7]

This paper considers the broad case for a migration-based Plan B.[8] We stress that our focus is not specifically on Pritchett's carefully crafted proposal for significantly scaled-up temporary migration, but instead we look at the broader case for using migration as an additional tool to alleviate poverty. A (too) pithy statement of the broader migration-based Plan B might be: *If you cannot bring good institutions to the poor, allow the poor to move to the good institutions.* Or, as Pritchett asks, "How long must *only* Bolivia figure on the international agenda and *not* Bolivians?"[9]

The importance of institutions enters our discussion of Plan B in a number of ways. First, to the extent that differences in institutional quality are significant determinants of differences in living standards and institutional improvements are hard to "buy" with foreign assistance, it is worthwhile to examine increased migration as an alternative way to increase living standards of migrants. Second, again assuming that institutional differences are key determinants of income differences, there is potential for large income gains to migrants resulting from "institutional arbitrage," as economically debilitating institutional structures are left behind (at least temporarily). Third, there are

5. The Millennium Development Goals (MDGs) are a set of measurable goals agreed upon by world leaders at the United Nations Millennium Summit in 2000 to improve the welfare of the world's poor by 2015. These include halving extreme poverty and hunger; achieving universal primary education; empowering women and promoting equality between women and men; reducing under-five mortality by two-thirds; reducing maternal mortality by three-quarters; reversing the spread of diseases, especially HIV/AIDS and malaria; ensuring environmental sustainability; and creating a global partnership for development with targets for aid, trade, and debt relief. See www.un.org/millenniumgoals/background.html.

6. Pritchett (2003a, p. 39).

7. Pritchett (2003b, p. 4). He also suggests that compensation could be paid to sending countries for tax losses and adverse development impacts and that sending countries could be allocated a quota for the stock of immigrants, with any failure of return leading to deductions from the allowed flow the following year.

8. We use the term "temporary migration" and "temporary labor flows" interchangeably. This focus of our paper should not be confused with immigration policies, which of course refer to the more permanent movement of people from one country to another.

9. Pritchett (2003a, p. 38, emphasis in original).

potential negative effects of increased migration in the destination countries, including the distributional harm of lowering the income of the less skilled, the fiscal harm from attracting individuals who impose net fiscal costs, and the harm to civic capital from less cohesive communities. Fourth, to the extent that rich countries disproportionately target the highly skilled, there is a risk that institutional development will be further harmed by the absence of institution builders in poor sending countries, suggesting a possible trade-off between the static gains to migrants (and their households in the country of origin) from institutional arbitrage and the dynamics of institutional reform (in the country of origin). And finally, given the weakness of institutions in sending countries, it is critical to pay attention to the design details of a large migration program to ensure that the benefits go to the intended beneficiaries rather than be dissipated in rent seeking.

Our argument is organized in six sections. In the next (or second) section, we trespass into political theory to consider the case for Plan B from a philosophical perspective. The debate between nationalists (who emphasize the priority of co-nationals) and cosmopolitans (who emphasize universal concern) has been an active one in political philosophy. We try to steer a middle course by suggesting a form of *partial cosmopolitanism* as a useful way for economists to think about Plan B. The approach we pursue is an application of Amartya Sen's idea of *consequence-based evaluation* (essentially consequentialism with evaluator relativity). This approach allows the evaluator (say a rich-country voter deciding on immigration policy) to give some priority to the interests of co-nationals, while also giving increasing weight to the interests of foreign-born individuals, the worse off their starting point is.

Our reading of the literature suggests that a significant Plan B would be challenged by a number of leading liberal philosophers. *Liberal egalitarian* philosophers, such as John Rawls and Thomas Nagel, would not extend the strong egalitarian demands for justice outside the boundaries of the state that Plan B requires. Although they might support expanded immigration on humanitarian grounds (such as for asylum), they would be averse to supporting substantially higher economically motivated migration, especially if it harmed the poor of the receiving countries. On the other hand, *liberal nationalist* philosophers, such as Michael Walzer and Will Kymlicka, would be likely to worry about the impact of Plan B on the domestic political community, though they might support the alternative of significantly expanded development assistance to meet the demands of global justice. The central motivation for thinking about a migration-based Plan B, however, is that standard development strategies have not worked in many countries precisely because even though the goal is to help poor people, the focus of development assistance continues to be poor countries, so the alternative may well be continued high levels of global poverty.

If one accepts our partial cosmopolitanism, the case for Plan B is then largely empirical. We review the empirical evidence on three central questions: How much would the migrants (more precisely, temporary workers) benefit? (Our answer: A lot.) Would rich-country residents be harmed? (Our answer: Probably not, though there is uncertainty about the effects of less-skilled labor inflows on less-skilled natives.) Would those remaining behind be harmed? (Our answer: The migrant's household will typically gain through remittances. However, if the relaxation of immigration restrictions has a strong bias toward skills, those remaining behind are likely to lose. But the negative effects will vary significantly by country and sector, with the public sectors in smaller countries being especially vulnerable.) Quite obviously, the precise answers to these questions would vary considerably depending on the relative magnitude of international labor flows.

The next three sections review the evidence regarding these three questions. In the third section, we document the extreme divergence in income levels among countries and argue that significant portions are explained by differences in institutions and physical capital per worker. Income gaps across countries are due more significantly to differences in the *places* than to differences in the *people*. Although the average endowments of human capital are certainly lower in poorer countries, and although much domestically acquired human capital does not travel well, the available evidence strongly suggests that there are large income gains (adjusted for purchasing power parity) following migration.

In the fourth section, we turn to the impact of migration on rich receiving countries. There appears to be fairly widespread acceptance that skilled migration in reasonable numbers is good for the recipient economies. The theoretical case is further strengthened when we move beyond the standard competitive model to consider such factors as the generation of innovation, knowledge spillovers, specialized skills, scale economies, and fiscal effects. Probably the best evidence for the acceptance of benefits of skilled immigration is the efforts many rich countries are making to better compete for the world's mobile talent. There is a great deal more skepticism about the benefits of less-skilled immigration, skepticism that has been strongly influenced by George Borjas's empirical work documenting the adverse effects of immigration on native wages.[10] However, Borjas's empirical conclusions are disputed, and economic theory also points to several mechanisms that suggest any adverse wage effects will wane over time. We also

10. For example, Borjas (2003).

briefly review some recent findings on the fiscal effects of immigration, noting that the results are sensitive to the composition of the immigration flows and the nature of the fiscal systems. To ensure political support for a Plan B that is focused on less-skilled workers, we argue that the fiscal rights of migrants should not be such that they impose fiscal burdens on natives.

We reach the fifth section with the case for Plan B looking reasonably strong. We focus on the impacts of Plan B on those remaining behind in the home country. We argue that the impacts of increased labor inflows are likely to be sensitive to its skill composition, with skilled emigration posing the greatest risk of harm to those who stay in the home country. This is a concern because present trends suggest that any loosening of immigration restrictions is likely to have a strong skill bias. However, even for skilled emigration, we argue that the effects are not all unwelcome, and the balance of effects is likely to vary by sector and by country. Not surprisingly, given our opening emphasis on institutional failure as the primary cause of development failure, we pay particular attention to the impact of skilled emigration on domestic institutional development. Although here again we note that not all of the effects are negative, we do worry that the loss of a significant fraction of scarce human capital will further undermine institutional development.

In the sixth section we continue our discussion of the impact of emigration on sending countries, subjecting the plan to the stress test of implementation, which will critically determine the degree to which Plan B will increase the incomes of the intended beneficiaries, that is, temporary migrants and their households in the country of origin. The sharply increased incomes of the latter will be a form of rents and is likely to attract rent-seeking behavior. We examine some possible implementation mechanisms and find that there are reasons to worry. Although this does not in principle undermine the case for Plan B, it does point to the critical importance of implementation mechanisms if it is to provide the sorts of benefits envisaged.

In the last section we conclude with an endorsement of the general idea behind Plan B. If the main reason for continued gross poverty in the world is an enduring failure to put in place growth-supporting institutions, *and* if the rich countries have better institutions and the capacity to absorb more workers without inducing significant distributional, fiscal, or civic harm, then the normative and positive cases for expanded labor inflows from poor countries is strong. Our main reservations relate to how Plan B may be implemented and whether a possible skill-bias as well as rent-seeking behavior would vitiate the benefits envisaged. But the answer is not to abandon Plan B. Instead, we suggest strategies to minimize the negative effects on those remaining behind.

Nationalism versus Cosmopolitanism

Partial Cosmopolitanism

How should we assess the case for Plan B? We start in this section by outlining and briefly defending what we call partial cosmopolitanism as a useful evaluative framework. The debate between defenders of nationalism and defenders of cosmopolitanism has been an active and sophisticated one in political theory.[11] As noted in the introduction, our excuse for trespassing on the terrain of political theory is that this debate has centered on a theoretical question that is fundamental for the evaluation of Plan B: What relative weight should we place on the interests of poor foreigners? In pursuing a partial cosmopolitanism, we try to steer a pragmatic course that allows for priority weighting of co-nationals but also allows for increasing priority for the globally less well-off, the worse off their starting point is. This middle course follows Appiah, "We need take sides neither with the nationalist who abandons all foreigners nor with the hard-core cosmopolitan who regards her friends and fellow citizens with icy impartiality."[12]

More specifically, the partial cosmopolitan approach we pursue is a form of the consequence-based evaluation explored by Sen.[13] Consequence-based evaluation is standard consequentialism extended to allow for evaluator relativity. Sen asks, "Must every person have the same outcome evaluation function $G(x)$ irrespective of differences in their positions vis-à-vis actions, beneficiaries, and the like?"[14] His answer is no: "There is . . . no compelling reason why a morality that is sensitive to the differences in the position of people vis-à-vis states (including the actions that bring those states about) should not permit—indeed require—that different people evaluate the same state differently."[15]

In the case of Plan B, we assume we are in the position of a rich-country voter deciding on immigration and other foreign assistance policies. The consequence-based approach allows for some priority to be given to co-nationals.[16] This is compatible, however, with increasing priority also granted to the globally less well-off.[17] A simple example of an additively separable

11. See Tan (2004) for an overview of the debate.
12. Appiah (2006, pp. xvi–xvii); Appiah continues, "The position worth defending might be called (in both senses) a partial cosmopolitanism" (ibid., p. xvii).
13. Sen (1982, 1983, 2000).
14. Sen (1982, p. 29).
15. Sen (1982, pp. 29–30). We leave open the interpretation of the outcome variable *x*. Outcomes could be measured, for example, as incomes, utilities, capabilities (see Sen 1992) or primary goods (see Rawls 1971).
16. See Miller (1995) for arguments for the "ethical significance" of national ties.
17. That is, the marginal social value of a unit increase in the situation (say, measured by income)

consequence-based evaluation function that allows for both forms of priority would be

(1)
$$G_i = \sum_{i=1}^{N} x_i^{1-\varepsilon} + \omega \sum_{j=1}^{M} x_j^{1-\varepsilon},$$

for which $0 \leq \omega \leq 1$ and $0 \leq \varepsilon < 1$,

where N is the number of nationals (before immigration) indexed $i = 1, \ldots, N$; M is the number of nonnationals (again before immigration) indexed $j = 1, \ldots,$ M; x is the measure of individual outcomes; ω is a priority discount given to non-nationals; and ε is a measure of inequality aversion. There is no priority given to co-nationals when $\omega = 1$ (pure cosmopolitanism), and there is complete priority when $\omega = 0$ (pure nationalism). There is partial cosmopolitanism (or partial nationalism if the reader prefers) when ω lies strictly between 0 and 1. Similarly, there is no priority for the less well-off when $\varepsilon = 0$ (pure aggregation), and there is increasing priority for the less well-off as ε converges toward 1.[18] It is important that the left-hand side is indexed by i, indicating that the evaluation is being done from the perspective of a national of the immigrant-receiving country.

The foregoing consequence-based approach allows—though it does not presuppose—a significant concern for nonnationals. This concern is not necessarily limited to humanitarianism or fulfillment of basic needs. Take, for example, a Filipino nurse who would experience a significant improvement in her living standard if given the opportunity to emigrate to a country within the Organization for Economic Cooperation and Development (OECD). We assume this nurse is neither living in poverty nor politically oppressed in the Philippines, and so the concern is not a humanitarian one as usually understood. Rather, the nurse would be a classic economic migrant, not a refugee fleeing a failed or oppressive state. The consequence-based approach could—though again need not—view this migration as leading to a social improvement.

Before proceeding to look at the empirical evidence on the effects of migration, in the remainder of this section we briefly examine some arguments of leading liberal egalitarians and liberal nationalists who have been skeptical about the claims of cosmopolitan justice and concomitantly have argued against eco-

---

of an individual of a given nationality is decreasing in the income of that individual.

18. One feature of this evaluation function is that, assuming that one is away from the extremes, a unit transfer from a national to a nonnational will always lead to a social improvement provided the nonnational is sufficiently badly off relative to the national. However, the extent to which the nonnational must be relatively worse off is increasing in the priority given to co-nationals.

19. We focus on philosophers with more liberal leanings because they might reasonably be

nomically motivated labor inflows.[19] It is thus important to ask if the case for Plan B can withstand their objections.

In his *Theory of Justice*, Rawls provides a nonutilitarian-based theory of justice that does not leave individuals vulnerable to the "calculus of social interests," of the kind inherent in equation 1.[20] As he argues: "Each person possesses an inviolability founded on justice that even the welfare of society as a whole cannot override."[21] Focusing on what he calls the basic structure of society or "the way in which the major social institutions distribute fundamental rights and duties and determine the division of advantages from social cooperation," he derives strongly egalitarian demands of justice for individuals *within* a given society.[22] However, in the extension of his theory to questions of global justice in his *The Law of Peoples*, he rejects a cosmopolitan view that focuses on the "well-being of individuals and not [on] the justice of societies."[23] In contrast to the strongly egalitarian demands of justice within a given society, he argues that what states are required to do as a result of the demands of justice to help individuals in other states is much more limited. This does not mean that states are not required to help what he calls "burdened societies," but what is required is that these societies be brought to some minimum level of development.

> Burdened Societies, while they are not expansive or aggressive, lack the political and cultural traditions, the human capital and know-how, and, often, the material and technological resources needed to be well-ordered. The long-term goal of (relatively) well-ordered societies should be to bring burdened societies, like outlaw states, into the society of well-ordered peoples. Well-ordered peoples have a *duty* to assist burdened societies. It does not follow, however, that the only way, or the best way, to carry out this duty of assistance is by following the principle of distributive justice to regulate economic and social inequalities among societies. Most such principles do not have a defined goal, aim, or cut-off point, beyond which aid may cease.[24]

Rawls clearly recognizes the importance of good institutions for societal success and also the challenges of putting good institutions in place. But he ultimately assumes that development assistance efforts will be successful in bringing burdened societies to the cut-off level. In *The Law of Peoples*, he briefly discusses the causes of immigration from burdened societies but claims "they

---

expected to support freedom of movement, all things equal. It is thus informative to explore their reasons for supporting extensive immigration restrictions—that is, what else they believe is given up with a more liberal international migration regime.

20. Rawls (1971, p. 4).
21. Ibid., p. 3.
22. Ibid., p. 7.
23. Rawls (1999, p. 119).
24. Rawls (1999, p. 106, emphasis in original).
25. Rawls (1999, p. 9).

would disappear in the Society of liberal and decent Peoples."[25] He does not, however, address the question of what to do if the normal forms of development assistance fail to put the institutional prerequisites for a successful society in place. It seems unlikely that Rawls would support the sorts of immigration levels that would occur under Plan B.[26] But what if the result of relying on the normal forms of development assistance is continued egregious levels of global poverty? In this case, continuing to resist immigration as a means of allowing the poor to escape failing institutions seems troublingly at odds with Rawls's focus on improving the situation of the least well-off within a given society as a central demand of justice. The partial cosmopolitan position we suggest allows a less sharp line to be drawn between the demands of justice *within* and *between* societies.

Plan B is also likely to be viewed with skepticism by those liberal theorists for whom the preservation of a vibrant political community is a matter of critical concern. As Michael Walzer eloquently states in his *Spheres of Justice*,

The distribution of membership is not pervasively subject to the constraints of justice. Across a considerable range of the decisions that are made, states are simply free to take in strangers (or not)—much as they are free, leaving aside the claims of the needy, to share their wealth with foreign friends, to honor the achievements of foreign artists, scholars, and scientists, to choose their trading partners, and to enter into collective security arrangements with foreign states. But the right to choose an admissions policy is more basic than any of these, for it is not merely a matter of acting in the world, exercising sovereignty, and pursuing national interests. At stake here is the shape of the community that acts in the world, exercises sovereignty, and so on. Admission and exclusions are at the core of communal independence. They suggest the deepest meaning of self-determination. Without them, there could not be *communities of character*, historically stable, ongoing associations of men and women with some special commitments to one another and some special sense of their common life.[27]

Indeed Walzer goes as far as to oppose even guest worker programs arguing that once communities choose to allow foreigners in, they cannot then reduce them to second-class citizens. This line of reasoning is a good example of how the best can be the enemy of the good. When a hypothetical guest worker is not allowed in, then his or her living standards in the country of origin may be worse than a third-class citizen's by the standards of the receiving country. But arguments such as Walzer's would appear to normatively prefer this state of

26. Regarding immigration, Rawls asserts that "an important role for government, however arbitrary a society's boundaries may appear from a historical point of view, is to be the effective agent of a people as they take responsibility for their territory and the size of their population, as well as for maintaining the land's environmental integrity" (Rawls 1999, p. 8).
27. Walzer (1983, pp. 61–62, emphasis in original).

affairs than one in which the guest worker (whose rights would be circumscribed relative to those of a citizen) would have a second-class status.

In the context of the U.S. debate over immigration, Samuel Huntington has argued that waves of generally less-skilled Hispanic immigrants on the one hand and globally mobile, skilled elites retaining dual loyalties—whom he disapprovingly calls "ampersands"—on the other are undermining the "Anglo-American culture that has been central to American identity for three centuries."[28] In response, one can question if the danger to domestic societies is as great as Walzer and Huntington seem to suppose. For example, diversity can be a source of economic strength and cultural vibrancy.[29] Transnational networks have also been shown to play a central role in overcoming informational and contractual barriers to international economic exchange.[30] More fundamental, individuals are capable of maintaining multiple identities, which often help enrich human interaction rather than undermine it.[31]

Will Kymlicka offers a more nuanced liberal nationalist position on immigration.

> For liberal nationalists . . . there is a tradeoff between the benefits of mobility and the desire to ensure the viability of one's national culture. At the moment, immigrants are almost always a source of enrichment, both culturally and economically, to national societies. But that is because the numbers of immigrants are limited, and those that are admitted are encouraged to integrate into the national political culture. A policy of open borders, however, could lead to tens of millions of new immigrants entering a country, exceeding the capacity of existing national institutions to integrate them. . . . On the liberal nationalist view, states have a legitimate right to limit the number of immigrants, and to encourage their integration, in order to protect the viability of existing national cultures.[32]

Kymlicka allows that this right to limit immigrants can coexist with strong demands for global justice.[33] For example, closed borders could be combined with generous development assistance, allowing for both the protection of national cultures and global distributive justice. Recalling the motivation for Plan B, however, the problem is that existing development assistance strate-

28. Huntington (2005, p. xvi).
29. Ottaviano and Peri (2004).
30. Rauch (2001).
31. As Amartya Sen (2006, pp. 4–5) puts it: "In our normal lives, we see ourselves as a member of a variety of groups—we belong to all of them. A person's citizenship, residence, geographic origin, gender, class, politics, profession, employment, food habits, sports interests, taste in music, social commitments, etc., makes us members of a variety of groups. Each of these collectivities, to all of which a person simultaneously belongs, gives her a particular identity. None of them can be the person's only identity or singular membership category."
32. Kymlicka (2001a, p. 219).
33. Kymlicka (2001b); see also Tamir (1993); Tan (2004).

gies are not working for a large number of poor countries. Consequently Kymlicka's solution does not square the circle, and Plan B would have to be entertained if the concerns of global poverty were to take precedence.

Attitudes toward Immigration

Thus far in this section, we have argued that a voter who places *some* weight on the well-being of poor foreigners *should* be interested in a migration-based Plan B. But what are the actual attitudes of voters in richer countries to immigration, and to less-skilled in particular? Unsurprising, voters attitudes are not very positive on this issue. Table 1, adapted from O'Rourke and Sinnott, reports responses from a cross section of countries from the 1995 International Social Survey Programme (ISSP) module on national identity.[34] Respondents were asked if the number of immigrants to their economy should (1) be increased a lot, (2) be increased a little, (3) remain the same, (4) be reduced a little, or (5) be reduced a lot. Each response was given a score corresponding to the number. The mean response exceeded 3 for every country, indicating a widespread preference for more restrictive immigration by a majority of the respondents. Since then, if anything, attitudes have hardened further that ranged from fears of the eponymous "Polish plumber" that contributed to the rejection of the European Union constitution in France to heightened security fears in the aftermath of bombings in London and Madrid.

A number of recent studies have probed the factors that predict an individual's attitude to immigrants. Not surprisingly, having to compete directly with immigrants in the labor market leads to more negative attitudes to immigration.[35] There is also evidence that attitudes are affected by how immigrants affect natives through public finance channels. Where immigrants impose a net fiscal cost, and that cost is primarily borne by higher-income tax payers, the support by higher-earning natives for immigration is tempered.[36] This may go some way to explaining the "dual policy paradox" identified by Hatton and Williamson, whereby the "median voter" in rich countries supports free trade but opposes immigration, since imports typically do not impose net fiscal burdens.[37]

34. O'Rourke and Sinnott (2004).
35. See, for example, Scheve and Slaughter (2001); O'Rourke and Sinnott (2004); Dustmann and Preston (2004); Mayda (2006). For example, Mayda (2006) finds a positive correlation in cross-country data between individual skill and pro-immigration attitudes where immigrants are relatively unskilled compared with natives.
36. Hanson, Scheve, and Slaughter (2005); Facchini and Mayda (2006).
37. Hatton and Williamson (2005). The other contributing factor identified by Hatton and Williamson is the reduced selectivity of immigrants because of the secular decline in the costs of migration.

Table 1. Average Sentiment Regarding Immigrants[a]

Hungary	4.402
East Germany	4.338
West Germany	4.226
Bulgaria	4.219
Latvia	4.182
Czech Republic	4.158
Italy	4.151
Britain	4.052
Slovak Republic	4.004
Sweden	3.961
Slovenia	3.939
Poland	3.888
United States	3.873
Norway	3.847
Netherlands	3.826
Austria	3.804
Philippines	3.796
Australia	3.768
New Zealand	3.742
Russia	3.717
Spain	3.401
Japan	3.391
Canada	3.317
Ireland	3.071
Mean	3.878

Source: Adapted from O'Rourke and Sinnott (2004). Original data from the International Social Survey Programme (ISSP) National Identify Survey 1995.

a. See text for explanation of scoring.

Although this research clearly establishes that self-interested concerns about labor market competition and fiscal burdens shape attitudes to immigration, there is evidence that noneconomic factors matter as well. Of particular interest given our discussion of partial cosmopolitanism are the findings of O'Rourke and Sinnott relating to the influence of nationalist sentiment.[38] Drawing on various questions relating to nationalist sentiment in the ISSP data set, they use factor analysis to construct variables that measure the extent of nationalist feelings. The first, which they label "patriotism," captures the strength of preference for and sense of superiority of one's own country. The second, which they label "chauvinism," captures the extent to which people hold an exclusive view of nationality and the extent to which they take an attitude of "my country right or wrong." This latter measure is of particular interest since it strikes us as being a good indicator of nationalist partiality in our partial cosmopolitan social wel-

38. O'Rourke and Sinnott (2004).

fare function. O'Rourke and Sinnott find that these measures of nationalism are strong and consistent predictors of anti-immigration attitudes, with the influence of the "chauvinism" variable being particularly strong.

This would all be discouraging to a supporter of freer immigration for the less skilled if nationalist sentiment were impervious to change. One reason for optimism comes from Hainmueller and Hiscox's findings relating to the importance of education for attitudes towards immigration.[39] Using European data, they find that more-educated individuals are more supportive of immigration regardless of the skill composition of immigration, which is not consistent with the explanations of pure labor market competition and fiscal burden. Their work also supports the intuitive view that education affects cultural values and beliefs, with more-educated respondents displaying lower propensities toward racism and placing more value on cultural diversity. In a related vein, Dustmann and Preston find evidence of a significant link between education and more positive attitudes toward immigration, with the effect coming in part through a more positive overall assessment of the effects of immigration and not just more benign assessments about the impact on labor market competition.[40]

To sum up this section, we stress that our goal has not been to adjudicate between the arguments of nationalist and cosmopolitan philosophers. Our goals were more modest. The first was to lay out an evaluative approach useful to someone who gives some degree of priority to the interests of co-nationals, but whose concern does not stop at national borders. This consequence-based approach should appeal to economists trained to think in terms of trade-offs. The second was to question a key assumption used by liberal theorists in their defense of restrictions on immigration and labor inflows—that development assistance strategies are sufficient to bring "burdened societies" to a threshold level of development, to meet the demands of global justice, or both, which would reasonably imply that a Plan B is not needed. The third was to argue that rich-country voters are capable of looking beyond their narrow interests concerning labor market and fiscal issues in forming their attitudes about immigration, notwithstanding their importance. We assume in the rest of the paper that the partial cosmopolitan evaluation approach captured by equation 1 is adopted by a voter, noting that the equation is general enough to encompass a wide range of value judgments about the relative priority to be given to nationals and foreigners and also the priority to be given to the less well-off. The case for Plan B will then depend on how the migrants, the receiving-country resi-

39. See Hainmuller and Hiscox (2006).
40. Dustmann and Preston (2004).

dents, and those remaining behind in origin countries are affected. We now turn to examine the evidence on each.

Benefits to Migrants

How large are the income gains that migrants experience when they migrate from poor to rich countries? On their face, the enormous gaps in average living standards suggest that these gains would be very large. However, if the observed gaps are mainly due to differences in human capital between countries, the gains would be modest. At the other extreme, if the differences in incomes are mainly due to differences in institutions and physical capital per worker, then the gains would be large. Using the terminology of Jasso, Rosenzweig, and Smith, it matters how much of the difference in incomes across countries is due to skill *differences* and how much is due to skill *prices*.[41] One further complication is that the human capital that migrants do have may "travel poorly," because it is poorly suited to or poorly rewarded in the labor market of the receiving country (for example, because credentials are not recognized). In this section we review the evidence on these questions to get a sense of how large the gains are likely to be.

Explaining Living Standard Differences across Countries

A strong consensus has formed in the literature on economic growth and development that differences in institutional quality explain a large part of the observed differences in living standards across countries. The evidence takes two main forms: accounting exercises that attempt to apportion the differences in living standards to differences in resources, treating the residual as a measure of total factor productivity (which in turn can be interpreted as a broad measure of institutional quality) and econometric exercises that attempt to identify the causal determinants of living standards.

Hall and Jones provided both forms of evidence.[42] Using an accounting exercise, they found that low total factor productivity played the most important role in explaining differences in living standards (for which output per worker serves as a proxy) between rich and poor counties. For example, when compared with output per worker in the United States, Kenya's relative output per worker was 0.056, which Hall and Jones showed can be decomposed as the

41. Jasso, Rosenzweig, and Smith (2002).
42. Hall and Jones (1999).

product of the relative (weighted) capital to output ratio (0.747), the relative human capital per worker (0.457), and the relative total factor productivity (0.165).[43] Clearly, low total factor productivity was the most important factor explaining Kenya's relative impoverishment. Similar results were found for other poor countries. The reason this is relevant to gains from migration is that poor total factor productivity can be "left behind" by moving to a rich country in a way that a lack of human capital cannot.

This accounting exercise leaves open the reason for the low total factor productivity. Hall and Jones went on to use instrumental variable techniques to establish that total factor productivity was causally related to measures of institutional quality, or what they call "social infrastructure." They further found that the two other components of output per worker (relative capital to output per worker ratio and relative human capital per worker) were also strongly influenced by the social infrastructure.[44]

Other authors have also highlighted the importance of institutions in explaining differences in living standards. Acemoglu, Johnson, and Robinson used settler mortality as an instrument to predict institutional quality.[45] The idea is that settlers are more likely to establish good institutions in the colonies if they have to live under those institutions themselves, and they are more likely to live under them in colonies where settler mortality is low. Rodrik, Subramanian, and Trebbi used instrumental variables (including the settler mortality variable from Acemoglu, Johnson, and Robinson) to disentangle the effects of institutions, geography, and integration into international markets and found that "the quality of institutions trumps everything else."[46]

The Transferability of Human Capital

The cross-country evidence points to large institutional differences across countries. One reasonable implication is that a worker with given skills would experience significant income gains as the worker moves from a weak institutional environment to a stronger one, since skill prices will be higher in better institutional environments. As noted above, however, a possible complication is that skills acquired in one country might transfer badly to other countries, weakening or perhaps even reversing the income gain.

---

43. Hendricks (2002) used an alternative measure of human capital based on the observed wages of immigrants to the United States and found similar results.
44. Hall and Jones (1999).
45. Acemoglu, Johnson, and Robinson (2001).
46. Rodrik, Subramanian, and Trebbi (2004, p. 135).

The literature on the earnings of immigrants does suggest less-than-perfect transferability. In a study of immigrant earnings in Israel, Friedberg found that education and experience acquired abroad were significantly less valued than such human capital acquired in Israel.[47] Indeed, the return to foreign experience was generally found to be negligible. However, foreign human capital was found to interact positively with domestic human capital, suggesting that the older investments can be made more valuable with additional investments in the receiving country.

Various studies of immigrant earnings in Canada also suggested significant discounting for foreign-acquired human capital. For example, Alboim, Finnie, and Meng reported substantial discounting of foreign education and experience, even after controlling for language skills.[48] Ferrer and Riddell also found evidence of discounting, although they showed the return to credentials—what they termed the "sheepskin effect"—was actually higher for immigrants than it was for nonimmigrants.[49] This suggests that foreign degrees are well-recognized in the Canadian labor market, contrary to often-heard complaints about the nonrecognition of foreign credentials.

One important question is whether the generally low return to foreign human capital reflects a general low quality of skills or poor transferability of those skills. The former should have a more limited negative effect on the gains from migration, since low-quality human capital should be poorly rewarded everywhere. Again using evidence from Canada, Sweetman found evidence of significant differences in how foreign human capital is rewarded on the basis of quality measures of source-country education systems.[50] This suggests that at least part of the discount observed simply reflects poor-quality human capital; an implication is that real skills will be rewarded in receiving-country labor markets.[51]

47. Friedberg (2000).
48. Alboim, Finnie, and Meng (2005).
49. Ferrer and Riddell (2004).
50. Sweetman (2004).
51. Using U.S. Census data, Özden (2005) also documented substantial variation across countries in the share of tertiary-educated immigrants that have a "skilled job." The share ranged from a low of 21 percent for Guatemala to a high of 76 percent for India. The differences across countries could be due to differences in immigrant selection or to differences in the quality of the underlying human capital. Özden found that both are important. His measures of quality are source-country education expenditures per student (adjusted for purchasing power parity) and a dummy variable for English being a commonly spoken language.

Longitudinal Evidence

Of course, the best evidence on migrant gains comes from directly observing a migrant's pre- and postmigration incomes. Unfortunately, such longitudinal evidence is very scarce. One important exception is data from the New Immigrant Survey, which surveys legal permanent residents in the United States. Using a pilot version of this survey, Jasso, Rosenzweig, and Smith reported measures of the average earnings gain to new permanent immigrants.[52] The reported gains were large, even after adjusting for purchasing power parity to account for lower costs of living in the source countries. For the 230 immigrants in their sample who had worked in the source country and in the United States, the average income gain was more than $20,000 (from $17,080 to $37, 989). It is noteworthy that these gains occurred despite evidence of weak transferability of skills across countries. They measured this transferability by regressing log earnings in the United States on log earnings in the source country. The coefficient of source-country earnings ranged from 0.17 to 0.34 in their regressions, suggesting a weak correlation between how their skills were rewarded in the source country and how they were rewarded in the United States. Although care should be taken not to push these findings too far, given the small size of the sample, taken together they suggest that the income gains from moving to a stronger institutional environment are large even when skills do not travel well. Put another way, skill-price differences appear to trump weak skill transferability, thereby allowing substantial gains to migrants.

Harm to Natives

The results in the previous section provide our partial cosmopolitan voter with a reason to support a substantial increase in immigration from poorer countries, recalling that this voter is assumed to value income increases for foreigners—especially less well-off foreigners. But in making the cosmopolitanism *partial*, we assume that voters care relatively more about the income effects on co-nationals. If co-nationals are significantly harmed by immigration—especially less well-off co-nationals—then our voters may have good reasons to view increased labor inflows unfavorably.

---

52. Jasso, Rosenzweig, and Smith (2002).

Distributional Harm

We first look to the impact of less-skilled immigrants on competing natives in the labor market. The recent debate over U.S. immigration reform reveals that the nature of the effects remains highly disputed. Both proponents and opponents of increases in legal immigration are able to point to econometric studies by well-known researchers to support their case. Somewhat surprising given the disagreement in the literature, the view that less-skilled natives have been significantly harmed by immigration flows over the last few decades has become close to conventional wisdom. For example, writing in the *New York Times*, Paul Krugman notes: "While immigration may have raised overall income slightly, many of the worst-off native-born Americans are hurt by immigration— especially immigration from Mexico. Because Mexican immigrants have much less education than the average U.S. worker, they increase the supply of less-skilled labor, driving down the wages of the worst-paid Americans."[53] In a similar vein, Martin Wolf writing in the *Financial Times* concludes: "Low-skilled immigration also has adverse distributional effects. If a dominant concern were with the welfare of the more disadvantaged of the native-born, the case for control over the current influx of illegal immigrants would be strong."[54] There is now overwhelming evidence that the lowest deciles of the native born in the United States have seen relatively little gains from the economic expansion over the last quarter century. But to what extent is that explained by inflows of less-skilled foreign-born workers as distinct from other important factors, be it changes in fiscal policies, skill-biased technical change, or increases in labor-intensive imports?

The most influential findings of harm to less-skilled natives come from George Borjas.[55] Borjas's method was to divide the U.S. workforce into skill classes based on education level and experience. He then measured the immigrant share in each skill class and showed that higher immigration in a particular skill class was associated with lower wages in that class; that is, he found the labor demand curve sloped downwards.[56] Cross-elasticities were also found to be negative within education branches (that is, the wages of classes with the

53. Paul Krugman, "North of the Border," *New York Times*, March 27, 2006, p. 19.

54. Martin Wolf, "How to Harvest the Disputed Fruits of Unskilled Migration," *Financial Times*, April 5, 2006, p. 17. Wolf goes on to suggest a solution that should appeal to a partial cosmopolitan worried about the harm to native-born, low-skilled workers: "If a desire to offer opportunity to poor foreigners tempered that concern, a case would exist for formal relaxation of controls, combined with wage-subsidies for native-born low skilled workers" (Ibid., p. 17).

55. See, for example, Borjas (2003).

56. Aydemir and Borjas (2006) applied the Borjas (2003) methodology to datasets for Canada, Mexico, and the United States, finding broadly similar elasticities.

same education but with different experience decline when immigration within a given skill class increases) but positive within experience branches (that is, the wages of classes with the same experience but different education increase when immigration within a given skill class increases). Overall, he found that immigration to the United States between 1980 and 2000 led to wage declines of 8.9 percent for high school dropouts, 2.6 percent for high school graduates, 4.9 percent for college graduates, and no significant change for those with some college. Borjas and Katz extended the empirical model to allow for long-run adjustments in the capital stock.[57] Looking just at Mexican immigration to the United States, they found that there was no change in the wage of the typical worker once they allowed for induced increases in the capital stock. However, the least-skilled workers continued to be negatively affected even after the long-run adjustment of the capital stock, although the extent of the negative effects was significantly reduced.[58]

An important assumption in Borjas's analysis was that immigrants and natives were perfect substitutes within a given skill class. Ottaviano and Peri showed that relaxing this assumption can lead to significantly different results.[59] It is widely agreed that immigrants of a given skill are substitutes for some workers while complements for others. Allowing for imperfect substitutability within skill classes allows for more extensive complementary effects.[60] Looking at the period from 1990 to 2000, Ottaviano and Peri found that immigration (8 percent of the labor force in 1990) actually led to an increase in the average wage of 2.0 to 2.5 percent. They did find the wages of high school dropouts were driven down, but only marginally (1 percent), while the wages of workers with more than a high school education rose by 3 to 4 percent.

The empirical challenge in identifying the wage effects of immigration is to find a plausibly exogenous source of variation in the level of immigration. The source of this variation for the previous two studies was differences in the immigrant share by narrowly defined skill class. A different approach is to use variation in immigration level by geographic area (usually in addition to broad skill level). Using this approach Card argued that the evidence suggests that "the new immigration" may not really be so bad. On the question of how less-skilled immigration has affected less-skilled wages, his empirical work pointed

---

57. Borjas and Katz (2005).

58. Looking only at Mexican immigration to the United States between 1980 and 2000, they estimated that the wages of high school dropouts were reduced by 8.2 percent assuming no induced changes in the capital stock. The fall in the dropout wage was 4.8 percent after long-run adjustments of the capital stock implied by their model.

59. Ottaviano and Peri (2005).

60. See also World Bank (2006a, chapter 2, box 2.4).

to "a surprisingly weak relationship between immigration and less-skilled native wages."[61]

Borjas pointed to two possible problems with an approach based on geographical areas.[62] The first is that immigrants may be drawn to regions experiencing positive labor demand shocks, which could mask the wage-reducing effect of increasing labor supplies. One solution is to instrument for low-skilled immigration using historical immigration patterns, on the assumption that the latter is correlated with current immigration but uncorrelated with demand shocks. The second is that the arrival of immigrants to a particular area may lead natives to move out, businesses to move in, or both, either of which would mitigate the local wage decline. The concern is that this mobility just spreads the wage decline around in a way that the area studies are unable to pick up.[63]

Card discussed two alternative explanations of the absence of wage impacts in the area studies.[64] The first applies the Heckscher-Ohlin model from trade theory to argue that the industry structure adjusts (and with it relative skill demands) to neutralize the relative supply shocks so that there is no change in relative wages. Intuitively, if there is an expansion in relative supply of less-skilled workers, industries that use less-skilled workers intensively will expand and in doing so will raise the demand for those workers. Looking at changes in industry composition in response to immigration, however, Card concluded that this was not the main adjustment mechanism. His preferred explanation is that technology adoption responds endogenously at the area level to changes in available factor supplies. So, for example, if the local supplies of less-skilled workers expand, local businesses adopt technologies that are more intensive in the use of less-skilled workers.[65]

What should we conclude about the impacts of increased immigration on natives? Although Borjas's findings certainly cannot be dismissed, there does seem to be reasonable grounds for believing that, once one allows for the less-than-perfect substitutability between immigrants and natives within skill classes, immigration has positive or more or less neutral effects. The results of the national studies that allow for this imperfect substitutability are generally rein-

61. Card (2005, p. 11).
62. Borjas (2003).
63. See Card (2001) for evidence against this explanation for why the impacts of wages in the area studies were so small.
64. Card (2005).
65. The question is why they do this without a decline in the relative cost of less-skilled workers. Here Card points to Acemoglu's (1998) model of endogenous technological change, which showed how firms innovated in a way that took advantage of locally available factors.

forced by the finding of immigration neutrality from the area studies. *It should be emphasized, however, that these results are based on limited increases in labor inflows.* These results, together with the results from the previous section, lead us to conclude that modest increases in temporary labor flows under Plan B are likely to lead to large gains for the migrants without undue harm to individuals in the receiving countries, at least over the longer run.

Even if it were true that less-skilled natives are harmed, the best way to respond is unlikely to be to block migration. Rodrik and Pritchett both point out that economists generally oppose blocking imports of less-skilled intensive goods, even though the distributional implications are similar to less-skilled immigration.[66] With earnings differences exceeding price differences across countries, the increase in global efficiency would be significantly greater with reduced migration barriers than it would be with reduced trade barriers.[67] When it comes to trade, most economists advocate direct policies to deal with the harm to certain workers (for example, wage subsidies or worker retraining). While it is fair to be skeptical that such compensation policies would actually be put in place, it is also fair to ask why they are an appropriate response to trade-induced distributional harm but not to migration-induced distributional harm.

Fiscal Harm

A second possible source of harm comes through the fiscal system and the fiscal burdens migrants might impose. Again, the concern is mainly focused on less-skilled migrants. Indeed, increased immigration of skilled migrants is often proposed as a way to deal with the looming fiscal imbalances caused by aging populations.[68] For the less skilled, there is a considerable debate about the extent of fiscal burdens and benefits, with estimates varying depending on the nature of the fiscal systems. For the United States, Borjas and Hilton found that immigrants are disproportionate users of welfare benefits, although the use of welfare declined after the 1996 reforms of the welfare system.[69] In the most widely cited analysis, the National Research Council provided both static (that is, annual) and dynamic (that is, long-horizon) estimates of the fiscal effects of immigration.[70] For the static estimates, detailed analyses of the effects for

66. Rodrik (2001); Pritchett (2003a).
67. Rodrik (2001).
68. See, for example, Storesletten (2000).
69. Borjas and Hilton (1996). See Bojas (2002) for a discussion of the decline in the use of welfare by immigrants. This drop is largely explained by a large drop in the welfare use by immigrant relatives of natives in California.
70. Smith and Edmonston (1997).

1989–90 in New Jersey and for 1994–95 in California pointed to per capita fiscal burdens of $232 and $1,178, respectively (both in 1996 dollars). In contrast, an analysis over a long horizon (300 years) that also allows for the fiscal contributions of the immigrants' descendents results in an estimate that the average net present value (NPV) of the fiscal impact of immigrants would be $80,000. The size of this NPV depends on the skill level of the immigrant. Immigrants with less than a high school education would impose a burden of $13,000 under the baseline scenario. However, immigrants with more than a high school education would yield a benefit of $198,000. Such estimates unavoidably require a large number of assumptions. Borjas pointed, for example, to the implications of the assumption that the debt to GDP ratio would be stabilized after 2016, requiring tax increases that would fall in part on the immigrants, thus increasing their fiscal contribution.[71] He noted that less optimistic assumptions about closing the fiscal imbalance—concerns that seem to have been borne out in the intervening years—can easily change the sign of the average immigrant contribution.

In Europe, the fiscal consequences of immigration are likely to be more significant given the relative generosity of its welfare states and higher tax levels, though care must be taken in generalizing, given the heterogeneity in fiscal systems. In a detailed review, Boeri, Hanson, and McCormick found that increased migration would increase fiscal costs in countries with more generous fiscal systems, but they concluded that the effects were generally moderate.[72]

Clearly, any generalization must be made with due caution, given the available evidence. However, it does seem reasonable to suppose that less-skilled immigrants entering into countries offering generous welfare benefits would impose fiscal burdens. Although Plan B envisions temporary increases in less-skilled labor flows, concerns about fiscal harm cannot be dismissed. But given that less-skilled workers will likely see income gains from access to rich-country labor markets, it would be a shame if increased access is blocked because of concern about fiscal burden under a regime where migrants receive the *same fiscal treatment* as natives. Although there are understandable reasons to worry about creating different classes of residents with different entitlements to benefits—a fear clearly captured in the earlier quote from Michael Walzer—insisting on equal access makes it likely that the *best* (that is, increased access on equal terms) will indeed be made the enemy of the *good* (that is, increased access on terms that avoid fiscal burdens). It is thus worth considering what

71. Borjas (1999).
72. Boeri, Hanson, and McCormick (2002).

Gordon Hanson calls a "rights-based approach," involving limited and phased eligibility for fiscal benefits.[73]

Impacts on Those Remaining Behind

This leaves one last group to worry about: those people who remain behind in the developing countries. While there is uncertainty about the extents of the gains to migrants and the impacts of immigration on receiving countries, the implications of emigration for developing countries are probably least understood of all. We first outline a simple framework that draws attention to the channels through which emigration affects development.[74] We then discuss what we see as an increasing trend towards skilled-focused legal immigration reform in rich countries and the likely impacts for institutional development in poorer countries.

Emigration and Development

We see emigration as affecting development through four main channels: prospect, absence, diaspora, and return. We briefly discuss each in turn.

The *prospect* channel captures how the simple prospect of emigration can affect the decisions of forward-looking individuals and governments in ways that impact a country's development. Most attention has been given to how a prospect of emigration affects decisions to acquire human capital. The typical story is that the return to skills is greater abroad than at home, so that the expected return to investments in human capital is greater the higher the probability of emigration. Suppose, for example, that rich countries relax their immigration restrictions. The increased probability of getting a visa would then increase the expected return on human capital, which would (provided the substitution effect outweighs the income effect) lead to increased investment. However, not all the human capital–enhanced individuals will actually get a visa—and indeed not all will end up choosing to go even if they do get a visa—so it is at least possible that the country will end up with a greater stock of human capital.[75] This has been referred to in the literature as "brain gain." The prospect of emi-

73. Hanson (2005).
74. This section draws heavily on Kapur and McHale (2005a).
75. Another mechanism might be that individuals invest in additional credentials so as to meet the admission criteria of receiving countries (especially those countries using skills-based points systems). The additional credentials might give these individuals the option of emigrating, but not all of these options will be exercised. The overall result *could* again be a large domestic stock of human capital.

grating is likely to also change the mix of human capital investments in the direction of more internationally marketable skills. This could bias the human capital stock away from the needs of the domestic economy given its industrial structure and also possibly bias investments away from skills with greater domestic social returns. On the other hand, the more forward-looking investment choices—for example, investments in programming skills—might help the country break out of less-dynamic patterns of comparative advantage.

Although the basic "brain gain" story has some plausibility given the clearly forward-looking nature of the demand for skills, it has come in for some strong criticism. Commander, Kangasniemi, and Winters as well as Schiff have argued, for example, that the highest-ability individuals will invest in skills regardless of the prospect of emigrating, but these individuals will be particularly prone to being recruited away when the prospect of emigration is opened up.[76] This is pure brain loss, and it may be very hard to recover through increased investments by more moderate-ability individuals. Another possible criticism is that the prospect of emigration is likely to affect the publicly funded supply of human capital as well as the private demand. Governments may be understandably less willing to invest scarce revenues in education if there is a high probability that the recipients will ply their skills elsewhere. We return to the possible impacts of the prospect of emigration on institutional development below.[77]

The *absence* channel measures the direct effects when some fraction of compatriots have emigrated. In most ways, these effects mirror the impacts of immigration with the sign reversed. For example, emigration with a given skill composition changes the size and composition of the domestic labor supply and with it the distribution of incomes among the people remaining behind. The standard competitive labor market model typically points to small changes in average incomes (although those changes are usually shown to increase with the square of the rate of emigration). But the model points to potentially larger changes in the distribution of incomes when that emigration is biased toward a particular skill level. For example, a relatively high rate of emigration of the highly skilled will lead to a relatively modest reduction in average incomes, but a significant increase in the skill premium. However, relaxing the assumptions of the competitive model to allow for such features as fiscal effects, specialized skills, knowledge spillovers, and scale economies allows for considerably larger effects on the average incomes as a result of significant

76. Commander, Kangasniemi, and Winters (2004); Schiff (2005).
77. The empirical results on the "brain gain" story have been mixed. Beine, Docquirer, and Rapoport (2001) found evidence of a positive effect on growth for countries with low rates of emigration of tertiary-educated workers. Schiff (2005) discussed evidence that skilled emigration lowers investments in tertiary education.

high-skilled emigration.[78] We pay particular attention to the implications of the loss of individuals who would have played key roles as institution builders below.

The *diaspora* channel captures the role emigrants play in development from afar. The central idea is that an emigrant retains certain connections to the home country and so should not be viewed as "just another foreigner" from the perspective of the home country. If we focus first on more-skilled emigrants, members of the diaspora are likely to show disproportionate willingness to transact with those back home, including information exchange, purchase of products, and investment in home-country businesses. Well-connected emigrants are also in a good position to act as "reputational intermediaries." The reputational function can take a number of forms: leveraging knowledge of the individuals and businesses in both countries to help match trading partners, using long-term relationships in both countries to support third party–based and reputation-based mechanisms of contract enforcement, and altering the "profile" or perception of compatriots in the country of origin through demonstration of capabilities in their new homes. A good (if sometimes exaggerated) example of the positive development role played by a skilled diaspora is the part played by India's Silicon Valley–resident diaspora in the development of India's information technology sector.[79]

Less-skilled emigrants can also play a critical role in home-country development from afar. The most important (though certainly not the only) mechanism is the sending of remittances. Burgeoning microeconometric research is establishing that remittances are helpful in reducing poverty.[80] There is also growing evidence that remittances respond positively to adverse shocks such as droughts and hurricanes, which is especially important when poor households have few other ways of managing risk.[81] The old conventional wisdom that remittances are "frittered away" on consumption is also changing, as evidence accumulates of a relatively high propensity to invest remittance income in assets such as education and working capital for small businesses.[82] However, the evidence in other contexts (for example, Afghanistan, Democratic Republic of the Congo, and Somalia) is less sanguine. It should be emphasized that no country has developed on the basis of remittances—hardly surprising given the reality that remittances result from migration, and the exit of substantial numbers of a population is a strong signal that there are serious problems in the country.[83]

78. See Kapur and McHale (2005a, chapter 6).
79. See Kapur and McHale (2005b); Saxenian (2002).
80. For a survey, see World Bank (2006a, chapter 5).
81. See, for example, Clarke and Wallsten (2004); Yang (2005).
82. See, for example, Cox and Ureta (2003); Woodruff and Zenteno (2001); Yang (2004).
83. Kapur (2005).

The final channel through which emigration affects development is the *return* channel. The focus here is on how emigrants might return with enhanced skills, savings, connections, and entrepreneurial ideas. In other words, emigrants may return "better" than they left. If the improvement in their economic assets is sufficiently great, it may more than compensate for any absence-related losses. The chances of this are even greater if the emigration occurs during depressed periods in the home country's economy, times when it may be hard to get an opportunity to make an economic contribution. Emigrants might then be seen as at least partly engaged in a form of intertemporal substitution: investing in various forms of capital when work opportunities at home are limited. One example of a country that appears to have prospered from such round-tripping is Ireland during the so-called Celtic Tiger boom years of the later 1990s. Surveys show that the emigration rate for male tertiary-level graduates peaked at around 25 percent in the late 1980s. This was a time of substantial job loss— with employment actually falling by 5 percent between 1982 and 1989—which led to unemployment rates that hovered in the mid-teens. With the dramatic turnaround in the economy in the 1990s, many of these emigrants were drawn back to the Irish economy. There is evidence that these returnees did come back with enhanced human capital relative to what they would have had if they had not left.[84]

The Skill Bias of Recent Immigration Reforms

Immigration reforms in many OECD countries are moving admission priorities in an ever-more skill-focused direction (embodied, for instance, in the "chosen immigration" legislation advocated by France's interior minister Nicolas Sarkozy). There is growing interest (for example, in the United Kingdom) in points-based systems for selecting immigrants on the basis of human capital characteristics of the kind pioneered by Australia and Canada in the 1960s and 1970s. Canada and Australia have at the same time been increasing the share of immigrants who qualify on the basis of skills in their overall immigrant intakes and reforming their temporary worker visa and student visa programs to better access the world's mobile talent. Although the United States has pursued some skills-focused reforms, such as increasing the number of green cards allocated on the basis of skills and temporarily tripling the number of H-1B temporary worker visas for highly skilled workers, the influx of less-skilled illegal immigrants have dominated recent debates in the United States.

---

84. Barrett and O'Connell (2001) found that returnees earned a 5 percent premium over observationally equivalent individuals who never left.

Various forces are driving the trend towards more skill-focused systems—forces from which the United States is unlikely to be immune. Such forces include the perceived importance of the access to international talent in the competitiveness of knowledge-based industries, the looming costs of paying the promised health and pension benefits of rapidly aging populations, and the belief that more-skilled elites will more easily integrate into host societies.[85]

The increasing skill bias in migration flows from poor to rich countries is evident when we look at emigration rates by skill level across countries. Table 2 draws from the database of Docquier and Marfouk on emigration rates to show the emigration rate for tertiary-educated individuals by region. This rate measures the ratio of the stock of tertiary-educated emigrants to total tertiary-educated stock (emigrants and domestic residents). Both numerator and denominator are restricted to those aged 25 years or older. Looking at the emigration rates for 2000, we see that 41 percent of the tertiary-educated individuals born in the Caribbean region were living in an OECD country—a startling number. The corresponding rates were 27 percent for West Africa, 18 percent for East Africa, 16 percent for Central America, and 13 percent for Central Africa. In four of these five regions, the tertiary emigration rate rose significantly between 1990 and 2000. Table 3 records emigration rates for countries facing the largest absence of their tertiary-educated stock. The table makes clear that it is small, poor countries that face the greatest risk of absence. For example, the tertiary emigration rate in 2000 was more than 80 percent for Guyana, Grenada, Jamaica, St. Vincent and the Grenadines, and Haiti. For these five countries, the average population was just 2.3 million, and the average GDP per capita in 2000 as a share of the U.S. level was just 13 percent. We next turn to the possible implications of skilled emigration for institutional development in the origin countries.

Skilled Emigration and Institutional Development

The role of human capital in institutional development has been a topic of interest in recent empirical and theoretical research. In two separate studies, Glaeser and colleagues and Glaeser, Ponzetto, and Shleifer presented evidence that improvement in economic and political institutions was strongly influenced by initial human capital endowments.[86] Acemoglu and Robinson developed a theory of institutional change in which the de facto political power to change institutions depends, in part, on the distribution of endowments, including the

85. See Kapur and McHale (2005a, chapters 3 and 4).
86. Glaeser and colleagues (2004); Glaeser, Ponzetto, and Shleifer (2006).

Table 2. Tertiary-Educated Emigration Rates to OECD Countries, by Region[a]

Region	Tertiary Emigration Rates			
	1990	2000	Difference	2000/1990
Caribbean	41.4	40.9	–0.5	0.99
Western Africa	20.7	26.7	6.0	1.29
Eastern Africa	15.5	18.4	2.9	1.19
Central America	12.9	16.1	3.2	1.25
Central Africa	9.8	13.3	3.5	1.36
Southeastern Asia	10.3	9.8	–0.5	0.95
Northern Africa	6.8	6.2	–0.6	0.91
Western Asia	6.9	5.8	–1.1	0.84
South America	4.7	5.7	1.0	1.21
Southern Africa	6.9	5.3	–1.6	0.77
South-central Asia	4.0	5.1	1.1	1.28
Eastern Europe	2.3	4.5	2.2	1.96
Eastern Asia	4.1	4.3	0.2	1.05

Source: Docquier and Marfouk (2004).

a. The emigration rate measures the ratio of the stock of tertiary-educated emigrants to total tertiary-educated stock (emigrants and domestic residents) for the population aged 25 and older.

distribution of human capital.[87] Rodrik stressed the importance of "local knowledge" in the search for institutions that are effective under local conditions.[88] Fukuyama and separately Pritchett and Woolcock focused on the importance of human and social capital in providing public services, particularly those services that are transaction intensive and that require discretion on the part of providers (for example, judges) to properly respond to specific circumstances.[89] Easterly emphasized the importance of properly motivated "searchers" to finding the best way to organize activities given the local conditions.[90]

It is easy to imagine that skilled emigration could directly undermine the *effectiveness* of institutions by thinning the ranks of those qualified to design and staff key institutional functions. Skilled emigration could also indirectly change the *politics* of institutional reform. One useful way to think about the latter effects is in terms of the "exit" and "voice" mechanisms for institutional improvement explored by Hirschman.[91]

Returning to our four-channel framework, skilled emigration could affect institutional change through all four channels. On the one hand, the prospect of emigration may give more productive members of society an exit option that improves their threat point in bargaining with predatory rulers, leading to insti-

87. Acemoglu and Robinson (2006).
88. Rodrik (2000).
89. Fukuyama (2004); Pritchett and Woolcock (2004).
90. Easterly (2006).
91. Hirschman (1970).

Table 3. Emigration Rates, 1990 and 2000ᵃ

Country	2000 Population (000s)	2000 Share of U.S. GDP per capitaᵇ	1990 Emigration rate total	1990 Emigration rate tertiary	2000 Emigration rate total	2000 Emigration rate tertiary
Guyana	744	0.120	0.33	0.91	0.42	0.89
Grenada	101	0.222	0.46	0.78	0.54	0.85
Jamaica	2,589	0.107	0.30	0.85	0.35	0.85
St. Vincent and the Grenadines	116	0.157	0.29	0.81	0.37	0.85
Haiti	7,939	0.053	0.07	0.79	0.12	0.84
Trinidad and Tobago	1,285	0.264	0.20	0.78	0.25	0.79
St. Kitts and Nevis	44	0.330	0.45	0.78	0.49	0.78
Samoa	177	0.143	0.46	0.97	0.51	0.76
Tonga	100	0.193	0.38	0.96	0.47	0.75
St. Lucia	156	0.165	0.19	0.68	0.23	0.71
Cape Verde	451	0.143	0.25	0.57	0.25	0.67
Antigua and Barbuda	77	0.295	0.33	0.65	0.38	0.67
Belize	250	0.173	0.28	0.67	0.29	0.65
Dominica	71	0.175	0.45	0.69	0.41	0.64
The Gambia	1,316	0.051	0.02	0.80	0.03	0.63
Fiji	811	0.146	0.16	0.66	0.21	0.62
The Bahamas	301	0.500	0.11	0.57	0.12	0.61
Malta	390	0.537	0.31	0.69	0.27	0.58
Mauritius	1,187	0.283	0.11	0.65	0.11	0.56
Seychelles	81	0.529	0.20	0.66	0.20	0.56
Sierra Leone	4,509	0.014	0.01	0.34	0.02	0.53
Ghana	19,867	0.056	0.01	0.38	0.02	0.47
Mozambique	17,911	0.026	0.01	0.27	0.01	0.45
Lebanon	3,398	0.124	0.17	0.44	0.15	0.39
Kenya	30,689	0.030	0.02	0.43	0.02	0.38
Lao PDR	5,279	0.046	0.08	0.30	0.10	0.37
Uganda	24,309	0.037	0.01	0.44	0.01	0.36
Cyprus	786	0.598	0.21	0.32	0.17	0.31
El Salvador	6,280	0.135	0.14	0.33	0.20	0.31
Sri Lanka	19,359	0.107	0.02	0.29	0.03	0.30
Nicaragua	4,959	0.096	0.08	0.30	0.09	0.30
Ireland	3,813	0.899	0.28	0.36	0.23	0.29
Hong Kong, China	6,665	0.759	0.08	0.32	0.09	0.29
Papua New Guinea	5,299	0.068	0.01	0.39	0.01	0.28
Vietnam	78,523	0.059	0.02	0.25	0.03	0.27
Rwanda	8,025	0.031	0	0.17	0	0.26
Honduras	6,424	0.074	0.04	0.22	0.08	0.24
Guinea-Bissau	1,366	0.023	0.01	0.09	0.02	0.24
Guatemala	11,166	0.117	0.06	0.20	0.09	0.24

Sources: World Bank (2006b); Docquier and Marfouk (2004).
a. Countries are ranked by their tertiary emigration rate in 2000.
b. Share of U.S. GDP per capita based on 2000 purchasing power parity dollars.

tutional and policy concessions such as less extortionary taxation. As Douglas North puts it,

> The ruler always has rivals: competing states or potential rulers within his own state. . . . The closer the substitutes, the fewer the degrees of freedom the ruler possesses, and the greater the incremental income that will be retained by the constituents. The opportunity cost of each of the various constituents will be different and will dictate the bargaining power each group has in the specification of property rights, and well as the tax burden it will incur. Opportunity costs will also dictate the allocation of services provided by the ruler to the degree they are not pure public goods, since the ruler will provide greater services to those with closer alternatives than to those with none.[92]

On the other hand, having an option to emigrate could also make younger people less willing to invest in skills that are most relevant to local institutions, preferring instead to invest in private-sector skills that are more internationally marketable—such as becoming programmers rather than lawyers.

The absence of talented individuals affects the *supply* of institution builders. As Fukuyama notes, "Public agencies with poorly trained staff and inadequate infrastructure will have difficulty delivering services."[93] But for Fukuyama the implications of the loss of educated individuals, scarce in number, may go beyond the loss of their narrowly defined human capital: "The kinds of internalized norms that motivate workers to do more than the minimum in exchange for their wages do not come naturally in any society; they are the result of education, training, and a socialization process that is partly specific to a particular profession and partly absorbed from the surrounding society."[94] This suggests that the loss of scarce talent does more than thin the available supply of human capital; it also undermines social capital and with it the more informal parts of the country's institutional infrastructure. In addition, absence can also impact the *demand* for better institutions. Although it is certainly possible that highly talented individuals have a stake in the continuation of bad institutions that allow them to extract rents, in general we would expect talented individuals to have a relatively strong interest in productivity-supporting institutions. Emigration can thus rob the country of influential voices for reform, especially those with internationally marketable talents and those who are not in the business of rent extraction at home.

Finally, looking at the diaspora and return channels, we must not forget that emigrants are not necessarily lost to the country from the point of view of institution building. Many skilled emigrants will remain connected to their former

92. North (1981, p. 27).
93. Fukuyama (2004, p. 66).
94. Fukuyama (2004, p. 66).

homes and can be a source of ideas on best practices and possibly even a source of funding for improved public services at the local level. (However, they can also be a source of funding for opponents of the government, thereby perpetuating civil strife that weakens a country's institutions.) Their fortunes made and their skills acquired, some returning emigrants will come back highly motivated to move their home-country institutions toward the norms that allowed them to achieve their success.

Implementation—the Achilles Heel of Plan B?

The possibility that Plan B could be undermined by skill bias in labor flows from poor countries points to the need to examine implementation mechanisms more closely. The history of development is replete with good ideas floundering on the shoals of implementation, and the degree to which Plan B will increase the incomes of the poor will depend on the manner of implementation. In this section we look at some examples of possible implementation mechanisms and find that there are more devils in the details than may be first apparent.

At the outset it must be recognized that labor mobility is one of the few global issues over which poorer countries have some bargaining power. After all, illegal migration is an issue that is of far greater concern to richer countries. The status quo favors poor countries in that all they have to do is do what they do well—simply do nothing. This is especially true of geographically contiguous countries who have limited incentives to reach bilateral deals, since any feasible negotiated number is likely to be swamped by illegal workers.

How will Plan B work in practice? Ideally one might envisage a lottery-like arrangement—a random drawing from a poor country's population that gives the winners an opportunity to work in sector X in country Y (or where skills are more specialized, such as in the health care field, in a specified subset). In practice, of course, the selection and matching problems in labor markets require specific institutional mechanisms.

Will the gains accrue to poor countries or poor people? The many contentious issues surrounding migration notwithstanding, on one issue the evidence is unambiguous. International migration from poor countries (even from Mexico) is positively selected compared with those workers remaining behind. Those migrants who are more likely to avail of the opportunities of Plan B will not be the illiterate but those with some schooling. Indeed the greater the economic travails of the country, the greater the likelihood that those trying to avail of Plan B will be the more educated and skilled. Although many of the latter may also be close to the poverty line and this would still be helpful to the poor country, one should not expect significant gains accruing to the poorest groups.

Political economy consequences. The biggest weakness in implementation is likely to occur at the sending country end, a consequence of two realities in the scheme: most gains accrue to migrants; and rationing will inevitably occur concerning who gets to go—and where. If there is one truism about countries with weak institutions, it is that where there are rents there is rent-seeking behavior. How much of the hypothesized income gains will actually reach the poor?

One possible implementation mechanism is similar to what prevails in labor flows to the Persian Gulf countries. A certified labor contractor recruits labor in the developing country and then supplies the labor to an employer in the industrialized country, relieving the latter of search costs and any legal obligations save those to protect the basic rights of workers. The rent-seeking hierarchy works as follows: the worker pays the labor contractor for the privilege of being hired; the labor contractor in turn has to pay the bureaucracy to obtain and maintain his certification; and the bureaucrats have to share these spoils with the politicians to remain in these lucrative posts (figure 1). This increases the fixed costs of going abroad, which are met either through debt obligations or by selling land (and whose recovery often necessitates a longer stint abroad).[95]

Although it is easy to construct hypothetical obstacles, it is not too hard to foresee the emergence of a political economy of rent seeking through labor exports of the sort we have schematically outlined. And if that occurs, there is a possibility of moral hazard. The very weakness of the institutions that prompted this scheme will also result in rent seeking, undermining the incentives to improve the institutions. Of course, one can design alternative institutional mechanisms ranging from labor contractors being certified by the labor-receiving country, to forced savings schemes for migrant workers, and so forth. Although space does not permit us to discuss them in detail here, our point is principally to highlight the reality that all mechanisms will have some unintended behavioral implications that must be carefully understood.

Ethnic bias redux? In practice it is pretty obvious that a Plan B will not be negotiated through the World Trade Organization (with attendant most favored nation [MFN] obligations). Labor-importing countries will insist on negotiating agreements with poor countries on a bilateral basis, given the fact that if

---

95. For an example from Bangladesh see Rahman (2001).

Figure 1. The Dissipation of Worker's Rents

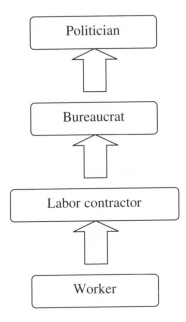

the richer countries cannot control *who* gets in (as distinct from *how many*), they will in all probability reject Plan B.

But bilateral deals are likely to result in one disturbing consequence: they will reverse hard-earned successes of reducing ethnic bias in immigration policies and by implication restrict the international mobility of different peoples. Until the 1960s immigration policies in most industrialized countries had strong ethnic biases, the result of blatant racism in the past. These policies were largely dismantled, but a Plan B would risk a de facto ethnic bias in international labor mobility. Imagine two of the most impoverished countries in South Asia—Afghanistan and Nepal. How many industrialized countries would prefer sourcing labor from the former compared with the latter? While we are likely to see Japan reaching agreements with the Association of Southeast Asian Nations, and the European Union with East Europe and Latin America, we are skeptical that there will be any takers for labor from Chad and Sudan—countries whose peoples are perhaps most in need of access to global labor markets.

Furthermore, on the source-country side, governments might also simply favor certain ethnic groups or areas that are politically important. Ethnic conflict and bias are fairly common in precisely those countries for whom Plan B is most intended—which may be amplified when rents are substantial.

Conclusion

Imagine a situation is which the global community is faced with helping the population of an impoverished and ravaged country—an Armenia or an East Timor, for example. It could either pour billions of dollars over the next few decades into these countries (which it has already done and will continue to do). Alternatively, it could give a significant number of residents one-way tickets out of the country. Which of the two alternatives is likely to have greater welfare implications if our numeraire is people rather than countries?

Although Lant Pritchett's Plan B is different, focusing on temporary (rather than on permanent) labor mobility, the underlying idea is similar: *If you cannot bring good institutions to the poor, allow the poor to move to the good institutions.* Since permanent moves of any significance will be politically unacceptable, Plan B proposes a pragmatic middle ground: allow labor circulation from poor to rich countries that will modestly increase the labor supply in industrialized countries without the attendant concerns of permanent settlement.

But if all parties gain (albeit to varying degrees), what explains the opposition to expanded labor inflows into rich countries? Pritchett critically discusses what he calls four "immovable ideas": (1) nations exist and nation states are a reasonable and just foundation of an international system, (2) all that matters for moral obligations is proximity, (3) labor mobility is bad for the poor in rich recipient countries, and (4) labor movements are not necessary to raise living standards.[96]

In considering the case for Plan B, we pragmatically accepted the first. We did not accept the second in its strong form, though we accepted that rich-country voters will typically give substantially greater priority to co-nationals. We found normative arguments by liberal philosophers against labor inflows wanting, a case of the best being the enemy of the good. In immigration policy, the insistence on multiculturalism in Western Europe may have contributed in the long run to increasing the resistance of the native born to further immigrant inflows (through the creation of unassimilated ghettoized immigrant communities). Similarly, setting standards that are too high for guest workers, for instance, thus making it hard to enforce the return requirements, simply means that the programs do not expand, thereby shutting out newer beneficiaries from poor countries.

We recognized that the evidence is mixed on the third point, with careful econometric studies on both sides. We argued, however, that the case for the

96. Pritchett (2003a).

poor in rich countries being harmed is less well established than the conventional wisdom supposes. And even if there is some harm, better ways to deal with that harm are available than to block efficiency and welfare-enhancing international labor flows. In casting doubt on the universal applicability of the last point, we drew on recent work that stresses the importance of the quality of institutions to development and the difficulties that many countries have putting those institutions in place.

We thus come down broadly in agreement with Pritchett on the importance of thinking now about a Plan B. (Or, to answer the question in the paper's title: not a lot.) In closing, however, we further discuss one lingering concern about the effects of Plan B—the effects on poor people remaining behind—and how Plan B might be designed to deal with it.

As discussed above in the section discussing the impact on the poor people remaining behind, immigration policies of rich countries are increasingly focusing on skills. There is a danger that any politically acceptable scaling up of immigration flows will have a significant skill bias. We also drew attention to the possibility that the loss of scarce talent—and especially potential institution builders in the upper tail of the talent distribution—could undermine domestic institutional reform. This is a particular concern for public institutions in small, poor countries. This means development advocates will have to work hard to ensure that a development perspective gets heard along with more nationally focused concerns (such as competitiveness in innovation-intensive sectors, paying the fiscal costs of an aging society, among others). In practical terms, the development voice must be heard to ensure that the less skilled are not shut out of rich countries.

Being realistic, however, we have to accept that governments in rich countries will continue to target the more skilled. It is thus important to enhance mechanisms that allow the poor remaining behind to share in the gains, a point also emphasized by Pritchett. These include mechanisms that help compensate poor sending countries as well as mechanisms that enhance home-country connections with the disapora. On the compensation side, rich countries could help fund essential institutional capacity-building in such sectors as education and health care. On the connections side, receiving countries could make it easier for emigrants to engage in beneficial interactions with family members remaining behind (that is, reduced regulatory policies and barriers to the sending of remittances, cooperation with sending countries that wish to impose a Bhagwati tax on emigrants that retain citizenship, and removing obstacles to back-and-forth movements).[97]

97. Concerning reduced regulatory policies and barriers regarding remittances, see the World

Finally in all plans, the "rubber hits the road" only during implementation. In examining possible implementation mechanisms, our analysis raised concerns about the political economy, in particular distributional conflicts and rent-seeking behavior arising from the rents that will accrue to those lucky enough to work outside the country. This means that we need to subject possible implementation mechanisms to much greater scrutiny to ensure that the benefits of Plan B indeed accrue to those for whom it is intended.

Bank's *Global Economic Prospects 2006* (chapter 6) for a detailed discussion of the options. The required cooperation with sending countries (wishing to impose a tax on emigrants) could simply be the validation of the emigrant's tax return by the tax authorities in the receiving country. This would occur at the request of the emigrant seeking to stay in good standing for the retention of his or her home-country citizenship. See McHale (2005).

Comment
and Discussion

Gary Burtless: The papers in this volume emphasize cross-border movement of people rather than goods and services. The essay by Devesh Kapur and John McHale asks whether cross-border migration can and should be an alternative route to raising the incomes of people who now reside in poor countries.

Lant Pritchett's paper in this volume suggests that the elimination of cross-border barriers to migration can contribute to the equalization of regional incomes in the barrier-free zone. I think his evidence is persuasive in showing that cross-regional differences in average income are much narrower where the legal impediments to migration flows are small. Inward and outward migration makes it possible for regional income differences to shrink in a way that is harder to achieve solely with free cross-border movements of tradable goods and services.

Comparing the Dakotas in the 1920s or 1930s with the Dakotas today, one would not claim free migration has been an engine of economic growth or development. On the other hand, it is hard to disagree with Pritchett that free migration has prevented Dakotans' relative incomes from falling as fast as would have been the case if all of them had been fenced in on the short-grass prairie.

It may have been a mistake for nineteenth-century Europeans to try to make a living in semiarid grasslands, but given the technology and agricultural prices of the time, the settlers probably enjoyed levels of real income that compared favorably with incomes obtainable elsewhere in the North Atlantic economy. Unfortunately for residents in Divide, Burke, and Mountrail Counties, North Dakota, those days are past. Laborers can now make a better living in places that in the late nineteenth century had much worse prospects than did the northern prairies—places like the Carolinas, Georgia, and south Florida.

The message of Pritchett's paper is that, while cross-border mobility may not be an engine of development in lagging areas, it is a driver of cross-region income equalization. Cross-border mobility has been good for Dakotans, whether they left or stayed in the Great Plains.

The paper by Kapur and McHale makes another point. Cross-regional income differences are not only a by-product of economic shocks, like the ones that drained comparative advantage out of the northern prairies. Persistent income differences are also produced by regional and national differences in institutions. I would add they are also the result of differences in social norms, including trust and honest dealing in the market place. Unlike tradable goods and services, which in theory can flow freely across national boundaries, institutions and social norms are pretty much stuck in place. If you want to change institutions or norms, you essentially have two options. You can make revolution where you live. Or you can move someplace else. From the perspective of an individual, the second option is much easier to accomplish than the first.

We come now to the modern nation-state, which regards cross-border mobility with deep suspicion. Some countries make it hard for their own citizens to leave, and almost all countries place restrictions on the entry of strangers. I cannot think of a single democracy that prevents its free citizens from leaving, but every modern democracy with the power to do so polices its border to keep the door closed on undesired aliens. "Undesired" for many countries simply means that the entrant wants to stay awhile and make a living. Most countries are happy to entertain well-heeled tourists, the idle rich, and carefully vetted students. They are less happy accepting foreigners who want to dig ditches, pick up garbage, build cars, or compete with their own professors, accountants, and plumbers. Rich democracies do not make a big distinction between migrants who want to work for a few years and those who want to stay indefinitely. Both kinds of immigrants are unwelcome.

The wide adoption of barriers to free entry raises the question of their moral legitimacy. Kapur and McHale summarize the debate between political philosophers who argue for different weighting schemes to take account of the interests of citizens and foreigners. Some theorists argue that a state's policy ought to be determined solely by the interests of its own citizens. The other view is that the welfare of other countries' citizens also deserves some weight in a nation's decisionmaking process. The authors favor a position somewhere between extreme nationalism and extreme cosmopolitanism.

The authors' discussion of political philosophy leads them to a straightforward conclusion. It would be a good idea to take account of the interests of people in other countries as well as the interests of one's own fellow citizens. The authors are particularly interested in helping poor people, especially poor residents of poor countries. For employees of universities, international organizations, and philanthropic nongovernment organizations (NGOs), these views do not seem particularly unusual or radical. The median rich-country voter is not at a university and is not the employee of an international organization or NGO, however. The median voter has never heard of John Rawls, Michael Walzer, or Amartya Sen. The conclusions of these important scholars would probably not matter much to the average voter, even if their names and opinions were widely familiar. In thinking about the practicality of Plan B as a development strategy, it is vital to learn what the median voter thinks—in particular, about weighing the welfare gains to immigrants against the possible losses and the distribution of gains and losses among one's fellow citizens. As long as rich democracies have the power to keep out unwanted foreigners, the views of the median voter will matter more than those of Rawls, Walzer, or Sen. Even if it were true that cross-border mobility is an alternative route out of poverty for many Third World workers, the conclusion is not very interesting if voters in rich countries reject the idea of accepting more immigrants.

Ignoring for a moment the issue of political acceptability, is Plan B an alternative route to better Third World incomes? The authors consider the likely economic gains to people who leave poor countries and the gains or losses to the people in poor countries who remain behind. They also consider possible impacts on native people in the countries to which immigrants move. These countries are for the most part rich. The authors conclude along with everyone else that the people who leave poor countries and find jobs in rich countries enjoy big economic gains from the move. Of course, the gains may be diluted by the bribes migrants have to pay to intermediaries to find and keep a job in a rich country.

In this volume the most powerful evidence about the size of potential gains available to migrants is provided in figure 4 of Mark Rosenzweig's paper (see p. 74). The numbers in that chart show skill prices, measured in dollars, of high school and college graduates in six poor and rich countries. The rank of the countries from lowest to highest income is Nigeria, India, Indonesia, Mexico, Korea, and the United States. Rosenzweig's data show that Mexican high school graduates can increase their real earnings about sevenfold by leaving Mexico and finding a job in the United States. For a Mexican college graduate, real earnings can rise by a factor of nine as a result of crossing the Rio Grande. For Nigerians, Indians, and Indonesians, the earnings gains are bigger still. Whether these earnings gains last only two or three years, as they would in a temporary visa program, or indefinitely, as would be the case under the current immigration policies of most rich democracies, the potential welfare gains accruing to immigrant workers are very large.

The essential fact is that most Third World workers would enjoy tremendous income gains if they could cross the border unmolested and work in the United States. The actual income gains have been large for the immigrants who have made the move. The gains and losses for almost everyone else are doubtful. What is more, these gains and losses are very hard to estimate reliably. This is true whether you think "everyone else" includes only the residents of the immigrants' home country who do not emigrate or also includes residents of the destination country.

Some residents of the immigrants' home country enjoy sizeable consumption gains because they receive remittances from their migrant relatives. Others derive a benefit because even though they do not receive remittances themselves their luckier neighbors enjoy income gains, giving a boost to the local economy. Of course, other unlucky neighbors may feel worse off because their situation has declined in comparison with that of their fortunate neighbors who have a rich, out-of-country relative. No one knows whether outward migration helps or hurts local governance, entrepreneurship, education, or public health in developing countries. This paper does not shed much light on those questions. It might be useful for researchers to consider the effects of heavy outward migration in the nineteenth and early twentieth centuries, when international barriers to immigration were much lower. What happened in Britain, Norway, and Sweden, three countries that experienced a big population exodus?

Let me return to the political feasibility of Plan B as a route to better Third World incomes. Feasibility depends on the acceptability of immigration to voters in high-income countries. If rich-country voters do not want to accept more immigrants from poor countries, it is not easy to see how international immigration can be a key policy that promotes income improvement. The political feasibility of Plan B depends on two things: the *actual* effects of immigration on rich-country citizens and the *perceived* effects on them. I optimistically assume these two effects are correlated.

The authors offer an overview of the empirical debate on whether and on how much unskilled immigrants hurt native-born workers who have below-average skills. They also describe evidence on whether immigrants improve or hurt the balance of government services and tax payments faced by rich-country citizens. They pay less attention to whether high-skilled immigrants help or hurt the incomes of high-skilled natives.

Their conclusion about the effects of unskilled immigrants on unskilled native-born workers is based on a wide reading of the relevant literature. Their conclusion from this literature, while well supported, is not terribly precise: "The case for the poor in rich countries being harmed is less well established than the conventional wisdom supposes. And even if there is some harm, better ways to deal with that harm are available than to block efficiency and welfare-enhancing international labor flows." The authors suggest that the immigration-induced losses of native-born unskilled workers are analogous to the trade-induced losses of workers in import-competing industries. Since economists typically recommend that compensation be offered to workers who are hurt by trade liberalization, the authors ask why rich countries ought not to adopt the same kind of measures to compensate workers who are hurt by immigration.

There is a crucial difference between the efficiency gains occurring from freer migration, on the one hand, and the gains from eliminating trade barriers, on the other. Economists have argued for more than two centuries that trade liberalization almost always improves the welfare of *both* trading partners. When Canada eliminates trade barriers with the United States or Mexico, we can be fairly confident that Canada and its trading partner will both derive welfare-improving efficiency gains through the miracle of comparative advantage. I do not believe the same reasoning applies when migration barriers are removed. Migration barriers between Europe and the New World fell dramatically in the sixteenth and seventeenth centuries, but original inhabitants of the New World would be astounded to learn that the elimination of these barriers improved the well-being of residents on their side of the Atlantic.

It is certainly true that big efficiency gains can be achieved when migration barriers are eliminated. But often the only group that can reliably be identified as "beneficiaries" consists of the fortunate migrants who enjoy real income gains because they have moved to a place where their skills command a higher price. Their move may have reduced the wages earned by people with similar skills in the destination country, however. It may have increased tax burdens on destination-country natives if the migrants receive expensive government services that cost more than the taxes immigrants pay. When migration occurs on a large scale, it can be socially and politically disruptive, undermining the very institutions and social norms that originally gave an income advantage to the destination country.

It is also true that rich countries can establish transfer programs to compensate native citizens who suffer economic harm as a result of higher migration. But how can we reliably identify the destination-country losers? What specific transfer mechanisms would fairly compensate them for their losses? How can the government persuade voters that it makes sense to allow more immigration when the same voters will be asked to shoulder heavier tax burdens to compensate the citizens who are hurt as a result of higher immigration? Europe famously offers more generous compensation arrangements than does the United States, in the form of social assistance, subsidized housing, and long-term unemployment benefits. Many European voters believe migrants derive outsize benefits under the social protection programs, which is an important reason why many of them oppose more immigration.

On balance I think it is likely that immigration has improved the welfare, not only of migrants to the United States, but also of people who are born in the United States. Whether rich-county citizens actually derive positive economic benefits from higher immigration is an empirical question, however. Unfortunately, it is one that current evidence does not conclusively answer. Theory and evidence are persuasive in showing that migrants derive big economic benefits from migration. In the long run, the political feasibility of Plan B depends crucially on persuading rich-country voters either that they *ought* to accept more poor migrants for moral reasons or that they are *very likely* to derive economic benefits from doing so. Judging by the current state of the debate over immigration in the United States and western Europe, advocates of higher immigration are a long way from persuading voters of either proposition.

Discussion: This paper and the remarks of the discussants generated an extremely lively general discussion. A large number of points and perspectives were raised. However, as Devesh Kapur noted at the end of the session, many of these address broad issues related to migration. This is not in fact the topic of the paper, which focuses on Plan B that proposes temporary migration.

Beth Anne Wilson asked the authors whether their analysis presumes that institutions are static and unchanging, as their presentation had suggested to her. To the contrary, she believes that large influxes of people who come with different social norms, different cultures and familiarity with different institutions often have important impacts on the institutions of both the sending and the receiving countries. She noted two examples: the political systems in 1880 in Ames, Iowa, and Chicago, Illinois, were quite different from each other; and in her experience, U.S. graduate schools had been less likely to enforce U.S. norms against cheating when their student bodies included a substantial mix from diverse cultures and responded instead by increasing supervision during exams. For any type of Plan B to work, she argued that it would be important to have some system in place to bring large groups of immigrants up to speed in terms of U.S. institutions. In her view, this is a difficult issue, but one that should receive much more attention than it seems to have had to date.

Doug Irwin agreed that Wilson had raised a challenging issue that warrants additional study. Irwin noted that work by Douglas North and others associates institutions with past dependence and great resistance to change in terms of fundamental norms. There is both conceptual and empirical work to be done to better understand incremental changes in institutions and how migration flows matter.

Johannes Linn raised three points. First, he agreed with the authors that institutions are extremely important. He found very illuminating their distinction between taking better institutions to people and taking people to better institutions. However, he would like to see this discussion extended to recognize the heterogeneity of institutions, particularly in large receiving countries. Are the migrants going to places where they reinforce weaker institutions in poorer areas? If so, the benefits to them are much smaller. Furthermore, such flows may exacerbate the perception or reality that immigrants are the reason that areas with concentrated populations have low institutional social capital, which in turn weakens institutions in host countries. Second, Linn thought it important to recognize that nationals do not always see all nationals as equals. In particular, people who have been citizens for generations may not see recent naturalized citizens as "equals," especially if they are a different color, religion, or culture.

Finally, Linn encouraged the authors to look more closely at the large and growing European literature on migration. He characterized it as extremely rich and focused directly on many of the issues the authors are addressing. In particular, it includes some quantitative estimates of costs and benefits to particular groups, as well as some specific proposals for temporary migration.

Gary Burtless followed up on the issue of how additional low-skilled immigrants would affect low-skilled American workers. He noted that there is a large literature studying the effects of both trade and migration on wages. In his view, there is a presumption that increasing the supply of those available to do low-skill jobs would adversely affect those already here doing those jobs. He saw abundant empirical support for this view in work by a number of economists, including George Borjas, Richard Freeman, and Larry Katz.

Mark Rosenzweig focused on the issue raised by Burtless about efficiency versus distribution. In his view, there is no question that there is a big gain in global efficiency associated with movements of people from places where their marginal productivity is currently very low to places where it is substantially higher. However, most of the gains seem to accrue to the people who are moving, with much more complex distributional implications for other groups. So the real problem is quite similar to that arising with trade—how do we redistribute some of those gains to those who lose? Finally, Rosenzweig noted that he would like to see more attention to the migration of high-skilled groups as well. He pointed out that there is a scarcity in the United States at both ends of the skill distribution and that the migration flow to the United States is also thick at both ends.

Susan Collins also commented on the issue of winners versus losers. As many have already noted, the actual migrants are clear winners. While their gains are often substantial, the much muddier implications for groups in the receiving country make it unsurprising that these countries often act to block entry. She noted that negotiating some type of bargain may provide a way to achieve an outcome enabling more migration. This perspective raises questions of what kinds of bargains may be effective and what their implications would be. She noted that, historically, part of the reason those in wealthy countries such as the United States have supported policies involving the transfer of resources to those in poorer countries related to other objectives—national security especially during the cold war and the war on terrorism more recently. She also noted that she was struck by the fact that, although the title of the paper is "Migration as the Alternative to Development," the discussants and many of the participants had frequently referred to migration as a route to development.

Many participants commented on the median voter framework raised in Burtless' discussion. Irwin noted that there is a tremendous demand in the United States for low-skilled workers. He thought that the median voter would be much more supportive of immigration if she or he were aware that preventing migration may imply making ones own bed in a hotel or being served by a robot in a restaurant. Collins highlighted the recent demonstrations that erupted in response to concerns that Mexican immigrants were being characterized as criminals. These demonstrations were much larger than many would have anticipated and were a testament to the effects of a changing U.S. population. She believes that these events are making many Americans rethink their views on immigration and that the position of the median voter may be evolving.

There was some discussion of the gains from immigration versus the gains from trade. Jeffrey Williamson stressed that his reading of the literature is that the gains from increased migration are likely to be very large, while the gains from trade are relatively trivial. The burning question this raises for him is why we are moving towards free trade, but migration flows remain so restricted. He was struck by the fact that it was the other way around 100 years ago, with much more restriction on trade than migration. Williamson strongly encouraged the authors to take a more historical perspective, which he argued would greatly inform the discussion. He stated that before 1913, 80 percent of the convergence of real wage across the Atlantic was driven by unrestricted migration (allowing for the interaction between global markets for capital and labor).

He discussed the long debate that took place in the United States, culminating in a revolution in attitudes around the time of World War I, after which U.S. immigration policy got tougher and tougher. He wondered what had changed and why—the median voter? The economic environment? In his view, Plan B is a nonstarter if we are not able to answer such questions.

Arvind Panagariya took issue with Williamson's claim that migration is clearly more beneficial than trade. In terms of the historical convergence of wages across the Atlantic, it was not clear to him that trade had been unimportant. More important, he pointed to the many recent examples of countries that had seen dramatic income expansions related to trade not migration—such as in China, India, Hong Kong, Korea, Malaysia, Taiwan, and Singapore. This has resulted in improved living standards for more than 2 billion people. Furthermore, in his view, there is no contest between Plan A (an available option through trade with proven success) and option B (which is only available at the margins).

References

Acemoglu, Daron. 1998. "Why Do New Technologies Complement Skills? Directed Technical Change and Wage Inequality." *Quarterly Journal of Economics* 113, no. 4: 1055–089

Acemoglu, Daron, and James A. Robinson. 2006. *Economic Origins of Dictatorship and Democracy.* Cambridge University Press.

Acemoglu, Daron, Simon Johnson, and James Robinson. 2001. The Colonial Origins of Comparative Development: An Empirical Investigation." *American Economic Review* 91, no. 5: 1369–401.

————. 2005. "Institutions as the Fundamental Cause of Long-Run Growth." In *Handbook of Economic Growth*, edited by Philippe Aghion and Steven N. Durlauf, pp. 385–464. Amsterdam: North Holland.

Alboim, Naomi, Ross Finnie, and Ronald Meng. 2005. "The Discounting of Immigrants' Skills in Canada: Evidence and Policy Recommendations." *Choices* 11, no. 2: 2–26.

Appiah, Kwame Anthony. 2006. *Cosmopolitanism: Ethics in a World of Strangers.* New York: W. W. Norton.

Aydemir, Abdurrahman, and George J. Borjas. 2006. "A Comparative Analysis of the Labor Market Impact of International Migration: Canada, Mexico, and the United States." NBER Working Paper 12327. Cambridge, Mass.: National Bureau of Economic Research.

Barrett, Alan, and Philip O'Connell. 2001. "Is There a Wage Premium for Returning Irish Migrants?" *Economic and Social Review* 32, no. 1: 1–21.

Beine, Michel, Frédéric Docquier, and Hillel Rapoport. 2001. "Brain Drain and Economic Growth: Theory and Evidence." *Journal of Development Economics* 64, no. 1: 275–89.

Boeri, Tito, Gordon H. Hanson, and Barry McCormick. 2002. *Immigration Policy and the Welfare System.* Oxford University Press.

Borjas, George J. 1999. *Heaven's Door: Immigration Policy and the American Economy.* Princeton University Press.

————. 2002. "Welfare Reform and Immigrant Participation in Welfare Programs." *International Migration Review* 36, no. 4: 1093–123.

————. 2003. "The Labor Demand Curve is Downward Sloping: Reexamining the Impact of Immigration on the Labor Market." *Quarterly Journal of Economics* 118, no. 4: 1335–374.

Borjas, George J., and Lynette Hilton. 1996. "Immigration and the Welfare State: Immigrant Participation in Means-Tested Entitlement Programs." *Quarterly Journal of Economics* 111, no. 2: 575–604.

Borjas, George J., and Lawrence F. Katz. 2005. "The Evolution of the Mexican-Born Workforce in the United States." NBER Working Paper 11281. Cambridge, Mass.: National Bureau of Economic Research.

Card, David. 2001. "Immigrant Inflows, Native Outflows, and the Local Market Impacts of Higher Immigration." *Journal of Labor Economics* 19, no. 1: 22–64.

———. 2005. "Is the New Immigration Really So Bad?" NBER Working Paper 11547. Cambridge, Mass.: National Bureau of Economic Research (August).

Clarke, George, and Scott Wallsten. 2004. "Do Remittances Protect Households in Developing Countries Against Shocks? Evidence from a Natural Experiment in Jamaica." Working Paper. Washington: World Bank.

Commander, Simon, Mari Kangasniemi, and L. Alan Winters. 2004. "The Brain Drain: Curse or Boon? A Survey of the Literature." In *Challenges to Globalization: Analyzing the Economics*, edited by Robert E. Baldwin and L. Alan Winters, pp. 235–78. University of Chicago Press.

Cox Edwards, Alejandro, and Manuelita Ureta. 2003. "International Migration, Remittances, and Schooling: Evidence from El Salvador." *Journal of Development Economics* 72, no. 2: 429–61.

Docquier, Frédéric, and Abdeslam Marfouk. 2004. "Measuring the International Mobility of Skilled Workers (1990–2000)." Policy Research Working Paper 3381. Washington: World Bank.

Dustmann, Christian, and Ian Preston. 2004. "Is Immigration Good or Bad for the Economy: Analysis of Attitudinal Responses." Centre for Research and Analysis of Migration Discussion Paper 06/04. University College London.

Easterly, William. 2006. *The White Man's Burden: Why the West's Efforts to Aid the Rest Have Done So Much Ill and So Little Good*. New York: Penguin Press.

Facchini, Giovanni, and Anna Maria Mayda. 2006. "Individual Attitudes towards Immigrants: Welfare-State Determinants across Countries." IZA Discussion Paper 2127. Bonn: Institute for the Study of Labor.

Ferrer, Ana, and W. Craig Riddell. 2004. "Education, Credentials, and Immigrant Earnings." Working Paper. University of British Columbia.

Friedberg, Rachel M. 2000. "You Can't Take it With You: Immigrant Assimilation and the Portability of Human Capital." *Journal of Labor Economics* 18, no. 2: 221–51.

Fukuyama, Francis. 2004. *State Building: Governance and World Order in the 21st Century*. Cornell University Press.

Glaeser, Edward L., Rafael La Porta, Florencio Lopez-de-Silanes, and Andrei Shleifer. 2004. "Do Institutions Cause Growth?" *Journal of Economic Growth* 9, no. 3: 271–303.

Glaeser, Edward L., Giacomo Ponzetto, and Andrei Shleifer. 2006. "Why Does Democracy Need Education?" NBER Working Paper 12128. Cambridge, Mass.: National Bureau of Economic Research.

Hainmueller, Jens, and Michael Hiscox. 2006 (forthcoming). "Educated Preferences: Explaining Individual Attitudes Toward Immigration in Europe. *International Organization*.

Hall, Robert E., and Charles I. Jones. 1999. "Why Do Some Countries Produce So Much More Output per Worker than Others?" *Quarterly Journal of Economics* 114, no. 1: 83–116.

Hanson, Gordon H. 2005. *Why Does Immigration Divide America? Public Finance and Political Opposition to Open Borders*. Washington: Institute for International Economics.

Hanson, Gordon H., Kenneth Scheve, and Matthew Slaughter. 2005. "Public Finance and Individual Preferences over Globalization Strategies." NBER Working Paper 11028. Cambridge, Mass.: National Bureau of Economic Research.

Hatton, Timothy J., and Jeffrey G. Williamson. 2005. "A Dual Policy Paradox: Why Have Trade and Immigration Policies Always Differed in Labor Scarce Economies?" NBER Working Paper 11866. Cambridge, Mass.: National Bureau of Economic Research.

Hendricks, Lutz. 2002. "How Important is Human Capital for Development? Evidence from Immigrant Earnings." *American Economic Review* 92, no. 1: 198–219.

Hirschman, Albert O. 1970. *Exit, Voice, and Loyalty: Responses to Decline in Firms, Organizations, and States.* Harvard University Press.

Huntington, Samuel P. 2005. *Who Are We? The Challenges to America's National Identity.* New York: Simon and Schuster.

Jasso, Guillermina, Mark R. Rosenzweig, and James P. Smith. 2002. "The Earnings of U.S. Immigrants: World Skill Prices, Skill Transferability and Selectivity." Working Paper. Princeton University, New Immigrant Survey. (http://nis.princeton.edu/papers.html [May 2, 2006]).

Kapur, Devesh. 2005. "Remittances: The New Development Mantra?" In *Remittances: Development Impact and Future Prospects*, edited by Samuel M. Maimbo and Dilip Ratha, pp. 331–60. Washington: World Bank.

Kapur, Devesh, and John McHale. 2005a. *Give Us Your Best and Brightest: The Global Hunt for Talent and its Impact on the Developing World.* Washington: Center for Global Development.

———. 2005b. "Sojourns and Software: Internationally Mobile Human Capital and High-Tech Industry Development in India, Ireland, and Israel." In *From Underdogs to Tigers: The Rise and Growth of the Software Industry in Brazil. China, India, Ireland, and Israel*, edited by Ashish Arora and Alfonso Gambardella, pp. 236–74. Oxford University Press.

Kymlicka, Will. 2001a. *Politics in the Vernacular: Nationalism, Multiculturalism, and Citizenship.* Oxford University Press.

———. 2001b. "Territorial Boundaries: A Liberal Egalitarian Perspective." In *Boundaries and Justice*, edited by David Miller and Sohail H. Hashmi, pp. 249–75. Princeton University Press.

Mayda, Anna Maria. 2006 (forthcoming). "Who is Against Immigration: A Cross-Country Investigation of Individual Attitudes towards Immigrants." *Review of Economics and Statistics* 88, no. 3.

McHale, John. Forthcoming. "Taxation and Skilled Indian Migration to the United States: Revisiting the Bhagwati Tax." Paper prepared for the conference on Skilled Migration Today: Prospects, Problems, and Policies. Council on Foreign Relations, New York, March 4–5, 2005.

Miller, David. 1995. *On Nationality.* Oxford University Press.

North, Douglas C. 1981. *Structure and Change in Economic History.* New York: W. W. Norton.

O'Rourke, Kevin H., and Richard Sinnott. 2004. "The Determinants of Individual Attitudes towards Immigration." Economic Paper 20042. Dublin: Trinity College.

Ottaviano, Gianmarco I. P., and Giovanni Peri. 2004. "The Economic Value of Cultural Diversity: Evidence from U.S. Cities." NBER Working Paper 10904. Cambridge, Mass.: National Bureau of Economic Research.

————. 2005. "Rethinking the Gains from Immigration: Theory and Evidence from the U.S." NBER Working Paper 11672. Cambridge, Mass.: National Bureau of Economic Research.

Özden, Çaglar. 2005. "Educated Migrants: Is There Brain Waste?" In *International Migration, Remittances, and the Brain Drain,* edited by Çaglar Özden and Maurice Schiff, pp. 227–44. Washington: World Bank and Palgrave Macmillan.

Pritchett, Lant. 2003a. "The Future of Migration: Irresistible Forces Meet Immovable Ideas." Paper presented at the conference on The Future of Globalization: Explorations in the Light of Recent Turbulence. Yale University, October 10.

————. 2003b. "The Future of Migration Part II." *YaleGlobal* (November 9). Available at YaleGlobal Online (http://yaleglobal.yale.edu/display.article?id=2774 [May 2, 2006]).

Pritchett, Lant, and Michael Woolcock. 2004. "Solutions When *the* Solution is the Problem: Arraying the Disarray in Development." *World Development* 32, no. 2: 191–212.

Rahman, Md. Mizanour. 2000. "Emigration and Development: The Case of a Bangladeshi Village." *International Migration* 38, no. 4: 109–30.

Rauch, James E.. 2001. "Business and Social Networks in International Trade." *Journal of Economic Literature* 39, no. 4: 1177–203.

Rawls, John. 1971. *A Theory of Justice.* Harvard University Press.

————. 1999. *The Law of Peoples.* Harvard University Press.

Rodrik, Dani. 2000. "Institutions for High-Quality Growth: What They Are and How to Acquire Them." NBER Working Paper 7540. Cambridge, Mass.: National Bureau of Economic Research.

————. 2001. "Comments at the Conference on 'Immigration Policy and the Welfare State.'" Trieste, Italy, June 23.

————. 2006 (forthcoming). "Goodbye Washington Consensus, Hello Washington Confusion?" *Journal of Economic Literature.*

Rodrik, Dani, Arvind Subramanian, and Francesco Trebbi. 2004. "Institutions Rule: The Primacy of Institutions Over Geography and Integration in Economic Development." *Journal of Economic Growth* 9, no. 2: 131–65.

Sachs, Jeffrey. 2005. *The End of Poverty: Economic Possibilities for Our Time.* New York: Penguin Press.

Saxenian, Annalee. 2002. *Local and Global Networks of Immigrant Professionals in Silicon Valley.* San Francisco: Public Policy Institute of California.

Scheve, Kenneth F., and Matthew J. Slaughter. 2001. "Labor Market Competition and Individual Preferences over Immigration Policy." *Review of Economics and Statistics* 83, no. 1: 133–45.

Schiff, Maurice. 2005. "Brain Gain: Claims about its Size and Impact on Welfare are Greatly Exaggerated." In *International Migration, Remittances, and the Brain Drain*, edited by Çaglar Özden and Maurice Schiff, pp. 201–26. Washington: World Bank and Palgrave Macmillan.

Sen, Amartya, 1982. "Rights and Agency." *Philosophy and Public Affairs* 11, no. 1: 3–39.

———. 1983. "Evaluator Relativity and Consequential Evaluation." *Philosophy and Public Affairs* 12, no. 2: 113–32.

———. 1992. *Inequality Reexamined*. New York: Russell Sage Foundation and Harvard University Press.

———. 2000. "Consequential Evaluation and Practical Reason." *Journal of Philosophy* 97, no. 9: 477–502.

———. 2006. *Identity and Violence: The Illusion of Destiny*. New York: W. W. Norton.

Smith, James P., and Barry Edmonston, eds. 1997. *The New Americans: Economic, Demographic and Fiscal Effects of Immigration*. Washington: National Academy Press, National Research Council.

Storesletten, Kjetil. 2000. "Sustaining Fiscal Policy through Immigration." *Journal of Poltical Economy* 108, no. 2: 300–23.

Sweetman, Arthur. 2004. "Immigrant Source Country Educational Quality and Canadian Labour Market Outcomes." Analytical Studies Branch Research Paper Series 234. Ottawa: Statistics Canada.

Tamir, Yael. 1993. *Liberal Nationalism*. Princeton University Press.

Tan, Kok-Chor. 2004. *Justice without Borders: Cosmopolitanism, Nationalism, and Patriotism*. Cambridge University Press.

UNDP (United Nations Development Programme). 2005. *Human Development Report 2005, International Cooperation at a Crossroads: Aid, Trade, and Security in an Unequal World*. New York: UNDP.

Walzer, Michael. 1983. *Spheres of Justice: A Defense of Pluralism and Equality*. New York: Basic Books.

Woodruff, Christopher, and Rene Zenteno. 2001. "Remittances and Microenterprises in Mexico." Working Paper. University of California–San Diego, Graduate School of International Relations and Pacific Studies.

World Bank. 2006a. *Global Economic Prospects 2006: Economic Implications of Remittances and Migration*. Washington.

———. 2006b. *World Development Indicators*. Washington.

Yang, Dean. 2004. "International Migration, Human Capital, and Entrepreneurship: Evidence from Philippine Migrants' Exchange Rate Shocks." Policy Research Working Paper 3578. Washington: World Bank, Research Program on International Migration and Development. DECRG.

———. 2005. "Coping With Disaster: The Impact of Hurricanes on International Capital Flows, 1979–2001." Working Paper. Ann Arbor: University of Michigan, Gerald R. Ford School of Public Policy.

SUZANNE DURYEA
Research Department at the Inter-American Development Bank

GUSTAVO MARQUÉZ
Research Department at the Inter-American Development Bank

CARMEN PAGÉS
Research Department at the Inter-American Development Bank

STEFANO SCARPETTA
Human Development Group of the World Bank

For Better or for Worse? Job and Earnings Mobility in Nine Middle- and Low-Income Countries

Recent evidence suggests that most market economies show significant dynamism. Many firms are created and destroyed every year, and surviving firms undergo a continuous process of transformation.[1] As a result, a substantial number of jobs are created and destroyed, and an even larger number of workers change status in the labor market, moving across jobs, from employment to unemployment and back to employment, and also entering and exiting the labor market.[2] Large, if not even larger, rates of mobility are also observed in developing countries.[3]

As noted by Haltiwanger and others, one of the most controversial debates on institutional design and economic policy has been sparked around the trade-offs associated with labor mobility.[4] On the one hand, mobility may promote efficiency and growth if economic forces induce the reallocation of resources toward the most productive uses. On the other hand, high mobility may imply that workers are uncertain and have concerns about income security.

This paper summarizes the findings of a study by the same authors titled "Mobility between Formal and Informal Jobs: Evidence from Transition and Latin American Countries."

1. Caves (1998); Bartelsman and Doms (2000); for surveys, see Bartelsman, Haltiwanger, and Scarpetta (2004).
2. See, for example, Davis and Haltiwanger (1999).
3. See IADB (2003); Rutkowski and Scarpetta (2005); Bartelsman, Haltiwanger, and Scarpetta (2004).
4. Haltiwanger and others (2004).

187

Such trade-offs between economic efficiency and job stability become particularly important in the context of middle- and low-income countries where limited safety nets do not insulate workers against economic risk. In the last fifteen years, many of these countries have seen rapid economic transformation led by structural reforms and trade integration. For example, in Latin America, trade as a percentage of GDP increased from 27 percent in 1995 to 44 percent in 2004, while in the same period in the transition economies (here defined as former socialist countries), it increased from 45 to 70 percent.[5] While such reforms have brought productivity gains, they have also increased labor reallocation.[6] Analyzing the welfare costs of such reforms is beyond the scope of this study. More modestly, we assess the nature of labor mobility in a sample of countries that underwent important—albeit different—structural reforms over the past decade that had significant impact on the magnitude and characteristics of labor mobility. This is an important first step to understanding the welfare effects of such reforms.

This article summarizes the findings of an ongoing study examining worker flows and, when possible, the associated earnings changes associated with such flows across different statuses in the labor market and across different types of jobs. The study focuses on three countries in Latin America and six transition economies of eastern Europe and the former Soviet Union. Although the selection of countries is driven by the existence of longitudinal data, essential for a study of worker mobility, this selection of countries has the bonus of spanning low- and middle-income economies, as well as transition and developing countries.

We address a number of questions. Central to the question of the nature of labor mobility is assessing to what extent workers transit quickly across jobs or become stuck in long periods of unemployment. Another central issue is to what extent mobility implies welfare gains or losses relative to those workers who did not change their status in the labor market. A third question, much discussed in the development literature, is to what extent workers in low- and middle-income countries experience barriers to entry into good (that is, "formal") jobs and thus become trapped in low-productivity and low-paying jobs. So far, few studies have directly examined mobility in low- and middle-income economies. Even fewer studies have examined mobility between different types of jobs.[7] In this study we define different types of jobs on the basis of whether

5. World Bank (2006).

6. For discussion of reforms and productivity gains, see Fernandes (2002); Pavcnik (2002); Eslava and others (2005). For discussion of reforms and labor reallocation, see Haltiwanger and others (2004); Eslava and others (2005).

7. See, for example, Maloney (1999); Gong, van Soest, and Villagomez (2004); IADB (2003).

they are salaried or not and whether workers have access to social security benefits, which we use as a proxy for whether such jobs are in compliance with the country's laws. To the extent possible we define common, harmonized categories to allow for cross-country comparisons.

The picture that emerges from our analysis is quite complex. There is a high degree of mobility in the labor market of all countries examined. Many workers move across jobs directly, while many others move in and out of the labor market and between jobs and unemployment. For most countries we do not find evidence of workers being trapped in unemployment for a long period, partly because of limited income-support schemes for the unemployed, which force workers to find a job quickly. We find large flows in and out of the labor market, however. Moreover, we find that mobility has important earnings consequences: positive for workers who move from informal salaried jobs to self-employment and negative for workers who move from formal to informal salaried jobs. However, individual heterogeneity and selection processes have a large role in shaping the earnings consequences of mobility.

Data

We focus our empirical analysis on six countries from eastern Europe and the former Soviet Union (Albania, Georgia, Hungary, Poland, Russia, and Ukraine) and on three Latin American countries (Argentina, Mexico, and Venezuela).[8] Although measurement problems and attrition bias are always potential issues in all studies based on longitudinal data, they do not seem to be more problematic in our selected group of countries than they are in the developed countries. We analyze transitions across one-year periods, because this periodicity is commonly available, with the exception of Georgia, where the longest time period between interviews is nine months. When more than two records of individual data are available for a country, an individual can, in theory, contribute multiple transitions, but we only consider the first transition per person in the analysis.

In our analysis, we consider six different statuses in the labor market: out of labor force, unemployed, formal wage employees, informal wage employees, self-employed, and farmers. Individuals not belonging to any of these categories (for example, employers or cooperative members) are excluded, because the number of observations for these two categories of owners of firms

8. See Duryea, Marquéz, Pagés, and Scarpetta (2006) for a full description of the data used in this study.

is not sufficient to perform a sensible dynamic analysis. Individuals are classified as out of the labor force when they did not work during the reference week and did not look for a job during the reference period. Unemployed are those who did not work in the reference week but had searched for a job. Formal wage employees are those who receive a salary as well as social security benefits (in Argentina, Mexico, Venezuela, Albania). In some cases, when information about social security is not available, formality is defined on the base of whether there is a written (or registered) contract (in Georgia, Ukraine), whether the firm is registered (in Hungary, Russia), or whether the contract is open ended (in Poland). Salaried workers who do not fall into these categories are considered informal. Self-employed are those who report to themselves (that is, business owners without employees). Following conventional definitions used by the ILO, we exclude self-employed persons engaged in professional activities, such as lawyers or doctors, from this category and hence from the sample. The self-employed are split into workers in agricultural activities (farmers) and workers in nonagricultural activities.

The nine countries examined are heterogeneous and have experienced different economic trends (see table 1). Albania and Georgia had the lowest per capita income of the group, with incomes of US$4,320 and US$1,766 (2000 U.S. dollars, purchasing power parity), respectively, but they experienced strong GDP growth during the two-year period studied as well as during the previous three years. Russia and Ukraine had higher GDP per capita levels in the period covered by the data. However, they also had quite different growth performances: Russia had very low growth, while Ukraine in the early part of the century had a high rate of growth. Hungary and Poland are higher-income countries, but they also experienced very different patterns of growth. During the period of study, Hungary underwent a major restructuring process, while Poland had higher growth at the beginning of the century.

The three Latin American countries experienced considerable volatility during the period of study. From 1995 to 2002, Venezuela underwent an exceedingly volatile period, experiencing major swings in growth from 10 percent per annum growth between 1995 and 1998, to the sudden decline of about 10 percent in 1999, to the subsequent recovery in 2001 by 8 percent, and the fall in 2002 of another 12 percent. At the same time, although it had the highest per capita income among the countries, the period covered by the analysis (1995–2001) was not stellar economically for Argentina. The severe economic crisis officially began in 2001, which was preceded since 1998 by slow growth and mounting debt. Average annual growth was less than 1 percent during the period of study, although it had been 7.9 percent in the previous three years.

Table 1. Economic Indicators

Country	Period of study	GDP per capita PPP[a]	GDP growth: annual percent change	GDP growth: annual percent change, prior 3 years	Trade/GDP: average annual change (1995–2004)
Albania	2002–2004	4,320	5.1	8.3	–1.02
Argentina	1995–2001	12,091	0.9	7.9	9.85
Georgia	1998–99	1,766	3.0	8.1	10.18
Hungary	1993–97	10,450	1.9	–6.2	4.5
Mexico	1990–2001	8,613	3.2	2.3	0.84
Poland	2000–02	10,501	2.5	5.2	6.56
Russia	1994–2003	6,896	0.9	–9.4	3.30
Ukraine	2003–04	5,544	10.7	6.8	5.38
Venezuela	1995–2002	5,860	0.3	1.3	0.82

Source: World Bank (2006).
PPP = Purchasing power parity.
a. Constant 2000 international dollars.

Mexico also had its share of volatility during its period of study from 1990 to 2001. The peso crisis occurred in 1995, with GDP declining by 6 percent. However, this was followed by strong growth of 5 percent annually, such that the period as a whole had an average growth rate of 3.2 percent.

Openness in trade increased substantially in most countries during the period of study. This was particularly true in eastern European countries, which with the exception of Albania underwent rapid growth in trade as a percentage of GDP. Trade openness also increased in Latin America, albeit to a lower extent. The fastest growth was in Argentina, although from a low base of 16 percent of GDP in 1995.

Our data indicate that approximately one-third of the individuals are not participating in the labor force, ranging from 29 percent in Albania to 41 percent in Mexico. Unemployment—as a share of the working-age population—varies significantly across the countries (about 3 percent of the working-aged in Mexico but about 12 percent in Georgia and Poland). Formal-sector workers constitute a large share of the population in Hungary but a much smaller percentage in Venezuela and Albania (21 percent and 14 percent, respectively). In comparison with their formal-sector counterparts, informal wage earners compose a much smaller share of the population in all countries—approximately half the size of the share of formal employees in Argentina and Mexico and even a smaller share in Georgia, Hungary, Poland, and Ukraine. The informal-wage sector comes closest in size to the formal sector in Albania and Venezuela. Self-employed workers in nonagricultural jobs represent 10 percent or less of the population in all countries. However, in the countries for which information on self-employment in agricultural sectors is available (in Venezuela, Albania, Georgia, and Poland), the share of this group is between 15 and 30 percent of the sample, except for Poland, which is at 10 percent.

Quite notably, in eastern European countries the transition to a market economy and the opening to the rest of the world have been accompanied by an increase in informal salaried employment. Among the Latin American countries, the same trend is observed in Argentina. Contrary to these observed increases, informal salaried employment as a proportion of the population declined in Mexico and Venezuela.

Labor Mobility

We describe labor mobility by calculating conditional probabilities of finding a worker in status j, in period $t + k$, conditional on being in status i at time t, or

$$p_{ij} = p(S_{t+k} = j/S_t = i)$$

for all labor statuses in the nine countries. This yields 6 by 6 transition matrices for each country (or 5 by 5 if the category self-employed in agricultural activities is not available).

When calculating transition probabilities, we obtain a number of interesting results (see table 2):

—*Unemployment is more persistent in the transition economies.* The differences in unemployment persistency are quite large. In Poland 67 percent of the unemployed workers had a spell of joblessness longer than one year. That figure is 50 percent in Georgia, around 39 percent in Hungary, but only 12 percent in Mexico. Lower unemployment insurance payments and lower duration of benefits in Latin America are likely to explain such differences.

—*Across countries, workers tend to stay in formal salaried jobs for longer periods of time than they do in informal salaried jobs.* In all countries workers are much more likely to remain in a formal job than in an informal one, with the highest differences being observed in Georgia and Hungary. This gap is still present in Mexico, although it is much smaller, where formal and informal salary jobs seem to be more similar. Self-employment shows an intermediate degree of persistence in all countries except in Russia. Self-employment activities in agriculture are more stable than are those in other economic sectors.

—*Contrary to what is sometimes assumed, informal salaried workers are more likely to end up unemployed than are formal salaried workers.* The likelihood that an employed worker will transit to unemployment is more than twice as high for an informal wage employee than for the formal counterpart. Such differences are more pronounced in Hungary, Poland, and Russia but less so in Mexico, where, as indicated above, there seem to be few differences between formal and informal salaried jobs. Instead, there are no common patterns among the nine countries relative to the exit from unemployment to salaried jobs. In Albania and Argentina unemployed workers are more than twice as likely to find an informal salaried job relative to a salaried one; in Ukraine and Hungary the tendency is the reverse. In the rest of the countries studied, transition probabilities from unemployment to the two types of salaried work are of similar magnitude.

—*Within employment, mobility between salaried jobs is much higher than mobility between salaried jobs and self-employment.* Thus it is quite remarkable that with the exception of Albania the probability of moving from an informal salaried job to a formal one is higher than the probabilities of moving to unemployment, self-employment, or out of the labor market. Of course, this only reflects transitions between one year and the year after. Workers may have spent some intermediate time in unemployment or other states, but we are unable to observe this. It is quite interesting, however, that moving to self-employment from informal salaried jobs is less prevalent than is moving to formal sector jobs. Strong preference for formal jobs, relative to self-employment; cumbersome procedures and regulations to starting new firms; or lack of access to capital may explain why many workers who are displaced or quit informal jobs end up in formal salaried employment.

Similarly, *workers who exit formal salaried jobs are in all cases much more likely to move to an informal salaried job than to self-employment*, suggesting again that preferences for salaried jobs, hurdles to firm creation such as administrative and legal procedures to register a business, or limited access to capital may limit entry into self-employment. But it is also noticeable that in countries with well-established safety nets (such as Poland and Hungary) workers are more likely to move to unemployment rather than to an informal salaried job.

What about mobility out of self-employment? The results here are quite diverse. In three out of the nine countries (Albania, Argentina, Ukraine), workers who exit self-employment are more likely to end up in an informal salaried job than in any other status. In Hungary and Russia they are more likely to move to a formal salaried job, while in Poland they are more likely to go to unemployment than to any other destination. In Mexico and Venezuela they are more likely to exit the labor force, followed soon after by moving to informal salaried jobs. In Georgia, workers who exit self-employment in nonagricul-

Table 2. Transition Matrices[a]

	Labor Market Status[b]						
	1	2	3	4	5	6	N
Albania							
1 Out of labor force	0.75 (0.008)	0.05 (0.004)	0.02 (0.003)	0.04 (0.004)	0.02 (0.003)	0.11 (0.006)	2,899
2 Unemployed	0.34 (0.022)	0.29 (0.021)	0.06 (0.011)	0.16 (0.018)	0.08 (0.012)	0.07 (0.012)	493
3 Wage formal	0.05 (0.006)	0.02 (0.004)	0.83 (0.011)	0.06 (0.008)	0.02 (0.005)	0.02 (0.004)	1,126
4 Wage informal	0.09 (0.011)	0.05 (0.008)	0.14 (0.013)	0.48 (0.020)	0.17 (0.014)	0.06 (0.009)	729
5 Nonagricultural self-employed[c]	0.08 (0.012)	0.02 (0.005)	0.04 (0.009)	0.12 (0.016)	0.69 (0.021)	0.05 (0.010)	513
6 Agricultural self-employed[c]	0.15 (0.007)	0.01 (0.002)	0.01 (0.002)	0.04 (0.004)	0.02 (0.003)	0.78 (0.008)	2,614
Share in each labor market status[d]	0.35	0.04	0.14	0.09	0.08	0.30	8,373
Argentina							
1 Out of labor force	0.78 (0.005)	0.08 (0.004)	0.03 (0.002)	0.07 (0.003)	0.04 (0.002)	n.a.	5,823
2 Unemployed	0.26 (0.010)	0.31 (0.011)	0.11 (0.007)	0.22 (0.011)	0.11 (0.008)	n.a.	1,579
3 Wage formal	0.03 (0.002)	0.05 (0.003)	0.84 (0.006)	0.07 (0.004)	0.02 (0.002)	n.a.	4,231
4 Wage informal	0.14 (0.008)	0.12 (0.007)	0.14 (0.008)	0.48 (0.011)	0.12 (0.007)	n.a.	2,123
5 Nonagricultural self-employed[c]	0.13 (0.009)	0.10 (0.007)	0.05 (0.005)	0.20 (0.010)	0.54 (0.012)	n.a.	1,553
6 Agricultural self-employed[c]	n.a.	n.a.	n.a.	n.a.	n.a.	n.a.	n.a.
Share in each labor market status	0.36	0.10	0.28	0.15	0.10	n.a.	15,309

	1	2	3	4	5	6	N
Georgia							
1 Out of labor force	0.78 (0.008)	0.07 (0.005)	0.02 (0.003)	0.02 (0.003)	0.01 (0.002)	0.10 (0.006)	3,197
2 Unemployed	0.24 (0.011)	0.50 (0.013)	0.07 (0.007)	0.06 (0.006)	0.04 (0.005)	0.08 (0.009)	1,404
3 Wage formal	0.03 (0.003)	0.02 (0.002)	0.89 (0.006)	0.03 (0.003)	0.01 (0.002)	0.03 (0.004)	2,650
4 Wage informal	0.05 (0.010)	0.04 (0.009)	0.26 (0.020)	0.46 (0.024)	0.06 (0.012)	0.13 (0.018)	457
5 Nonagricultural self-employed[c]	0.06 (0.013)	0.03 (0.009)	0.07 (0.013)	0.12 (0.018)	0.52 (0.029)	0.21 (0.022)	394
6 Agricultural self-employed[c]	0.07 (0.006)	0.02 (0.003)	0.03 (0.004)	0.02 (0.003)	0.03 (0.004)	0.83 (0.009)	2,607
Share in each labor market status[d]	0.29	0.10	0.26	0.05	0.04	0.26	10,709
Hungary							
1 Out of labor force	0.84 (0.668)	0.06 (0.438)	0.06 (0.422)	0.03 (0.330)	0.01 (0.165)	n.a.	3,344
2 Unemployed	0.23 (1.559)	0.39 (1.842)	0.23 (1.719)	0.11 (1.151)	0.04 (0.723)	n.a.	826
3 Wage formal	0.06 (0.334)	0.04 (0.275)	0.86 (0.469)	0.03 (0.254)	0.01 (0.129)	n.a.	5,184
4 Wage informal	0.18 (1.786)	0.14 (1.623)	0.23 (1.859)	0.40 (2.193)	0.05 (1.041)	n.a.	569
5 Nonagricultural self-employed[c]	0.11 (2.007)	0.05 (1.557)	0.13 (2.262)	0.08 (1.619)	0.63 (3.051)	n.a.	298
6 Agricultural self-employed[c]	n.a.	n.a.	n.a.	n.a.	n.a.	n.a.	n.a.
Share in each labor market status	0.34	0.08	0.49	0.06	0.03	n.a.	10,220
Mexico							
1 Out of labor force	0.81 (0.001)	0.02 (0.000)	0.06 (0.001)	0.07 (0.001)	0.04 (0.001)	n.a.	143,535

Table 2 (continued). Transition Matrices[a]

			Labor Market Status[b]				
	1	2	3	4	5	6	N
2 Unemployed	0.30	0.12	0.26	0.24	0.08	n.a.	9,098
	(0.005)	(0.003)	(0.005)	(0.004)	(0.003)		
3 Wage formal	0.07	0.02	0.75	0.13	0.03	n.a.	95,103
	(0.001)	(0.000)	(0.001)	(0.001)	(0.001)		
4 Wage informal	0.14	0.03	0.27	0.47	0.09	n.a.	57,325
	(0.001)	(0.001)	(0.002)	(0.002)	(0.001)		
5 Nonagricultural self-employed[c]	0.19	0.02	0.08	0.15	0.57	n.a.	33,115
	(0.002)	(0.001)	(0.002)	(0.002)	(0.002)		
6 Agricultural self-employed[c]	n.a.	n.a.	n.a.	n.a.	n.a.	n.a.	n.a.
Share in each labor market status	0.41	0.03	0.29	0.17	0.10		338,176
Poland							
1 Out of labor force	0.90	0.06	0.01	0.02	0.00	0.01	27,889
	(0.191)	(0.140)	(0.073)	(0.079)	(0.035)	(0.062)	
2 Unemployed	0.14	0.67	0.06	0.10	0.01	0.02	9,725
	(0.376)	(0.492)	(0.265)	(0.317)	(0.112)	(0.124)	
3 Wage formal	0.03	0.04	0.90	0.02	0.00	0.00	29,546
	(0.107)	(0.126)	(0.196)	(0.091)	(0.032)	(0.034)	
4 Wage informal	0.08	0.16	0.25	0.49	0.01	0.02	2,997
	(0.542)	(0.699)	(0.897)	(1.014)	(0.174)	(0.221)	
5 Nonagricultural self-employed[c]	0.04	0.06	0.03	0.01	0.86	0.01	2,109
	(0.419)	(0.552)	(0.474)	(0.251)	(0.848)	(0.149)	
6 Agricultural self-employed[c]	0.03	0.01	0.01	0.01	0.00	0.94	7,059
	(0.186)	(0.100)	(0.101)	(0.124)	(0.057)	(0.256)	
Share in each labor market status[d]	0.35	0.12	0.36	0.05	0.03	0.09	79,324
Russia							
1 Out of labor force	0.76	0.06	0.07	0.10	0.01	n.a.	2,777

	1	2	3	4	5	6	N
2 Unemployed	0.19 (0.008)	0.34 (0.004)	0.21 (0.005)	0.23 (0.006)	0.03 (0.002)	n.a.	756
3 Wage formal	0.02 (0.014)	0.03 (0.017)	0.82 (0.016)	0.10 (0.015)	0.03 (0.007)	n.a.	2,412
4 Wage informal	0.13 (0.003)	0.09 (0.004)	0.31 (0.008)	0.43 (0.007)	0.04 (0.005)	n.a.	1,672
5 Nonagricultural self-employed[c]	0.06 (0.008)	0.08 (0.007)	0.46 (0.012)	0.21 (0.013)	0.18 (0.005)	n.a.	310
6 Agricultural self-employed[c]	n.a.	n.a.	n.a.	n.a.	n.a.	n.a.	n.a.
Share in each labor market status	0.32	0.09	0.38	0.19	0.03	n.a.	7,927
Ukraine							
1 Out of labor force	0.76 (0.010)	0.10 (0.008)	0.09 (0.007)	0.04 (0.005)	0.01 (0.003)	n.a.	2,030
2 Unemployed	0.25 (0.019)	0.33 (0.019)	0.26 (0.018)	0.13 (0.014)	0.03 (0.009)	n.a.	658
3 Wage formal	0.06 (0.005)	0.04 (0.004)	0.86 (0.008)	0.03 (0.004)	0.01 (0.002)	n.a.	2,725
4 Wage informal	0.08 (0.020)	0.08 (0.020)	0.32 (0.041)	0.47 (0.044)	0.05 (0.017)	n.a.	184
5 Nonagricultural self-employed[c]	0.12 (0.042)	0.11 (0.038)	0.12 (0.041)	0.15 (0.047)	0.50 (0.062)	n.a.	71
6 Agricultural self-employed[c]	n.a.	n.a.	n.a.	n.a.	n.a.	n.a.	n.a.
Share in each labor market status	0.34	0.10	0.49	0.06	0.02	n.a.	5,668
Venezuela	1	2	3	4	5	6	N
1 Out of labor force	0.79 (0.002)	0.04 (0.001)	0.03 (0.001)	0.06 (0.002)	0.08 (0.001)	0.01 (0.002)	38,055
2 Unemployed	0.22 (0.008)	0.25 (0.009)	0.17 (0.006)	0.19 (0.007)	0.15 (0.002)	0.02 (0.007)	4,706

Table 2 (continued). Transition Matrices[a]

			Labor Market Status[b]				
	1	2	3	4	5	6	N
3 Wage formal	0.06	0.05	0.75	0.09	0.05	0.00	18,009
	(0.002)	(0.002)	(0.004)	(0.003)	(0.000)	(0.002)	
4 Wage informal	0.13	0.08	0.22	0.39	0.13	0.04	12,699
	(0.004)	(0.003)	(0.005)	(0.006)	(0.003)	(0.004)	
5 Nonagricultural self-employed[c]	0.17	0.05	0.06	0.11	0.58	0.04	14,243
	(0.008)	(0.005)	(0.004)	(0.011)	(0.015)	(0.006)	
6 Agricultural self-employed[c]	0.09	0.03	0.02	0.17	0.05	0.63	1,801
	(0.004)	(0.002)	(0.003)	(0.003)	(0.003)	(0.005)	
Share in each labor market status[d]	0.40	0.06	0.21	0.13	0.16	0.03	89,513

Source: Duryea, Marquéz, Pagés, and Scarpetta (2006).

n.a. Not available.

N denotes number of observations in sample.

a. Observed $P(i,j)$ matrices.

b. In countries for which the category self-employed in agricultural activities is not available, only 5 by 5 matrices are available. Bootstrapped standard errors are in parentheses.

c. Includes unpaid family workers.

d. Share in column 6 is rounded.

tural activities are more likely to become self-employed in agricultural activities (that is, they become farmers). However, it is quite noticeable that in all countries with the exception of Russia *the probability of moving to a formal salaried job is much higher for workers who exit informal salaried activities than it is for workers who exit self-employment.*

In addition to transition probabilities, one can compute additional measures that make use of the trace or determinant of such matrices to assess aggregate mobility—that is, which country displays the higher rate of mobility across all labor market statuses. We found that *despite the deep restructuring process that took place in the transition economies during the past decade, aggregate labor mobility is lower in these countries, compared with that in the three Latin American countries.*[9] Mexico and Venezuela are the countries that experience higher aggregate mobility, while at the other extreme Poland and Georgia exhibit the lowest.[10] Part of the explanation for this regional difference is due to the large mobility out of unemployment and movement in and out of the labor market in Latin America (particularly in Mexico and Venezuela) compared with the transition economies. This is due to different factors. First, there is a high mobility in and out of the labor market by youth. For example, the probability of moving from unemployment to out of the labor force among youth is around 30 percent in Argentina, Mexico, and Venezuela.[11] Second, mobility in and out of jobs—even in the formal sector—is higher in Latin America compared with transition economies.[12] Third, higher macroeconomic volatility in Latin America may further explain such regional differences.

These results for aggregate mobility refer to the average worker. While aggregate mobility is higher for youth (aged 15 to 24) than it is for the prime-age population (25 to 49), the latter also experiences substantial mobility.[13] For example, the probability of switching from a formal to an informal job is on average 12 percent for youth and 7 percent for the prime-age population (table 3). But adults experience a higher probability of moving from an informal to a formal job (24 percent compared with 19 percent for youth). By level of skill, Pagés and Stampini report higher mobility between formal and informal salaried jobs for unskilled workers relative to skilled ones.[14]

9. See Duryea, Marquéz, Pagés, and Scarpetta (2006) for aggregate mobility results.
10. These results do not include data for Russia.
11. See Borgarello and others (2006).
12. There is also high mobility from informal wage employment and inactivity (defined as out of the labor market) among youth in Latin America and, albeit lower, between self-employment and inactivity. See Borgarello and others (2006) for more details on youth mobility in the labor market.
13. Borgarello and others (2006).
14. Pagés and Stampini (2006).

Table 3. Transition Probabilities between Formal and Informal Salaried Jobs by Age

	15–24-year-olds		25–49-year-olds	
	$P(F,I)^a$	$P(I,F)$	$P(F,I)$	$P(I,F)$
Argentina	0.11	0.14	0.07	0.15
Albania	0.16	0.12	0.07	0.16
Georgia	0.05	0.09	0.03	0.29
Mexico	0.15	0.22	0.12	0.28
Ukraine	0.08	0.44	0.03	0.3
Venezuela	0.15	0.16	0.09	0.25
Average	0.12	0.19	0.07	0.24

Source: Duryea, Marquéz, Pagés, and Scarpetta (2006).

a. P(F, I) denotes transition probability from labor market status formal salaried to status informal salaried. P(I,F) denotes transition probability from informal to formal salaried.

Wage Changes

The results discussed above illustrate that workers undergo substantial labor mobility, but is this mobility conducive to income gains? Or rather do workers undergo important wage losses as they transit across labor market statuses?

To assess the effects of a job switch on earnings, we compare the change in earnings of workers who switch jobs with the change in earnings of those workers who did not switch jobs. To prevent such comparisons from being affected by differences in the characteristics of workers in different statuses, we also control for such differences in observable characteristics, such that these observable differences are not driving the wage changes.[15] The results listed below only address job-to-job transitions (including moving to self-employment) since we do not observe earnings for unemployed or out-of-labor-force workers. We therefore miss an important source of income instability associated with the income losses that result from periods of being unemployed or out of the labor force. In addition, results relative to earning changes cannot be obtained for all countries and employment statuses because in some countries either earnings for self-employed workers are not available or the number of workers

15. More formally, we estimate the following equation:

$$\Delta \ln(w_{mt}) = \alpha + \sum_{i=1}^{J}\sum_{j=1}^{J}\beta_{ij}\left(S_{mi(t)} \cdot S_{mj(t-1)}\right) + \sum_{i=1}^{J}\sum_{j=1}^{J}\delta_{ij}\left(S_{mi(t)} \cdot S_{mj(t-1)}\right)X_{mt} + \gamma X_{mt} + \sum_{t=2}^{T}\varphi_t D_t + \varepsilon_{it}$$

where W_m is hourly wage of individual m, $S_{mi(t)}$ represents the labor market status i of individual m in period t, $\mathbf{X}$ is a vector of individual characteristics that are assumed to affect not only the status in the labor market at any point in time but also the probability of moving across statuses in the labor market, D represents time dummies, and ε_{it} is the *iid* error term. Individual and job characteristics include age and age squared, education, occupation, and industry. From this, we predict the change in wage from moving from status i to status j. Finally, we assess the following difference-in-difference estimate: $\Delta\Delta w = \Delta w_{ij} - \Delta w_{ii}$.

observed transiting from one status to another is too small to make reliable estimates of wage changes. Nonetheless, the available data yield a number of insights:[16]

On average, Latin American workers who move from formal to informal salaried jobs suffer a decline in wages (compared with workers who remain in formal salaried jobs), while the evidence is more ambiguous in transition economies. In Argentina, Mexico, and Venezuela workers who move from formal to informal salaried jobs experience a decline in monthly wages; the reverse move results in an increase in wages. Similar results are found in Albania and Ukraine. When switching from formal to informal salaried jobs in Georgia, Poland, and Russia, workers experience an increase in monthly earnings (compared with workers who stay in formal salaried jobs), indicating better opportunities in the unregulated economy.

However, large individual heterogeneity exists among workers moving from formal to informal salaried jobs. Even in countries in which workers moving from a formal to an informal salaried job register a decline in earnings on average, a substantial share of workers experience wage increases associated with that change. For example, in Argentina 43 percent of the workers who move from the formal to the informal sector experience a wage increase. The corresponding numbers for Albania, Russia, Mexico, and Venezuela are 37, 35, 44, and 35 percent, respectively.

Workers who switch from formal to informal jobs may be negatively selected. In all countries, with the exception of Albania and Georgia, workers who remain in formal salaried jobs have, on average, higher initial wages than workers who move to informal salaried jobs. Significantly, the opposite is also the case for workers who switch from informal to formal salaried jobs: in most countries, the average starting wage of "switchers" (from the informal to formal sector) is higher than the average starting wage of "stayers." This is consistent with lower observed or unobserved abilities for workers who switch to the informal sector. This also indicates that traditional estimates of wage differentials between formal- and informal-sector workers may be overestimated: an important component of wage gaps between the formal and informal sector may be associated with negative selection.

The consequences for earnings of switching between formal salaried and self-employed jobs vary across countries. In Mexico and Venezuela moving from a formal salaried job to self-employment results, on average, in a decline in monthly earnings (relative to those workers who remain in their original sta-

16. See Duryea, Marquéz, Pagés, and Scarpetta (2006) for further description of the methodology and a full description of the results relative to wage changes.

tus), while the opposite move brings an increase. In Argentina switching from formal salaried employment to self-employment is associated with an increase in monthly earnings. However, moving from self-employment to a formal salaried job is also associated with higher monthly earnings, indicating that workers move when they see opportunities for improvement.

There are also indications of negative selection among those who move from formal salaried jobs to self-employment: Workers who make this shift have lower starting salaries on average than do workers who remain in formal salaried jobs. And when moving from self-employment to a full salaried job, those workers have, on average, higher starting wages than workers who remain in self-employment.

Workers who move from informal salaried jobs to self-employment experience an increase in earnings. In the few countries for which a sufficient number of observations are available for transitions from salaried informal jobs to self-employment, the evidence suggests that such a move leads to an increase in monthly earnings. The opposite transition tends to lead to a decline in earnings, but not in all cases. In Albania and Argentina a move from self-employment to a salaried informal job is associated with an increase in monthly earnings, suggesting again that workers move when opportunities for improvement are available.

There is evidence that those who move from salaried informal jobs to self-employment are positively selected: the starting earnings of workers who remain in salaried informal jobs are lower than the starting earnings of workers who move to self-employment. Conversely, workers who switch from self-employment to salaried informal jobs had lower starting earnings (when self-employed) than those who remain in self-employment.

Conclusions

Overall, the analysis suggests a complex picture of workers' mobility in the labor market. Mobility is quite high not only in and out of the labor market but also across different types of jobs. Contrary to what is commonly found, informal salaried workers are more likely to transit to unemployment than are formal salaried workers. This is at least partly explained by the much lower stability of informal salaried jobs, relative to formal salaried employment. Within jobs, mobility within wage employment (that is, formal to informal) is higher than that between wage employment and self-employment, suggesting that barriers to entry into self-employment or strong preferences for salaried employment reduce flows into self-employment. For workers who leave self-employment, transitions to informal salaried jobs, unemployment, or exiting the labor force entirely tend to be more common than moving into a formal salaried job.

The data also suggest important earning consequences of transitions. In some countries, there is evidence that, on average, workers who move from formal to informal salaried employment experience earning losses. Yet in some of the transition economies, switching from formal to informal salaried jobs improves workers' earnings. Similarly, for many, switching to self-employment is a way to improve earnings, particularly for informal wage workers. Within countries, there is significant individual heterogeneity in earnings changes associated with mobility: Even when workers lose earnings from switching across certain statuses on average, many workers gain in that process. Finally, there is evidence of selection among switchers: The data suggest that those who switch from formal to informal salaried activities are negatively selected, while those who move to self-employment from informal salaried activities are positively selected.

Comment
and Discussion

Carmen Reinhart: I will offer three areas of comment on the paper. The first concerns the macroeconomic environment in which the transitions discussed take place. Second, I want to focus on the methodology employed and suggest some directions where the authors might develop some interesting insights by further parsing the data. Finally, I have a few reservations concerning the quality of the data.

The paper reviews evidence on labor market mobility in nine countries. Three countries (Argentina, Mexico, and Venezuela) come from Latin America, while the remainder (Albania, Georgia, Hungary, Poland, Russia, and the Ukraine) are transition economies in Eastern Europe. The period of study ranges from as little as two years (Georgia and the Ukraine) to eleven years (Mexico). The paper uses longitudinal labor force survey data to construct a transition matrix for each country, with each cell representing the probability of having labor force status j in period $t + k$ conditional on having status i in period t. The authors consider six possible labor force outcomes (an issue I will return to later): out of the labor force, unemployed, formal salaried worker, informal salaried worker, self-employed, and farmer.

As a macroeconomist, I tend to think about the big picture when viewing issues of labor mobility. Table 1 in the paper and the subsequent discussion highlights the high level of macrovolatility in the countries studied. Many of the countries experienced large output swings during the sample period, and in others (Hungary and Russia) the period of analysis immediately followed a severe recession. I would additionally emphasize that other types of volatility, such as relative price movements between the traded and nontraded sector, can have important influences on labor market options beyond their effect on output.

Economic crises serve to highlight the effects of the kinds of macroeconomic volatility I have in mind. The sample includes episodes of currency, banking, debt, and inflation crises, so consideration of crisis dynamics is nontrivial. As an example, currency crises imply large changes in the real exchange rate, which can have a particularly adverse effect on the nontraded sector. If, say, a currency crisis precedes the collapse of the real estate and construction industries, we would likely see a large movement of the displaced workers from the formal to the informal sector. The authors should control for such macroeconomic effects in their analysis, and they might generate some useful observations by examining in detail certain crisis subperiods.[1]

My second suggestion involves looking more closely within the labor market movements reported. I again come back to big picture economic currents, here financial liberalization and privatization, which were prominent in all of the countries in the sample. I would like to see the authors expand their matrix to make it possible to study movements *within* a given labor market sector that could shed light on the effects of these big picture policies.

Financial liberalization has had a profound impact on the structure of the economies considered. I recall traveling in Indonesia in 1995, when overnight it seemed the country went from five banks to one hundred and five banks. Financial liberalization likely played an especially important role in the former Soviet states. As a result, a significant portion of these economies shifted from agriculture or manufacturing into finance. It would constitute a major contribution to document how the associated reallocation of resources affected labor market mobility. Importantly, this would require looking within the formal salaried sector to measure movement into financial firms.

The period of study also coincided with substantial privatizing of state-owned enterprises. Such privatizations occurred in all of the transition economies, as well as in Mexico and Argentina. A common feature of these privatizations was subsequent downsizing—newly private firms laying off surplus labor. I would like to know the extent to which transitions out of the formal salaried sector can be related to firms' privatizing. In Argentina, for example, privatization has been associated with rising macro-unemployment. Does this relationship hold at the microlevel, and how many of the laid-off workers wind up taking jobs in the informal sector? Note again that these questions require looking within a given cell of the matrix, in this case to focus on the transition probabilities for formal sector workers in formerly government companies.

Finally, a few points of reservation. The first concerns the quality of the data, particularly for the informal sector. The authors could do more to convince the reader that measurement errors are not systematic and therefore driving the results. Second, I advise caution when comparing Latin American countries to

---

1. Kaminsky and Reinhart (1999) and Frankel and Rose (1996) contain dates of currency crises, and Caprio and others (2005) list banking crises.

those in Eastern Europe. The period of study coincides with the transition from a centrally planned economy in the former Soviet states, which must have influenced flows between the formal and informal sector. Any conclusions regarding the disparate effects of labor market institutions in these two regions should be considered in this light.

I enjoyed this paper and learned much from it. I urge the authors to take greater consideration of the macroeconomic circumstances, particularly the implications of choosing a sample of countries prone to frequent crises. I also hope they pay more attention to transitions within sectors, as examining flows within the formal sector and from certain industries and types of firms may yield many fruitful insights.

Discussion: Susan Collins began by noting the rich nature of the findings on mobility. She suggested the possibility of probing the data sets for information about cross-border migration, in addition to internal migration, as a relevant extension of the research.

Carol Graham suggested that an analogue to Carmen Reinhart's focus on the macroeconomic picture, which was triggered by the high degree of variance in unemployment rates, would be an additional focus on social welfare institutions. She noted that cross-country differences in the extent of social support might help explain this variance in rates. In some contexts, such as in Latin America, where social welfare systems are much more limited than they are in Poland (which has the highest unemployment rates of any country in the data set), most individuals cannot afford to be formally unemployed and instead are self-employed or in the informal sector.

John McHale noted that the results in the paper shed new light on what it means to be formal and informal and how that meaning varies across countries. The paper provides a better sense of how wages vary across these sectors and in unexpected ways. In Eastern Europe, for example, wages are not that different in the informal sector. These very modest differences imply something very different about the structure of the economy and what that formal-informal distinction means as compared with a case in which there are very sharp distinctions in wages.

Lant Pritchett suggested that the paper should have made distinctions between the transition matrices of men and women from the outset. He noted that the behavior of men and women in the labor force was very different and thus pooling it in the same transition matrix may make little sense. In the same vein, he felt that young, prime-age, and old workers should also be separated. If eighteen-year-olds, for example, churn through six jobs, it is not particularly worrisome. Those same trends for a prime-age worker would be extremely unsettling.

Carmen Pagés responded by saying that she appreciated the comments and acknowledging that the paper was preliminary and very much part of ongoing research. She and her coauthors still have a great deal of data to analyze, and they are trying to organize them according to a model that will enable them to account for many of the issues raised by the commentators. She also agreed with Carmen Reinhart on the importance of going beyond the microlevel and looking at macro trends.

References

Bartelsman, Eric J., and Mark Doms. 2000. "Understanding Productivity: Lessons from Longitudinal Microdata." *Journal of Economic Literature* 38, no. 3: 569–95.

Bartelsman, Eric J., John C. Haltiwanger, and Stefano Scarpetta. 2004. "Microeconomic Evidence of Creative Destruction in Industrial and Developing Countries." Policy Research Working Paper 3464. Washington: World Bank (December).

Borgarello, Andrea, Suzanne Duryea, Analia Olgiati, and Stefano Scarpetta. 2006. "Early Work Experience for Youth: Stepping Stones or Traps." Working Paper. Washington: World Bank (June).

Caprio, Gerard, Daniela Klingebiel, Luc Laeven, and Guillermo Noguera. 2005. "Banking Crisis Database." In *Systemic Financial Crises*, edited by Patrick Honohan and Luc Laeven, appendix: pp. 307–40. Cambridge University Press.

Caves, Richard E. 1998. "Industrial Organization and New Findings on the Turnover and Mobility of Firms." *Journal of Economic Literature* 36, no. 4 (December): 1947–982.

Davis, Steven, and John Haltiwanger. 1999. "On the Driving Forces Behind Cyclical Movements in Employment and Job Reallocation." *American Economic Review* 89, no. 5 (December): 1234–258.

Duryea, Suzanne, Gustavo Marquéz, Carmen Pagés, and Stefano Scarpetta. 2006. "Mobility between Formal and Informal Jobs: Evidence from Transition and Latin American Countries." Working Paper. Washington: World Bank (June).

Eslava, Marcela, John Haltiwanger, Adriana Kugler, and Maurice Kugler. 2005. "Factor Adjustments after Deregulation: Panel Evidence from Colombian Plants." NBER Working Paper 11656. Cambridge, Mass.: National Bureau of Economic Research.

Fernandes, Ana M. 2002. "Trade Policy, Trade Volumes, and Plant-Level Productivity in Colombian Manufacturing Industries." Policy Research Working Paper 3064. Washington: World Bank.

Frankel, Jeffrey, and Andrew Rose. 1996. "Currency Crashes in Emerging Markets: An Empirical Treatment." *Journal of International Economics* 41, nos. 3-4 (November): 351–66.

Gong, Xiaodong, Arthur van Soest, and Elizabeth Villagomez. 2004. "Mobility in the Urban Labor Market: A Panel Data Analysis for Mexico." *Economic Development and Cultural Change* 53: 1–36.

Haltiwanger, John C., Adriana Kugler, Maurice Kugler, Alejandro Micco, and Carmen Pagés. 2004. "Effects of Tariffs and Real Exchange Rates on Job Reallocation: Evidence from Latin America." *Journal of Policy Reform* 7, no. 4 (December): 191–208.

IADB. 2003. *Good Jobs Wanted: Labor Markets in Latin America: 2004 Economic and Social Progress Report*. Washington: Inter-American Development Bank.

Kaminsky, Graciela L., and Carmen Reinhart. 1999. "The Twin Crises: The Causes of Banking and Balance of Payments Problems." *American Economic Review* 89 no.4 (June): 473–500.

Maloney, William F. 1999. "Does Informality Imply Segmentation in Urban Labor? Evidence from Sectoral Transitions in Mexico." *World Bank Economic Review* 13, no. 2: 275–302.

Pagés, Carmen, and Marco Stampini. 2006. "Skill Level, Mobility, and Labor Market Duality: Evidence from Latin America and Transition Economies." Working Paper. Washington: World Bank.

Pavcnik, Nina. 2002. "Trade Liberalization, Exit, and Productivity Improvements: Evidence from Chilean Plants." *Review of Economic Studies* 69, no. 1: 245–76.

Rutkowski, Jan J., and Stefano Scarpetta, with others. 2005. *Enhancing Jobs Opportunities: Eastern Europe and the Former Soviet Union.* Washington: World Bank.

World Bank. 2006. *World Development Indicators.* Washington.

MICHAEL KREMER
Harvard University

Globalization of Labor Markets and Inequality

In thinking about the impact of the globalization of labor markets on inequality, economists naturally turn to the Hecksher-Ohlin model. While in many contexts the effects of trade and migration can presumably be well understood through this model, in other contexts it may be less appropriate. I argue below that considering models other than the Hecksher-Ohlin model may suggest very different implications regarding the effects of the globalization of labor markets on inequality. I first discuss Kremer and Maskin, which looked at the impact of trade on inequality in poor countries, and then discuss Kremer and Watt, which examines the impact of immigration on inequality in rich countries.[1]

Trade

Consider a standard Hecksher-Ohlin model with two complementary factors of production: skilled labor and unskilled labor. Suppose there is a rich country with a high ratio of skilled to unskilled labor and a poor country with a low ratio of skilled to unskilled labor. Under the Hecksher-Ohlin model, allowing trade will equalize factor prices, and therefore skilled wages will rise in the rich country and fall in the poor country. Unskilled wages will fall in the rich country and rise in the poor country. This result of trade increasing inequality in the rich country resonates with many in the United States and in Europe.

However, the model also implies that trade will decrease inequality in the poor country. Many, however, are not convinced that this implication of the model is consistent with the experience of poor countries. People opposed to

The author thanks the editors for useful comments. This version has been changed from the original because of revisions to the model.
1. Kremer and Maskin (2003); Kremer and Watt (2006).

globalization often see it as benefiting elites in the rich world and the poor world at the expense of the poor in each world. The moderate left often argues that for poor countries to take advantage of globalization they need to educate their labor force, an argument that seems difficult to reconcile with the standard Hecksher-Ohlin model.[2]

Kremer and Maskin argue that there are empirical problems with the Hecksher-Ohlin model's predictions regarding the effects of trade in poor countries and then propose a model that could account for some of these effects.

Empirical Problems with the Hecksher-Ohlin Model

There are at least two problems with the standard Hecksher-Ohlin model. First, the standard model would predict that when factor endowments are most different, trade should be greatest. However, there is not much trade between the rich countries and the poorest countries.

Second, there is little evidence that globalization decreases inequality in developing countries, while there is some evidence that globalization in fact increases inequality in these countries. The evidence is from episodes of trade liberalization and also cross-country regressions. Several studies suggest that wage inequality increased when Mexico joined the General Agreement on Tariffs and Trade (GATT) in 1985 and embarked on a broad liberalization of trade and foreign investment.[3]

Time series studies that found that wage inequality increased after globalization in developing countries include work on Argentina, Chile, Colombia, Costa Rica, and Uruguay.[4] Wood surveyed the literature and concluded that increased openness was associated with reduced wage inequality in the Asian Tiger economies in the 1970s and 1980s but with increased inequality in Latin America in the 1990s.[5]

Lindert and Williamson argued that the limited evidence available for other countries indicated that liberalization tends to be followed by increases in inequality, but causality is doubtful, particularly since in several large countries (India, China, Russia, and Indonesia) liberalization had been only partial.[6]

---

2. Clinton (2000).

3. Feliciano (2001); Cragg and Epelbaum (1996); Feenstra and Hanson (1996); Aitken, Harrison, and Lipsey (1996); Pavcnik (2000).

4. Argentina (Robbins, Gonzales, and Menendez 1995); Chile (Robbins 1995a); Colombia (Robbins 1996a); Costa Rica (Robbins and Gindling 1998); Uruguay (Robbins 1995b, 1996b).

5. Wood (1997).

6. Lindert and Williamson (2001).

Most of the recent panel data literature either found that trade liberalization was positively associated with inequality in poor countries or found no strong association. Barro's survey of inequality and growth in a panel of countries found that the relationship between openness and inequality was positive for low-income countries and negative for high-income countries, with the turning point occurring at a GDP per capita level of $13,000.[7] Kapstein and Milanovic found a similar result, with a turning point around $6,000.[8] Lundberg and Squire found in panel data (which included developed and developing countries) that the income share of the lowest two quintiles was negatively affected by openness, while that of middle and upper quintiles was positively affected.[9] Others found insignificant results or found that results were sensitive to the particular specification used.[10]

The Model: Globalization of the Production Process

Kremer and Maskin formulated a model that suggested that little trade existed between the richest and poorest countries and that globalization might have increased inequality in poor countries.[11] We modeled globalization of the production process rather than globalization of trade in produced goods. This work used a production function explored earlier by Kremer and Maskin and used by Piketty to make a similar argument on the impact of immigration.[12] Our work differs from Piketty's in that our model suggests that there may be limited trade between the richest and poorest countries, and because while Piketty suggests that immigration may increase inequality in poor countries, our work suggests that trade may increase inequality in both rich and poor countries.[13]

Kremer and Maskin assumed that when a production process is globalized a single product is manufactured out of components made and assembled in different countries.[14] Thus the people working on the product are in effect work-

---

7. Barro (2000).

8. Kapstein and Milanovic (2003). When regional dummies are included in regressions, openness reduces inequality in rich and transition economies, increases it in Latin America, and has no significant effect elsewhere. However, since there is a correlation between income levels and region membership (Latin American countries are more similar to other Latin American countries than they are to African countries in income level), it is not clear that including regional dummies does not throw the baby out with the bath water.

9. Lundberg and Squire (2003).

10. Rama (2001); Dollar and Kraay (2001a, 2001b); Li, Squire, and Zou (1998); White and Anderson (2001); Garrett (2001).

11. Kremer and Maskin (2003).

12. Kremer and Maskin (1996); Piketty (1997).

13. Kremer and Maskin (2003).

14. Kremer and Maskin (2003).

ing together. For example, workers in rich countries may design and market shoes, while those in poor countries may stitch the shoes.

Suppose, to consider as simple an example as possible, that two workers are needed to produce a product, a manager and an assistant. Suppose that output depends on the skill of each of those workers but is more sensitive to the skill of the manager than it is to the skill of the assistant. In particular, suppose that output is equal to the quality of the manager squared times the quality of the assistant, $Q_m{}^2Q_a$. The key assumptions here are that workers of different skill levels are imperfect substitutes, that output is more sensitive to skill in one task than it is in the other task, and that different tasks within the same production process are complements. These two tasks could be, as mentioned above, designing a sneaker and actually stitching a sneaker.

Suppose that there are four workers who need to be organized into two production teams, each with two workers. Two of the workers have skill H, and two of them have skill L, where $H > L$. If one production team is composed of high-skilled workers and the other is composed of low-skilled workers, output is then $H^3 + L^3$. However, if the high-skilled workers are the managers and the low-skilled workers are the assistants, so that each production team has one high-skilled worker and one low-skilled worker, then output in each production process is H^2L, and total output is $2H^2L$. There are no externalities here. The decentralized equilibrium is efficient, so in equilibrium, production will be organized to maximize output.

Cross-matching, in which the high-skilled workers are the managers in each production team and the low-skilled workers are the assistants in each production team, yields more output if

$$\frac{H}{L} < \frac{1+\sqrt{5}}{2}$$

in this simple example. Thus if skill levels of the high- and low-skilled workers are not too different, it is more efficient to match them together in the same production teams.

If the difference in skill between high- and low-skilled workers is too great, then it is more efficient for the workers of different skill to work in separate production teams. Intuitively, if the difference in skill is too great, then high-skilled workers will not want to work with low-skilled workers. For example, a very good sneaker designer does not want to have the sneaker stitched by someone who is going to do a poor job. However, if the skill gap is only moderate, then it is beneficial to take advantage of the cross-matching.

To get a sense of how wages are determined, consider a simple example. Normalize output prices to 1. Suppose that there are more L workers than H workers, so that there are not enough H workers to be matched with each L worker. Suppose also that the skill levels are close enough that it is optimal to cross-match if possible. Since there are not enough H workers to pair with all L workers, some of the low-skilled workers will be self-matched. This ties down the wages of L workers at

$$w_L = \frac{L^3}{2}.$$

Since total output for a cross-matched production process is H^2L,

$$w_H + w_L = H^2L$$

These two equations together determine the wages of high-skilled workers.

To understand the effect of globalization, consider a simple two-country example: there is a rich country and a poor country and one good. The rich country has workers of skill A and B. The poor country has workers of skill C and D. Assume $A > B > C > D$. Suppose that globalization consists of a change in technology that allows workers to match across borders. Before globalization it was not technologically feasible to produce across borders. Thus the only possible (though not necessary) cross-matches were A with B or C with D. Now suppose that fax machines, the Internet, and cheap airline tickets make it possible to match across borders. After globalization has occurred, A can match with C and B can match with C. Trade here is defined as cross-border production.

Kremer and Maskin showed that if C and D are sufficiently low relative to A and B, no one in the rich country wants to work with people in the poor country.[15] This will be the case if

$$\frac{B}{C} > \frac{1+\sqrt{5}}{2}.$$

If C is higher and D is lower, so that

$$\frac{B}{D} > \frac{1+\sqrt{5}}{2} > \frac{B}{C},$$

then the highest-skilled workers in the poor countries will work with workers in rich countries, and globalization will increase inequality in the poor country.

Thirty years ago Indian engineers worked as engineers in garment factories, steel factories, and auto factories. These factories hired a lot of lower-skilled

15. Kremer and Maskin (2003).

Indian workers. Thus there was a fair supply of skilled workers who were presumably complementary with unskilled workers in India.

Today, many Indian engineers are working on projects together with engineers in Silicon Valley. This potentially raises the wages of Indian engineers but leaves unchanged the wages of lower-skilled Indians who are left out of the globalized production process. Wages for these lower-skilled workers remain constrained by the condition that some of them will have to self-match. Higher-skilled workers can therefore do no worse than continue to work at the autarky wage rate, but under some parameter values they may earn more, because of the option of cross-matching with workers in developed countries. For the case in which there are more D-workers than C-workers,

$$w_D = D^3/2, \; w_C \geq \max\{C^3/2, DC^2 - D^3/2\}.$$

Thus in this model, trade could actually increase inequality in the poor country. Note that trade could also increase inequality if there are more C-workers than D-workers. The key insight is that the globalization of the production process may benefit only those in the developing country with a skill level sufficiently close to that of their rich country collaborators, thus marginalizing low-skill workers in the developing country. The effect on inequality in the rich country is ambiguous, but for some parameter values, it will increase.

It seems plausible that there are different types of trade in the world, some of which are well modeled by the Hecksher-Ohlin model but others which might be modeled along the lines described above. Below I discuss how moving beyond the Hecksher-Ohlin model similarly suggests that some types of migration may have very different effects on inequality than conventionally believed.

Migration

Migration restrictions are arguably the largest distortion in the world economy and the most costly for the world's poor. From the point of view of people in developing countries, it would likely be highly beneficial to abolish these restrictions. However, as highlighted in the recent debate over immigration in the United States, rich countries are unlikely to remove migration restrictions for low-skilled workers. There are three main political obstacles. The first is concern that low-skilled workers migrating into the country will drive down wages for low-skilled natives. Second, there are concerns that migration may create drains on the welfare state. Finally, there are concerns about the effect that removing migration restrictions would have on native culture.

**Table 1. Foreign Private Household Workers and Female Labor
Force Participation**

Percent

Country	FPHW as share of labor force	Female labor force participation 1970	Female labor force participation 1990
Kuwait	19.9	12.5	23.2
Bahrain	10.1	7.6	47.2
Saudi Arabia	8.9		
Singapore	7	26.7	74.6
Hong Kong	6.8	39.6	75.5
Greece	1	34	64.7
Taiwan	0.8		
Israel	0.8	44	58.7
United States	0.3	47.5	76.3
United Kingdom	n.a.	43.9	73.5
Germany	n.a.	53.5	73.3
France	n.a.	61.8	68.8
Japan	n.a.	46.1	63.9
Korea	n.a.	36.6	48.9

Source: Kremer and Watt (2006).
n.a. Not available.

Borjas showed that a Hecksher-Ohlin approach suggests a very big distributional impact of low-skilled migration on natives and a very small increase in social surplus for natives.[16]

This model is appropriate for some types of migration, but not all. In particular, it may not apply to a certain form of migration that is growing rapidly. In the past 20 years, there has been rapid growth in migration of foreign private household workers (FPHWs) to do domestic work in countries that have recently become wealthy (see table 1). In Hong Kong and Singapore, FPHWs represent approximately 7 percent of the labor force. The percentages are even bigger in the Persian Gulf countries. In Taiwan, Greece, and Israel, FPHWs represent almost 1 percent of the labor force. The workers are overwhelmingly female.

Some receiving countries, such as Hong Kong and Singapore, have special visa programs for foreign private household workers, which restrict them to working in that sector and do not allow them to bring in family members. In other countries, many FPHWs work "under the table," so few statistics are available to quantify the extent of this phenomenon. For example, Chile has many domestic workers from Paraguay. Italy and Spain also have significant numbers of illegal domestic workers.

16. Borjas (1995).

Kremer and Watt argue that immigration of foreign private household workers will not be subject to the three political obstacles to migration to rich countries discussed above, although it raises a different set of ethical and political constraints.[17] In particular, we argue that migration of FPHWs raises wages for native low-skilled workers and creates large fiscal and welfare gains for the receiving countries. When families in Hong Kong and Singapore hire nannies from the Philippines, educated native women are potentially able to either enter the labor market or supply more labor and move into a higher-powered job. Hong Kong and Singapore have extremely high female labor force participation now, which they did not have before large-scale implementation of these FPHW programs. To the extent that high-skilled women move into the formal-sector labor force and out of home production, this increases the ratio of skilled to unskilled workers in market labor. This tends to drive down the wages of skilled labor relative to unskilled labor, thus decreasing native wage inequality.

This form of migration also creates a large fiscal benefit. There is a big tax distortion in favor of home production because home production is not taxed while market labor is. Thus if a high-skilled woman, who in most countries would face a fairly high marginal tax rate, enters the labor force after hiring a FPHW, all of her labor income is taxable, and the taxes she pays are a pure benefit to the rest of society.

Finally, Singapore- or Hong Kong–style programs avoid fears that migration will change the culture of the host society in the long run, because immigrants are overwhelmingly female and are not allowed to bring their families. (As noted below, this raises other concerns, of course.)

The rest of this paper is structured as follows: the next section will discuss the model used in Kremer and Watt, followed by a discussion of the results of a calibration of the model designed to estimate the impact of a Singapore- or Hong Kong–type FPHW program in the United States. The last section discusses ethical issues and leakage of FPHWs into other sectors.

The Model: Immigration of FPHWs

Kremer and Watt assume that there are three types of agents: native high-skilled workers, native low-skilled workers, and foreign private household workers. We normalize the native population to 1 and assume that a fraction, h, are high skilled, leaving $1 - h$ as the fraction of low-skilled natives. Each agent is endowed with 1 unit of labor.

17. Kremer and Watt (2006).

Agents consume two types of private consumption goods: a general good, denoted as A, and a domestic good like cooking, cleaning, or childcare, denoted as C. All native consumers must consume a required R units of the domestic good. The domestic good can be self-produced, purchased from day care centers, or purchased from private household workers. Natives also consume a public good paid for by the government, which is discussed later.

The production function for good A is $A = H^\beta L^{1-\beta}$, where H is high-skilled native labor, L is low-skilled native labor, and $0 < \beta < 1$. We assume immigrating foreign private household workers are legally excluded from entering this sector under the terms of their visa, as in Hong Kong and Singapore.[18] We will consider the case in which some foreign private household workers leak into the general economy and substitute for low-skilled workers in production of good A later in this section.

Day care centers produce good C with production function $C_{dc} = kH^\beta L^{1-\beta}$. They assume day care centers have the same factor intensity as good A. If anything, this is a conservative assumption, as Kisker and colleagues found that 47 percent of teachers in U.S. day care centers have completed college.[19] This is considerably more than the 24.1 percent of workers with college degrees in the general economy.[20]

Day care centers only produce certain types of the domestic good. We therefore assume that there is an upper limit denoted by $\bar{c} < R$ as to how much of the domestic good consumers can purchase from day care centers. Most day care centers are open only during limited hours, are closed on holidays, and send sick children home. Consumers employing day care centers must still drop off and pick up their children, find alternative child care on holidays, and care

---

18. The assumption that low-skilled immigrants and low-skilled natives are not perfect substitutes and that these types of immigrants have a comparative advantage at producing the domestic good is necessary for our results. Imperfect substitutability of immigrants and native low-skilled workers may arise because of differences in skills between these workers; or government policies that restrict immigrants' ability to work outside the domestic sector, as in the Hong Kong foreign domestic helpers program or in the U.S. and U.K. au pair programs; or differential enforcement of immigration restrictions across workers in different sectors. Some evidence that immigrants have a comparative advantage in domestic work is provided by the fact that in 1998 in the United States, noncitizens were almost five times more likely to work in the personal service–private household category as were U.S. citizens—3.6 percent of noncitizens were employed in those occupations as opposed to 0.7 percent of U.S. citizens, and 2.7 percent of foreign-born U.S. residents (including naturalized citizens) work in personal service occupations. Cortes and Tessada (2006) found specifically that 25.8 percent of low-skilled female immigrants are employed in private households, a number much larger than that for the native population.

19. Kisker and colleagues (1991).

20. Kominski and Adams (1994).

for sick children themselves. Day care centers also do not perform other domestic tasks such as cooking and cleaning.

We also assume a third type of technology for good C production—private household workers. In most of the developed world, we observe very few natives working as private household workers. In the United Kingdom in 1990, only 0.05 percent of the working population were employed as domestic housekeepers. In the United States, only around 1 percent of the entire employed population (which includes natives and nonnatives) are employed in the personal services–private household industries. To account for this, we also assume that working conditions and social stigma associated with private household work cause people to dislike working in the private household sector and that households prefer or are more efficient at producing their own domestic good, because they know their own tastes in food, enjoy taking care of their own children, and so forth. This will mean that there will be a wedge between the after-tax wage of potential employers and the wage in alternative jobs open to potential employees.

Although foreign household workers experience a utility penalty when working as private household workers, we assume that their other options are even less attractive. Thus we assume a potentially inelastic supply of foreign private household workers and that the supply of foreign private household workers is only limited by the number of visas that the host government will provide.

With the creation of a FPHW program, the host nation admits low-skilled immigrants who can provide the full R units of domestic good production for exactly one household.[21] These workers are prohibited from working in the production of good A and are only permitted to work as private household workers in the receiving country.

The government taxes the labor income of all natives at tax rate τ and spends all tax revenue on a public good that is only enjoyed by natives. To abstract from debates about whether immigrants pay more in taxes than they receive from the government in social services, we assume that foreign private household workers neither are taxed nor enjoy the benefits of the government good. (In fact, foreign private household workers are most likely to be net contributors to the welfare system.)

21. We assume that native private household workers need at least $1 - R + \bar{c}$ units of their time to produce R units of domestic good for one household. As a result, native private household workers need to purchase child care service from day care centers or hire private household worker for themselves to be able to work as private household workers. This assumption is not crucial to our results, and it is made for the sake of simplicity. The opposite assumption that private household workers have enough time to fully produce their own domestic services would simply lead to changes in certain cutoffs.

High-skill households, with their high opportunity cost of time, will be the first to employ these FPHWs. This may allow high-skilled native workers to move from domestic work to market work. (In practice women provide the bulk of child care in the absence of PHWs, and it is, therefore, women who primarily move from work at home to work in the market.) Thus the labor supply of the high-skilled increases, and as a result the relative native low-skilled wage increases. The high-skilled labor freed up by FPHWs is also taxable, resulting in a fiscal benefit and a reversal in the tax-induced distortions against market production.

Calibration of the Model:
Impact of an FPHW Program in the United States

A difficult issue in estimating the ultimate impact on the host country's welfare is determining just how many high-skilled women are freed up for each private household worker who immigrates. To the extent that employing foreign private household workers leads to increases in leisure or fertility or to simply more consumption of home services, these effects will not be large.

In Israeli data, women with youngest children aged 2 to 4 who employ household helpers for more than 16 hours per week have approximately 21.6 percentage points or 29.0 percent higher labor force participation than those who do not hire care givers. Using microdata from Israel in 2002, we can make rough estimates of the private household workers' impact on the intensive margin. Using self-reported weekly hours, college-educated women with children younger than 4 who hired a private household worker had 34.4 percent higher reported hours worked last week.[22] Cortes and Tessada found very big effects of immigration on female labor supply using time use data from the United States.[23] They use past migration as an instrument for current migration, arguing that social networks are important determinants of future patterns of immigration. The authors estimated that a 10.0 percent increase in the number of workers with less than a high school education will increase the labor supply of all women by about 10.0 percent.[24] The point estimate was arguably implausibly large, but the lower bound of the 10.0 percent confidence interval

---

22. Kremer and Watt (2006). Self-reported usual weekly labor hours were 17.5 percent greater. These estimates come from the authors' regressions of the labor supply of college-educated women with children younger than 5 using Israeli data from 2002. The point estimates are the coefficients on a dummy indicating whether the women employed a foreign private household worker for more than 40 hours a week.

23. Cortes and Tessada (2006).

24. Khananusapkul (2004) also attempted to estimate the labor supply effect of low-skilled

of the estimate implied that each immigrant in an occupation that arguably largely substitutes for domestic production increased native labor supply to the market by the equivalent of 0.34 workers.[25] These results were largely due to differences on the intensive margin.

Evidence consistent with the hypothesis that taking care of children leads to lower wages is provided by Ellwood, Wilde, and Batchelder who use a panel data set to estimate that high-ability women suffer net hourly wage losses of 30.0 percent ten years after the birth of a child, relative to counterparts who did not give birth.[26]

Other empirical studies that have investigated the relationship between child care prices and mothers' workforce participation have found that decreases in child care costs increased the likelihood of mothers joining the labor force at elasticities ranging from –0.74 to –0.2.[27]

Rough calibrations suggest sizeable changes in wages and welfare for natives. We estimate the welfare effect by assuming that for every immigrating PHW, 0.2 high-skilled women are able to join the labor market (or equivalently each native high-skilled woman employing a FPHW increases labor supply by 20.0 percent—for example, moving from a forty-hour work week to a forty-eight-hour work week.)

To estimate the welfare gains and wage effects of foreign private household workers, we also need information on the share of high-skilled workers, their

---

immigrants, but since she lacked time use data on the intensive margin of labor supply, she was unable to find strong results.

25. Only 12.9 percent of the U.S. labor force had less than a high school education. A 10 percent increase in the number of people without high school education because of immigration corresponded to a 1.29 percent increase in the overall labor force. In the United States 20.7 percent of all immigrants with less than a high school education found employment in industries we classify as likely to displace substantially native household production (private household services, landscaping services, child care services, restaurant services, drinking establishments, car washes, barber shops, beauty salons, nail salons, dry cleaning and laundry, and taxi and limousine services, according to the Public Use Microdata Samples 2000). This implies that a 10 percent increase in the population of workers without high school education due to immigration would correspond to a 0.207 x 0.0129 = 0.27 percent increase in the native labor force. (Cortes and Tessada [2006] assumed that low-skilled immigrants and low-skilled natives are not perfect substitutes and are aggregated with a constant elasticity of substitution [CES] aggregator. For simplicity, we assume that they are perfect substitutes as their assumption will not change the figures by much.)

Using Cortes and Tessada's 10.0 percent lower confidence interval for the impact on female labor means that this increase in immigration would lead to about a 0.2 percent increase in native, female labor supply, equivalent to a 0.09 percent increase in total native labor supply, which suggests that each immigrant in occupations that affect native labor supply increases native labor supply by 0.09/0.27 = 34.1 percent of a native worker.

26. Ellwood, Wilde, and Batchelder (2004).

27. Blau and Robins (1988); Connelly (1992); Ribar (1995); Kimmel (1998).

wages, and the deadweight loss of taxation. If one treats workers with a college education as high-skilled, then $h = 0.24$ for the United States. On the basis of data from Hong Kong, we assume that high-skilled workers employing private household workers earn twice the average wage in the economy.[28]

The extra tax revenue from the increased labor supply of the employers of private household workers creates an externality benefit equal to the amount of high-skilled labor entering the labor market times the wage of high-skilled workers times the tax rate times the marginal cost of funds.

In this case, if each private household worker frees up 20.0 percent of a high-skilled worker, and these high-skilled workers earn twice the average wage in the economy as suggested by the Hong Kong data, and households face a marginal tax rate of 51.6 percent, and the marginal cost of raising 1 dollar in tax revenue is 1.4 dollars, then each private household worker creates an externality benefit equal to $0.2 \times 0.5 \times 1.4 \times 2 = 0.28$ times the average wage in the economy. This implies that it is possible to raise welfare by about 1.96 percent of wages by admitting 7.0 percent of the labor force as foreign private household workers, taking into account only the benefits associated with the fiscal externality. If we assume that wages make up 60.0 percent of GDP, welfare increases by just under 1.2 percent of total GDP.[29] Our estimated welfare effects are thus two orders of magnitude larger than those found by Borjas who estimated that immigration of 10 percent of the workforce raised national income by at most 0.01 to 0.02 percent when the supply of capital was perfectly elastic.[30]

We can do a similar calculation for wages. Under a constant elasticity of substitution (CES) production function, the effect of foreign private household workers on relative wages of native low-skilled and native high-skilled workers depends on the proportionate increase in each type of labor supply. Suppose again that each private household worker frees up 20.0 percent of a high-skilled worker.

If 7.0 percent of the labor force consists of foreign household workers, high-skilled labor increases by 0.2×7.0 percent = 1.4 percentage points. Given that high-skilled natives make up about 24.0 percent of the native labor force, high-

28. According to the Hong Kong Census and Statistics Department, in January 1996 median monthly household income of households hiring domestic helpers in Hong Kong was 40,000 HK dollars. In the fourth quarter of 1995, median monthly household income of all Hong Kong households was 15,700 HK dollars. Ideally, we would have data on relative wages of freed-up workers as opposed to the household as a whole, but we do not have this yet but expect to have better data in the future.

29. The model does not allow for capital. To the extent that capital is mobile or otherwise adjusts over time, the estimates may be reasonable in the long run, but in the short run, overall increases in output will not be as sharp. The pattern in changes and returns to factors will depend on the patterns of complementarity and substitutability among skilled labor, unskilled labor, and capital.

30. Borjas (1999).

skilled labor increases by about 1.4/24 = 5.8 percent. Although private household workers will displace native workers in day care centers, because we assume that the skill intensity of day care centers is the same as that of the general economy, the proportion of low-skilled natives displaced in day care centers will be exactly offset by the proportion of high-skilled natives displaced in day care centers. Under a Cobb-Douglas production function, the elasticity of substitution is 1 and

$$\frac{W_L}{W_H} \approx \frac{h}{(1-h)}.$$

This implies that the ratio of low-skilled to high-skilled wages increases by about 5.8 percent. If we assume an elasticity of substitution of 1.5, this ratio decreases by about two-thirds to 3.9 percent.

Even under the extreme assumption that day care centers are wholly staffed by low-skilled natives, wages of low-skilled natives will rise. To measure the percentage increase in the number of low-skilled workers, we need to compare the number of native day care center workers freed up with the total low-skilled population. For day care centers, we assume that each immigrant replaces a native day care worker at a ratio of 5:1. (The usual ratio of staff to child in day care facilities is 1:9, but some private household workers may care for more than one child.[31]) We also assume that 75.1 percent of natives who hire foreign private household workers would utilize day care centers in the absence of migration. This is the labor force participation rate of Israeli women who do not hire household workers. We thus assume that for every 100 foreign private household workers hired, 75.1 will replace native day care center workers, but only at a rate of 5 to 1. In this case, the increase in low-skilled labor would be $0.07 \times 0.751 \times 0.2 = 1.05$ percentage points, which is about 1.42 percent of the low-skilled native labor force (76 percent). This would increase the ratio of low- to high-skilled wages by 4.4 percent (5.8 percent – 1.4 percent) under a Cobb-Douglas assumption. With an elasticity of substitution of 1.5, the ratio would increase by 2.9 percent.

Leakage and Other Issues Surrounding
Adoption of this Program by "Old Rich" Countries

The discussion above raises the question of whether foreign private household worker programs could ever move beyond newly rich countries, such as Singapore and Hong Kong, to countries such as the United States or countries in the European Union. As discussed above, many countries electively enforce

31. Blau (2003).

immigration restrictions against firms but do little to enforce restrictions against FPHW migration, so to some extent this is happening already.

Could rich countries go further and adopt Singapore- or Hong Kong–style programs? While Hong Kong and Singapore may be able to enforce visa restrictions against foreign private household workers entering the general economy, in other countries, foreign private household workers might leak at a higher rate into the general economy and compete with low-skilled natives. People might come to the United States through a program for FPHWs and then stay and move into the general economy, where they would compete with low-skilled natives.

It is straightforward to calculate the largest fraction of immigrants who can leave the foreign private household program for the general economy without reducing the relative wages or welfare of the native low-skilled. Define the variable F as the amount of high-skilled labor freed up by each private household worker. Note that if the number of low-skilled immigrants leaking into the general economy for each 1 immigrant who remains in the foreign private household sector is

$$\frac{(1-h)F}{h},$$

then the proportional increase in high-skilled labor from foreign private household workers is exactly equal to the increase in low-skilled labor from immigrants leaking into the general economy. If F is 0.2 as previously assumed and $h = 0.24$, then as long as fewer than 0.62 immigrants leak into the general economy for each foreign private household worker, the relative wages of the native low-skilled would increase. Even at a leakage rate of 0.62, however, low-skilled natives would experience welfare gains because of the extra tax revenue received by the government.

Leakage can be limited by having migrants post a bond or having employment agencies keep some proportion of earnings in escrow.

There is a paradox here because ex ante FPHW programs result in welfare gains for the host country and also presumably make the migrants better off. Ex post, however, social norms in societies with a long history of immigration may be inconsistent with the idea of restricting long-term residents to the domestic work sector and prohibiting them from bringing family members.

Programs with temporary nonrenewable visas may be less subject to this criticism. Au pair programs work on this basis. There may, however, be an efficiency cost to making visas nonrenewable.

If the United States did adopt an FPHW program, the resulting financial flows to poor countries from remittances from the foreign private household workers could be very large. If each worker saves or remits $5,000 a year, and the foreign private household workers make up 7 percent of the labor force, then they would remit over $40 billion a year, four times the U.S. official development assistance.

Whatever one thinks of the merits of Singapore- and Hong Kong–style foreign private household worker programs, to the extent that a significant fraction of migrants from poor to rich countries are working, legally or illegally, as domestic workers or in other jobs that free up high-skilled native workers from household production, such as gardening, the Hecksher-Ohlin model will yield an incomplete picture of the consequences of migration on native labor markets.

References

Aitken, Brian, Ann Harrison, and Robert E. Lipsey. 1996. "Wages and Foreign Ownership: A Comparative Study of Mexico, Venezuela, and the United States." *Journal of International Economics* 40, nos. 3–4: 345–71.

Barro, Robert J. 2000. "Inequality and Growth in a Panel of Countries." *Journal of Economic Growth* 5, no. 1: 5–32.

Blau, David. 2003. "An Economic Perspective on Child Care Policy." *Journal of Population and Social Security: Population Study* I, Supplement (June): 423–42.

Blau, David, and Philip Robins. 1988. "Child-Care Costs and Family Labor Supply." *Review of Economics and Statistics* 70, no. 3: 374–81.

Borjas, George. 1995. "The Economic Benefits from Immigration." *Journal of Economic Perspectives* 9, no. 2: 3–22.

———. 1999. "The Economic Analysis of Immigration." In *Handbook of Labor Economics*, vol. 3A, edited by Orley Ashenfelter and David Card, pp. 1697–760. Amsterdam: North-Holland.

Clinton, Bill. 2000. Address to a Joint Session of the Indian Parliament. New Delhi (March) (www.indianembassy.org/indusrel/clinton_india/clinton_parliament_march_22_2000.htm).

Connelly, Rachel. 1992. "The Effects of Child Care Costs on Married Women's Labor Force Participation." *Review of Economics and Statistics* 74, no. 1: 83–90.

Cortes, Patricia, and Jose A. Tessada. 2006. "Cheap Maids and Nannies: How Low-Skilled Immigration is Changing the Time Use of American Women." Working Paper. Massachusetts Institute of Technology, Department of Economics.

Cragg, Michael I., and Mario Epelbaum. 1996. "Why Has Wage Dispersion Grown in Mexico? Is It the Incidence of Reforms or the Growing Demand for Skills?" *Journal of Development Economics* 51, no. 1: 99–116.

Dollar, David, and Aart Kraay. 2001a. "Trade, Growth, and Poverty." Policy Research Working Paper 2615. Washington: World Bank.

―――. 2001b. "Growth Is Good for the Poor." Policy Research Working Paper 2587. Washington: World Bank.

Ellwood, David, Ty Wilde, and Lily Batchelder. 2004. "The Mommy Track Divides: The Impact of Childbearing on Wages of Women of Differing Skill Levels." RSF Working Paper. Harvard University and New York: Russell Sage Foundation (March).

Feenstra, Robert C., and Gordon H. Hanson. 1996. "Globalization, Outsourcing, and Wage Inequality." *American Economic Association Papers and Proceedings* 86, no.2: 240–45.

Feliciano, Zadia. 2001. "Workers and Trade Liberalization: The Impact of Trade Reforms in Mexico on Wages and Employment." *Industrial and Labor Relations Review* 55, no. 1: 95–115.

Garrett, Geoffrey. 2001. "The Distributive Consequences of Globalization." Leitner Working Paper 2001-02. Yale University Leitner Program in International and Comparative Political Economy.

Kapstein, Ethan, and Branko Milanovic. 2003. *Income and Influence: Social Policy in Emerging Market Economies.* Kalamazoo, Mich.: Upjohn Institute.

Khananusapkul, Phanwadee. 2004. "Do Low-Skilled Female Immigrants Increase the Labor Supply of Skilled Native Women?" Working Paper. Harvard University.

Kimmel, Jean. 1998. "Childcare Costs as a Barrier to Employment for Single and Married Mothers." *Review of Economics and Statistics* 80, no. 2: 287–99.

Kisker, Ellen, Sandra L. Hofferth, Deborah Phillips, and Elizabeth Farquhar. 1991. "A Profile of Child Care Settings: Early Education and Care in 1990." Report prepared for the U.S. Department of Education by Mathematica Policy Research.

Kominski, Robert, and Andrea Adams. 1994. "Educational Attainment in the United States: March 1993 and 1992." *Current Population Reports* P20-476. Washington: U.S. Department of Commerce, Bureau of the Census (May).

Kremer, Michael, and Eric Maskin. 1996. "Wage Inequality and Segregation by Skill." Working Paper 5718. Cambridge, Mass: National Bureau of Economic Research (August).

―――. 2003. "Globalization and Inequality." Working Paper. Harvard University, Department of Economics.

Kremer, Michael, and Stanley Watt. 2006. "The Globalization of Household Production." Working Paper. Harvard University Center for International Development.

Li, Hongyi, Lyn Squire, and Heng-fu Zou. 1998. "Explaining International and Intertemporal Variations in Income Inequality." *Economic Journal* 108, no. 446: 26–43.

Lindert, Peter H., and Jeffrey G. Williamson. 2001. "Does Globalization Make the World More Unequal?" Working Paper 8228. Cambridge, Mass.: National Bureau of Economic Research.

Lundberg, Mattias, and Lyn Squire. 2003. "The Simultaneous Evolution of Growth and Inequality." *Economic Journal* 113, no. 487: 326–44.

Piketty, Thomas. 1997 "Immigration et justice sociale." *Revue Economique* 48, no. 5: 1291–309.

Pavcnik, Nina. 2000. "What Explains Skill Upgrading in Less Developed Countries?" Working Paper 7846. Cambridge, Mass.: National Bureau of Economic Research.

Rama, Martín. 2001. "Globalization, Inequality and Labor Market Policies." Paper prepared for the European online Annual World Bank Conference in Development Economics (ABCDE-Europe). Washington: World Bank, Development Research Group.

Ribar, David. 1995. "Structural Model of Child Care and the Labor Supply of Married Women." *Journal of Labor Economics* 13, no. 3: 558–97.

Robbins, Donald. 1995a. "Earnings Dispersion in Chile after Trade Liberalization." Cambridge, Mass.: Harvard University Institute for International Development.

————. 1995b. "Trade, Trade Liberalization, and Inequality in Latin America and East Asia: Synthesis of Seven Country Studies." Cambridge, Mass.: Harvard University Institute for International Development.

————. 1996a. "Stolper-Samuelson (Lost) in the Tropics: Trade Liberalization and Wages in Colombia 1976–94." Cambridge, Mass.: Harvard University Institute for International Development.

————. 1996b. "HOS Hits Facts: Facts Win. Evidence on Trade and Wages in the Developing World." Cambridge, Mass.: Harvard University Institute for International Development.

Robbins, Donald, and Thomas Gindling. 1998. "Educational Expansion, Trade Liberalisation, and Distribution in Costa Rica." In *Poverty, Economic Reform, and Income Distribution in Latin America*, edited by Albert Berry and R. Albert Berry. Boulder, Colo.: Lynne Rienner.

Robbins, Donald, Martin Gonzales, and Alicia Menendez. 1995. "Wage Dispersion in Argentina, 1976–93: Trade Liberalization amidst Inflation, Stabilization, and Overvaluation." Cambridge, Mass.: Harvard University Institute for International Development. Processed.

White, Howard, and Edward Anderson. 2001. "Growth versus Distribution: Does the Pattern of Growth Matter?" *Development Policy Review* 19, no. 3: 267–89.

Wood, Adrian. 1997. "Openness and Wage Inequality in Developing Countries: The Latin American Challenge to East Asian Conventional Wisdom." *World Bank Economic Review* 11, no. 1: 33–57.

ARVIND PANAGARIYA
Columbia University

Migration: Who Gains, Who Loses

Analytically as well as politically, migration is a more complex phenome-non than international trade. The latter involves two-way flows of goods and services that allow the real aggregate income to grow in each country involved. Therefore, the arguments for protection against imports typically rest on the detrimental effects on the income distribution or the existence of prior distortions in other markets.

Migration involves one-way flows, which calls for a distinction to be made between the "source" country and the "destination" country. In addition, one must separately consider the welfare of the migrant and also decide whether his or her welfare constitutes a part of the welfare of the source country or destination country. In turn, since the migrant physically resides in the country of destination and cannot be excluded from consuming public goods, society is confronted with the issue of fiscal burden imposed by the migrant on the native population.

The literature on the brain drain saw explosive growth in the 1970s and has been elegantly surveyed by Bhagwati and Rodriguez. This literature continues to provide a useful framework for analyzing many of the current issues in the migration debate.[1] Therefore, my discussion below draws heavily on that literature. I begin with the introduction of the basic issues with the help of the conventional one-good, two-factor model.

The Simple Welfare Economics of Migration in a One-Good Model

The one-sector, two-factor model offers us the simplest framework within which we can introduce the key issues that migration raises. The model has the

---

1. Bhagwati and Rodriguez (1975).

obvious limitation that it does not admit international trade. As such, it is to be viewed as only the starting point for the introduction of the basic issues.

With this qualification, I call the two factors capital (K) and labor (L) and divide the world into two countries: the capital-abundant North and labor-abundant South. In figure 1, the horizontal axis $O_S O_N$ represents the total supply of labor worldwide. I measure labor employed in the South to the right from O_S and that employed in the North to the left from O_N. Using the only good in the economy as the numeraire, MPL_S and MPL_N represent the marginal product curves of labor in the South and the North, respectively.

Suppose now that point R gives the initial allocation of labor between the North and the South. It is then immediately clear that the initial northern wage, W_N, exceeds the initial southern wage, W_S. The area under each country's marginal product curve up to the labor-allocation point gives its total income. The rectangle formed by the height of the wage and the length of labor allocation determines the wage bill with the rest of the income going to capital.

Next, allow just one worker to migrate. Given the higher wage in the North, this migration will be from the South to the North. Assume for simplicity that the migrant does not own any capital either before or after migration. Under such circumstances, since the volume of migration is infinitesimally small by assumption, neither the welfare of those left behind in the source country nor that of the native population in the destination country is altered. Only the migrant benefits, who now receives the higher northern wage. Before emigration from the South, he added W_S to the GDP and received W_S; after immigration into the North, he contributes W_N to the income and receives W_N.

If migration is finite, however, the welfare of those left behind in the source country and of the native population in the destination country is affected. This is shown by the movement of RR' workers from the South to the North in figure 1. Continuing to assume that migrants do not own any capital either before or after migration, this change leads to a loss of the triangular area FGH by those left behind in the South and the gain of the triangular area ABC by the native population in the North. Migrants themselves gain the rectangular area $BCFG$. The world income as a whole rises by the area $ACHF$.

Migration also leads to an income distribution effect. In the South, reduced endowment of labor raises the wage. In the North, the labor endowment increases and the effect on the wage is the opposite. If the ownership of factors were specialized so that capital was owned entirely by "capitalists" and the "workers" derived their entire income from labor, the changes would effectively improve the income distribution in the South, worsen it in the North, and improve it worldwide.

Figure 1. Migration in the One-Good Model

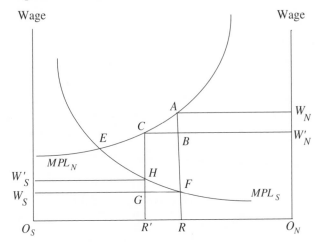

Note that so far I have avoided any reference to the effect of migration on "national" welfare. This is because the answer here critically depends on whether the welfare of the migrant is included in the welfare of the source country or the destination country. If migration is temporary, it makes sense to continue to include the welfare of the migrant in the welfare of the source country. In this case, since the welfare of the migrants rises by more than the decline in the welfare of those left behind, national welfare of the source country rises. Since the native population in the destination country also benefits, migration improves national welfare in both countries.

If migration is permanent, however, the answer is less clear-cut. The reason is that the welfare of the migrants cannot automatically be made a part of the welfare of the destination country. Even permanent migrants rarely cut their ties with the source country, and a case can still be made for at least a partial inclusion of their welfare in the source country welfare. This case is further strengthened if the migrants remit a part of their income to the relatives in the source country.

Figure 1 also helps us understand some of the political economy implications of migration. It is evident that if migration is driven exclusively by the wage difference and is entirely free, it will equalize the wages internationally. From the political economy standpoint, the precise wage at which the marginal product curves of the North and of the South intersect is crucial. The closer this intersection is to the initial wage in the North, the more likely that the wages in New Delhi (South) will be determined in New York (North). On the contrary, the closer the intersection is to the initial wage in the South, the more likely that the wages in New York will be determined in New Delhi. Migration is likely to be feared less by the North and desired more by the South in the former than in the latter case.

Based on the one-good model, the analysis up to this point is simple. However, complications arise as the model is made richer to allow for international trade. Complications also arise when distinctions are made between unskilled and skilled migration. Before I consider these features, however, let me take up an issue raised recently in the literature with respect to the welfare of the migrant.

Global Care Chains and the Welfare of the Migrant

The analysis in the previous section suggests that the proposition that the migrant benefits ought to be rather uncontroversial. Even when one introduced more goods into the model and allowed for international trade or formally distinguished between skilled and unskilled labor, the migrant would likely move only in response to a higher wage in the destination country and would therefore benefit.

One possible objection, however, is that migration in response to the higher wage may require the movement of a nonworking spouse who may find her welfare declining with the loss of the richer social life in the source country. But since the decision of the household to migrate is voluntary, it is reasonable to argue that the household taken as a whole must see its welfare rise with the costs of social hardship to the spouse more than offset by the financial benefits reaped.

Sociologist Arlie Russell Hochschild forcefully makes a closely related argument in the context of the global care chains. She argues that the global care chains that bring the Third World mothers to care for the First World children hurt the former and their children. She writes, "Most of the migrant workers . . . interviewed talked of going back, but . . . it was their wages that went home while they themselves stayed on in the USA or Italy." She further states that being in the care chain is "a brave odyssey . . . with deep costs" and that the poor migrant mother's "child may be getting less motherly care than the First World child." Hochschild concludes in favor of policies that will discourage the global care chains and hence the associated migration.[2]

2. Hochschild (2000), pp. 133, 136.

The argument made by Hochschild is readily countered. For instance, in my review of the book in which the article by Hochschild appeared, I noted,

"Arguably, this is wrong diagnosis and, hence, wrong prescription. It is entirely possible that while the migrant mother brings her loving care to the First World children, not available from their super-busy mom, her own children back home are reared under the loving care of her extended family that is so common in traditional cultures. Moreover, even when this is not true, one must ask whether the educational and other opportunities opened up by the migrant mother's earnings do not outweigh the cost of the children being reared by someone else."[3]

I may further add that insofar as Third World mothers voluntarily decide to take advantage of better economic opportunities in the First World, they are effectively voting with their feet in favor of migration. Since they are free to return but choose not to do so despite the social and psychological costs of separation from their own children, the presumption has to be in favor of migration improving their lot over the alternative.

The Source Country

I focus on two issues in this section: temporary migration as a development strategy and some asymmetries in the welfare economics of emigration.

Temporary Emigration as a Development Strategy?

The analysis associated with figure 1 suggests that if North-South wage differences are large, as is indeed the case currently, potential gains from temporary migration to the source countries are large. Using a simple simulation model more than two decades ago, Hamilton and Whalley concluded that the gains from freeing up migration of labor worldwide were larger than the existing world income at the time. Because North-South wage differences have remained large, these large gains from migration are still possible.[4]

In an article in 1999, I had proposed that if developed countries insist on a multilateral agreement on investment as a part of the next negotiating round of the World Trade Organization (WTO) developing countries should symmetrically demand an agreement on the temporary movement of workers.[5] My broad

---

3. Panagariya (2000). In his recent celebrated book *In Defense of Globalization*, Jagdish Bhagwati (2004) also wrote critically of the thesis advanced by Hochschild.

4. Hamilton and Whalley (1984).

5. See Panagariya (1999). The bid for a multilateral agreement on investment seemingly succeeded at the WTO Ministerial Conference at Doha in 2001, but it eventually failed at the Cancun Ministerial Conference in 2003.

argument was that when a factor market is liberalized internationally, the bulk of the benefit goes to the owner of the migrating factor, which receives the higher return prevailing in the destination country. In the case of investment, developed countries are the source countries and developing countries are destination countries. Therefore, the benefit of the higher return on investment in the latter would accrue largely to the former. The situation is reversed with respect to labor: here the developing countries are the source countries and will therefore benefit from the higher wage in the developed—destination—countries. The calculations by Hamilton and Whalley suggest that these gains would be large.[6]

With the removal of the multilateral investment agreement from the negotiating agenda of the Doha Round, my original basis for demanding an agreement for temporary movement of workers no longer exists. Moreover, Congress has now taken the view that the temporary movement of natural persons is an immigration issue and has forbidden the U.S. Trade Representative to negotiate any agreements on migration issues. Nevertheless, many, including Rodrik and Stiglitz and Charlton, have subsequently embraced the proposal and have been calling for an, what is now politically unviable, agreement on opening the rich-country labor markets to temporary migration from the poor countries as a part of the Doha negotiations.[7]

In addition, Pritchett and Kapur and McHale have offered variants of "development" strategies based on temporary migration.[8] The premise underlying each of their proposals is that somehow the conventional development strategies centered on trade openness have failed and we must try something different. And that something may well be temporary migration of workers from the poor to the rich countries.

In my judgment, this is a largely flawed view for two reasons. First, as documented systematically in another article of mine, virtually every successful growth experience during the last half decade has taken place in the presence of rapidly expanding trade and either low or declining trade barriers.[9] As such the premise that the conventional strategy has failed is itself on very shaky grounds. Second, and more important, whereas the world markets to trade are open so that a strategy based on outward-oriented trade policies is readily available, one based on opening the rich-country markets to either temporary or permanent migration on a scale significant enough to make a dent in poverty in the vast majority of the poor countries can only be viewed as a pie in the sky.

6. Hamilton and Whalley (1984).
7. Rodrik (2002); Stiglitz and Charlton (2005).
8. Pritchett (2003a, 2003b); Kapur and McHale (2006).
9. Panagariya (2004).

Thus, leaving aside the exceptional cases, an example being Mexico, which have a vast common border with a rich country and can count on a large number of their citizens to cross the border illegally if not legally, most developing countries cannot hope to gain significant access to rich-country labor markets. The most they can hope for is a modest expansion of opportunities for skilled emigration as the populations age in the United States, Europe, and Japan. Therefore, any development strategy that relies on the emigration of a significant population—skilled or unskilled—to the rich countries has far poorer chances of success than the one that relies on the conventional approach. In the case of sub-Saharan Africa, which is the region in the greatest need of help, it is simply not likely that the rich countries will accept significant numbers of their unskilled workers in the foreseeable future.[10] And insofar as skilled workers are concerned, given their extreme shortage in the region in the first place, it is even doubtful whether their emigration is a plus for the source countries in the first place (more on this below).

The Welfare Economics Once Again: Some Asymmetries

It is useful to clarify further the analytics of the impact of emigration on the source country. The discussion in the first section showed that, absent remittances, finite migration within the one-good, two-factor model worsens the welfare of the population left behind. This result need not extend to a model with more goods. Thus, consider the two-good, two-factor (capital and labor), small-country model. We know that the factor prices in this model are tied to commodity prices as long as both goods are produced. Therefore, assuming both goods continue to be produced before and after migration and remembering that the goods' prices are set from the world market, even finite emigration leaves the factor prices unchanged. With the rate of return on capital and the wage rate entirely unchanged, those left behind are neither worse off nor better off in the postmigration equilibrium. In this case, even small remittances by migrants will suffice to strictly improve the welfare of those left behind.

If the source country is large, however, migration will change the terms of trade, which will in turn change the factor prices and hence the welfare of those left behind. The direction of the change in welfare will depend on the direction of the change in the terms of trade. I will have the occasion to elaborate on the implications for welfare of the changes in terms of trade in the context of the host country problem in the next section. Here let me focus on some

10. In a world in which almost fifty years of exhortations have failed to induce most of the rich countries to raise development assistance to 0.7 percent of their respective GDPs, any expectation that they will open their labor markets to assist developing countries is unrealistic.

asymmetries with respect to skilled versus unskilled migration and large versus small countries in the context of the source country problem.

Because unskilled labor is plentiful in most developing countries, few of them view its outflow with disfavor. Any losses along the lines of figure 1 are more than compensated by remittances. This is true, for example, of Mexico, which actively seeks access to the U.S. market by its unskilled workers. It is also true of the emigration of workers from countries such as India and Pakistan to the oil-rich Middle Eastern countries.

This conclusion turns weaker, however, when it comes to skilled migration, especially from smaller countries from sub-Saharan Africa or the Caribbean. When skilled workers leave, the country loses not only the triangular area such as *FGH* in figure 1 but also the costs incurred on their education and training. Additional loss can arise if there are significant externalities from these workers to the rest of the population or if their wages happen to be below the value of their social marginal product.[11]

These factors could be particularly relevant to some of the smaller countries in which emigration of skilled workers makes up an extremely high proportion of their in-country total. For example, consider table 1, taken from Mishra.[12] It shows the percentages of the labor force that has migrated from various Caribbean countries to the United States between 1965 and 2000 at various levels of education. The last column shows that the proportion of the population with tertiary education migrating to the United States has ranged from 18 percent for the Dominican Republic to 80 percent for Guyana.[13]

If one assumes that skilled workers such as doctors and engineers generate external economies for the rest of the population, their emigration would lead to losses that can be much larger than the triangular loss of *FGH* in figure 1. In effect, emigration reduces the available externality and therefore productivity of labor. In terms of figure 1, the marginal product of labor (*MPL*) curve shifts downward, making the loss bigger than the triangular area *FGH*.

Assuming plausible externality parameters, Mishra computes the loss in production from emigration for the Caribbean countries.[14] Combining this cost with the cost of education, she finds that the total cost imposed by emigration

11. Externalities arise, for example, if emigrating workers are a source of know-how for those left behind.

12. Mishra (2006), annex table 1.

13. Similarly high emigration rates to the countries of the Organization for Economic Cooperation and Development are observed for some African countries, for example, 47 percent for Ghana (see "Fruit That Falls Far from the Tree," *Economist,* Finance and Economics section, Economic Focus column, November 3, 2005).

14. Mishra (2006).

Table 1. Percentage of Labor Force that Has Migrated to the United States, by Level of Schooling, 1965–2000

Country	Primary	Secondary	Tertiary
Antigua and Barbuda	3	57	56
Bahamas, The	2	10	58
Barbados	4	20	46
Belize	4	54	62
Dominica	6	56	49
Dominican Republic	5	28	18
Grenada	7	61	75
Guyana	7	35	80
Haiti	2	27	79
Jamaica	5	29	78
St. Kitts and Nevis	8	31	65
St. Lucia	2	13	53
St. Vincent and the Grenadines	4	23	71
Trinidad and Tobago	3	17	68
Average	4	33	61

Source: Mishra (2006, table 2).

on these countries more than outweighs the remittances. Thus, despite remittances, emigration leaves these countries worse off.

An important cost imposed by skilled emigration on those left behind in the source country, which has been entirely ignored in the literature and is perhaps more significant than the externality, is the loss of the transfer of income from emigrating skilled workers to the rest of the population. This transfer takes at least two forms. First, skilled workers are likely to contribute disproportionately to the tax revenues that finance the spending on public goods. Second, for a variety of reasons, most notably government regulation, wages of skilled workers in the developing countries are held well below market wages. For example, many developing countries regulate doctors' fees, setting them well below the market rate. Alternatively, one can imagine that the market demand curve for the services of skilled workers, such as doctors, itself understates the social marginal benefit of those services. Because the poor lack purchasing power, their ability to pay falls well short of the social value of providing treatment to them. Either way, the wages paid to the skilled workers do not reflect their true social marginal product. It is then easy to show that emigration leads to a larger loss than the triangular loss of *FGH* in figure 1.

Thus, in figure 2, suppose *SMB* represents the social marginal benefit of the doctors' services, as a function of the volume of such services measured along the horizontal axis. Suppose further that the initial supply of doctors is given by point *L* and that the doctors' fees are set at W_S, which is below the social

Figure 2. Losses from Skilled Emigration

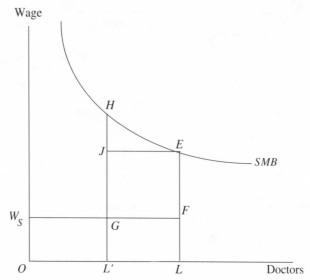

marginal benefit of the service. If *LL'* doctors now emigrate, the loss to those left behind is not just the triangular area *EJH* but additionally includes the rectangle *EFGJ*.

While losses such as these from the emigration of skilled workers can be significant for smaller developing countries, they are unlikely to swamp the benefits from skilled emigration accruing to the larger developing countries. The obvious example here is that of India: even the large absolute emigration of skilled workers represents only 4.3 percent of its total skilled labor force.[15] Nevertheless, because of its large absolute size in the United States, the Indian diaspora has generated significant benefits for India.

Benefits from the emigration of Indian skilled workers have accrued in at least five dimensions. First, the Indian diaspora in the United States has contributed significantly to the rapid advancement of the information technology (IT) industry in the United States. In turn, this advancement has benefited the Indian IT sector. Second, many Indian immigrants are employed in top positions in leading U.S. companies and have played an important role in bringing these companies to India as potential buyers of Indian goods or as investors. Third, the Indian diaspora has also turned into a significant political force within the United States and has been instrumental in promoting better political ties between the two countries. Fourth, the success of the Indian diaspora

15. "Fruit That Falls Far from the Tree," *Economist* (2005).

also generates an "inspiration" effect on those left behind. In particular, it encourages the young in India to seek higher education and to excel. In the long run, this effect promises to improve the quality of the Indian labor force. Finally, the Indian diaspora has also contributed significantly through remittances. Currently, remittances contribute more than $20 billion annually to the national income of India.[16] Not all of these remittances come from skilled workers, but the share of the latter is very substantial.

The Host Country

Whereas the smaller developing countries feel threatened by the emigration of the skilled, the developed countries fear the immigration of the unskilled. Recent literature has pointed to two sources of concern. First, immigration undercuts the wages of the native unskilled and thus has a detrimental effect on income distribution. Second, unskilled immigrants often enter illegally and do not pay taxes. Yet they consume public services such as education and health for which the native population pays through taxes. These immigrants, thus, effectively lower the overall welfare of the native population. Let me consider each of these concerns in turn.

Immigration and Unskilled Wages

Harvard economist George Borjas is the leading voice among economists expressing both concerns. In a 2003 article, he worked with a one-good model in which workers with different skill (education) levels, whether native or immigrant, were imperfect substitutes for one another.[17] Also, he assumed that native and immigrant workers with the same skill levels were perfect substitutes for one another. Within this broad framework, he estimated that the effect of immigration into the United States between 1980 and 2000 was to lower the average wages by 3 percent and unskilled wages by 8 percent.

This finding was based on the assumption that immigration had no effect on the stock of capital. But because an increased labor force through immigration raises the return to capital, it must also lead to an increase in the stock of capital through either faster accumulation or larger inflows of foreign capital. Borjas found that once this effect was included, immigration had no effect on the average wage, while it lowered unskilled wages by less than 5 percent.

16. Reserve Bank of India (2005), table 146.
17. Borjas (2003).

Subsequently, Ottaviano and Peri have argued that even these estimates by Borjas are on the larger side.[18] These authors argue that even within the same skilled category natives and immigrants are imperfect substitutes and end up in very different jobs. For instance, unskilled Mexican workers are found predominantly in gardening, housework, and construction, while unskilled natives are concentrated in logging. Allowing for such imperfect substitutability, they found that immigration between 1980 and 2000 raised the average wage of native workers by 2 percent and that its effect on unskilled wage was either nil or moderately negative.

These findings complement those of Card who took an altogether different approach to measuring the effects of immigration on wages.[19] He hypothesized that if immigrants have an adverse effect on unskilled wages, it must show up in lower unskilled wages in the cities where immigrants are disproportionately located. He found no such effect.

An important objection to these studies is that they all assume a one-good economy. This assumption has the unrealistic implication that the economy does not engage in international trade. Once two or more goods are allowed for, however, the negative relationship between immigration and wages may not hold even qualitatively. Indeed, this fact may be behind relatively weak evidence linking immigration to reduced wages.

To see why, consider the two-good, two-factor, capital-labor model. Suppose there are two countries, a capital-abundant North and labor-abundant South, and tastes are identical and homothetic across all individuals. Assume further that the North has a superior technology for the production of a labor-intensive good in the Hicks-neutral sense. In this setting, free trade in goods equalizes the goods' prices but not factor prices. In particular, the return to labor is higher in the North. Relaxing slightly the restriction on labor mobility leads some workers to move from the South to the North. At the original goods' prices, increased labor endowment leads to expansion of the labor-intensive sector and contraction of the capital-intensive sector in the North. Because the South loses labor, the opposite change takes place there. In general, it cannot be determined, however, whether these changes lead to a reduction or increase in the relative supply of the labor-intensive good. Therefore, the relative price of the labor-intensive good may rise or fall. If it rises, wages will rise in both the source and destination countries, and if it falls, wages will fall in both countries. In either case, the effect of migration on wages as predicted by the one-good model will necessarily be false in one of the two

18. Ottaviano and Peri (2006).
19. Card (2005).

countries. If the price of the labor-intensive good rises, wages would paradoxically *rise* in the country of immigration, and if it falls, wages will paradoxically *fall* in the country of emigration.

An alternative way to understand this ambiguity is to consider the effect of immigration on trade. When more labor comes into the country via immigration, at the original goods' prices, the labor-intensive good expands. Assuming the country is an importer of the labor-intensive good, this expansion of labor reduces the need for imports. This means less labor is imported indirectly through trade. Thus increased supply of labor from abroad through immigration is counteracted by reduced supply of labor through trade. This is one possible reason why labor economists have had great difficulty in finding large effects of immigration in the data.

This point remains valid when nontraded goods are allowed for and immigrant workers are concentrated in these goods. In the source country, emigration leads to the contraction of the labor-intensive good and expansion of the capital-intensive good, as before. In the destination country, suppose that the immigrant worker is employed in housework. If a member of the household who previously did this work is now freed up to enter the labor force, at the initial prices, the effect of this entry is to expand the traded labor-intensive good and contract the traded capital-intensive good. The eventual effect on the factor prices still depends on the changes in the traded goods' prices induced by these output (and possibly expenditure) changes.

In an alternative scenario, the member of the household may choose to take greater leisure time instead of adding to the labor supply—this will be the likely case if the immigrant is employed in a task such as gardening that was previously done by the member of the household. In this case, the perverse outcome is likely in the destination country, whereby the decreased supply of the labor-intensive good in the source country would raise the price of the latter and push the wages up everywhere.

More realistically, distinctions may be made between skilled and unskilled labor. Replacing capital by skilled labor in the two-factor model accomplishes this task most simply. In the housework example, imagine then that the immigration of unskilled labor makes it possible to expand the supply of skilled labor by releasing, for example, a mother from child care duties. In this case, the effect of immigration is even more likely to raise unskilled wages.

Access to Public Services and the Welfare of the Native Population

Concerns have also been expressed that immigrants access welfare benefits at substantially higher rates than do natives and that they also use education and health services disproportionately more than is accounted for by their tax contributions so that there is a net transfer from the native population to the immigrant population.[20] According to Smith and Edmonston, the net fiscal deficit for providing services to immigrants in 1996 was $1,174 and $229 per native family in California and New Jersey, respectively.[21] Hanson and colleagues discussed various aspects of this issue in detail in their long survey article.[22]

A key factor that has received virtually no attention in this context, however, is that, while immigrants may impose this fiscal burden on the native population, they also generate benefits for it. For instance, when immigrants perform gardening services for the native households, they generate consumers' surplus for the latter. Likewise, when they perform housework that allows members of the native families to participate more fully in the labor force, they help the latter earn income. These gains can be particularly large if the wage at which natives would perform the services provided by the immigrants is prohibitively high so that the households would end up doing their own gardening or housework. A proper evaluation of the impact of immigrants on the native population must take into account this benefit side and not just the cost side on which the literature to date has focused.

Concluding Remarks

Perhaps the most robust proposition on the welfare effects of migration is also the most obvious one: the migrant generally benefits. Once we get past the migrant and focus on the welfare of those left behind in the source country or the native population in the destination country, generalizations are hard to make. For example, on the one hand, some of the small countries that have lost 50 percent or more of their skilled labor force have probably been hurt by emigration on balance. On the other hand, the conventional losses from skilled emigration in the case of the larger countries (India) have most likely been more than offset by benefits in the form of faster development of the IT industry, increased incentives to seek technical education, and a variety of "diaspora effects."

As regards the destination country, the dominant theme in the empirical literature has been that immigration has depressed the wages, worsened the

20. Camarota (2001).
21. Smith and Edmonston (1997).
22. Hanson and colleagues (2002).

income distribution, and imposed fiscal costs on the native population. I have argued that a closer examination raises serious doubts about the validity of each of these themes. The theoretical basis for the proposition that immigration depresses wages or worsens the income distribution is rather fragile. Unsurprisingly, upon close examination, the empirical evidence available from various studies reaches conflicting conclusions as well.

Finally, I have taken a skeptical view of the proposals for temporary migration being the centerpiece of a development strategy for the poor countries. For one thing, the evidence simply does not support the premise that the conventional model has failed to deliver positive results. In fact, virtually every successful case has followed the conventional strategy of relying on outward-oriented policies. Moreover, leaving aside some exceptional cases such as Mexico, an emigration-based strategy is simply not available. Thus most sub-Saharan African countries currently face a shortage of skilled workers, so that their emigration will actually make matters worse. They could benefit from the emigration of unskilled workers, however, but few rich countries are open to accepting them.

References

Bhagwati, Jagdish. 2004. *In Defense of Globalization*. Oxford University Press.

Bhagwati, Jagdish, and Carlos Rodriguez. 1975. "Welfare-Theoretical Analyses of the Brain Drain." *Journal of Development Economics* 2, no. 3 (September): 195–221.

Borjas, George. 2003. "The Labor Demand Curve Is Downward Sloping: Reexamining the Impact of Immigration on the Labor Market." *Quarterly Journal of Economics* 118, no. 4 (November): 1335–374.

Camarota, Steven A. 2001. "Immigrants in the United States—2000: A Snapshot of America's Foreign-Born Population." *Backgrounder*. Washington: Center for Immigration Studies (January) (www.cis.org/articles/2001/back101.html).

Card, David. 2005. "Is the New Immigration Really So Bad?" NBER Working Paper 11547. Cambridge, Mass.: National Bureau of Economic Research (August).

Hamilton, Bob, and John Whalley. 1984. "Efficiency and Distributional Implications of Global Restrictions on Labour Mobility: Calculations and Policy Implications." *Journal of Development Economics* 14, no. 1: 61–75.

Hanson, Gordon H., Kenneth F. Scheve, Matthew J. Slaughter, and Antonio Spilimbergo. 2002. "Immigration and the U.S. Economy: Labor-Market Impacts, Illegal Entry, and Policy Choices." In *Immigration Policy and the Welfare State*, edited by Tito Boeri, Gordon Hanson, and Barry McCormick, pp. 169–285. Oxford University Press.

Hochschild, Arlie Russell. 2000. "Global Care Chains and Emotional Surplus Value." In *On the Edge: Living with Global Capitalism*, edited by Will Hutton and Anthony Giddens, pp. 130–46. London: Jonathan Cape.

Kapur, Devesh, and John McHale. 2006. "What is Wrong with Plan B? International Migration as an Alternative to Development." See this volume of *Brookings Trade Forum 2006*, pp. 137–172.

Mishra, Prachi. 2006. "Emigration and Brain Drain from the Caribbean." In *The Caribbean: From Vulnerability to Sustained Growth*, edited by Ratna Sahay, David O. Robinson, and Paul Cashin, pp. 225–57. Washington: International Monetary Fund.

Ottaviano, Gianmarco I. P., and Giovanni Peri. 2006. "Rethinking the Effects of Immigration on Wages" (www.econ.ucdavis.edu/faculty/gperi/Papers/perott_august_2006.pdf).

Panagariya, Arvind. 1999. "The Millennium Round and Developing Countries: Negotiating Strategies and Areas of Benefits." Paper presented at the conference "Developing Countries and the New Multilateral Round of Trade Negotiations." Harvard University, November 5–6. Also as G-24 Discussion Papers Series, no. 1, UN Conference on Trade and Development and Center for International Development, Harvard University (March 2000).

———. 2000. "Why Did the Chicken Cross the Globe." Review of *On the Edge: Living with Global Capitalism. Times Higher Education Supplement* (September 29): 30.

———. 2004. "Miracles and Debacles: In Defense of Trade Openness." *World Economy* 27, no 8 (special issue on Global Trade Policy, August): 1149–171.

Pritchett, Lant. 2003a. "The Future of Migration: Irresistible Forces Meet Immovable Ideas." Paper presented at the conference "The Future of Globalization: Explorations in the Light of Recent Turbulence." Yale University, October 10.

———. 2003b. "The Future of Migration–Part 2: Immovable Ideas Help Prevent Migration." YaleGlobal Online (September 9) (yaleglobal.yale.edu/display.article?id=2774).

Reserve Bank of India. 2005. *Handbook of Statistics on Indian Economy*. Mumbai.

Rodrik, Dani. 2002. "Feasible Globalizations." Discussion Paper 3524. London: Centre for Economic Policy Research.

Smith, James P., and Barry Edmonston, eds. 1997. *The New Americans: Economic, Demographic, and Fiscal Effects of Immigration*. Washington: National Academy Press, National Research Council.

Stiglitz, Joseph E., and Andrew Charlton. 2005. *Fair Trade for All: How Trade Can Promote Development*. Oxford University Press.

ISABEL SAWHILL
Brookings Institution

Do Open Borders Produce Greater Happiness? An Underanalyzed Question

When Carol Graham and Susan Collins asked me to do this, I was a little reluctant since I am not an expert on global labor markets. However, I have recently been exposed to some interesting work that is going on right here at Brookings. This work has stimulated me to suggest a relatively loose mega-hypothesis for which I think there are at least some pieces of supportive evidence. However, I present these ideas to provoke discussion rather than to argue the case in any dispositive way.

I come at this from what you might call a rich-country perspective, and more specifically from a U.S. perspective. It seems to me that there is good news and bad news from this perspective. The good news is that the United States has more flexible and open labor markets than do some other rich countries, such as those in Europe. That is commonly thought to be one reason why we have a lower rate of unemployment, less inflation, and more growth. Our strong economy in turn has attracted capital and labor from the rest of the world. Some people argue this is because a glut of savings and of labor exists in the rest of the world and that these flows of capital and labor to the United States are a result of the fact that this country is a very attractive place to work or invest. So that is the good news.

The bad news with respect to this inflow of capital is the fact that we have become extremely dependent on foreigners to pay for the excess of imports over exports; we are consuming more than we are producing and borrowing the difference. It is ironic, if not immoral, that the wealthiest country in the world is borrowing from poorer countries such as China to support its excess consumption. More than half of our publicly marketable debt is now owed to foreigners, many of them in less-developed nations. If such capital were invested instead

245

Figure 1. Real and Nominal Wage Rigidity by Country[a]

Percent

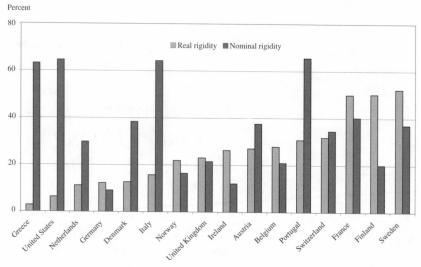

Source: Dickens (2006).
a. Estimates of the percentage of workers potentially affected by downward nominal wage rigidity versus downward real wage rigidity.

in improving standards of living in the home countries of the debt holders, it might help to reduce global poverty. In the meantime, these global imbalances are likely to be unsustainable. So whatever prosperity the United States is experiencing at the present time is built on a very uncertain foundation.

The bad news with respect to the inflow of labor is that it has produced a fractious debate about immigration and its effects on the U.S. economy and on American society. Opinions differ about the effects of immigration on wage rates for the native born and on the incidence of poverty. But it is likely that immigration has contributed somewhat to wage inequality, which is growing and which is higher than in other industrialized countries. In addition, it has swollen the ranks of the U.S. poor in a discernible way.

As partial evidence for the above mega-hypothesis, I have drawn on a few pieces of research done by my colleagues at Brookings. Figure 1 is from a research project directed by William Dickens of the Brookings Institution and Erica Groshen of the Federal Reserve Bank of New York. The figure focuses on wage rigidity and therefore on the question of whether the United States has more flexible labor markets than do other advanced countries (as argued above). The evidence here seems clear. With the exception of Greece, the United States has less downward real-wage rigidity than other countries. As Bill Dickens along with George Akerlof of the University of California–Berkeley and George

Figure 2. Male and Female Log Hourly 90/50 and 50/10 Earnings Ratios

Log hourly wage ratio

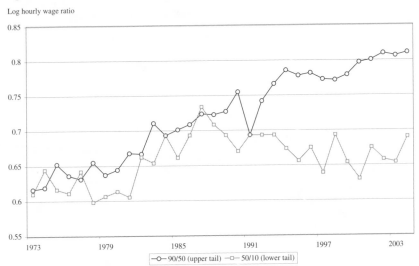

Source: Autor, Katz, and Kearney (2006), citing Current Population Survey May and monthly files, 1973–2004.

Perry of the Brookings Institution have shown, the unemployment caused by downward nominal rigidity can be overcome if the central bank is willing to tolerate moderate inflation (in the 2 to 3 percent range).[1] This option is not available to countries that face substantial downward real-wage rigidity, in which the only way to consistently reduce unemployment is to increase productivity growth.

A second piece of evidence comes from research done by another colleague, in this case Melissa Kearney in a study done jointly with David Autor of MIT and Lawrence Katz of Harvard University.[2] Their study looks at two measures of wage inequality, as shown in figure 2. The first is the ratio of hourly earnings at the 90th percentile to that at the 50th percentile. The second looks at the ratio of the 50th percentile to the 10th percentile. Looking at the trends in these measures, from the early to the mid part of the period, from 1973 to about 1987, one sees growing inequality in both measures. From the 1990s, inequality at the top of the distribution continues in a strong way, but at the bottom half, it more or less levels off. So given that immigration of low-skilled workers, especially from Mexico, increased during this latter period, one might have expected to see a growing gap between the middle and the bottom, but this does

1. Akerlof, Dickens, and Perry (2001).
2. Autor, Katz, and Kearney (2006).

Figure 3. International Estimates of Father-Son Earnings Elasticity

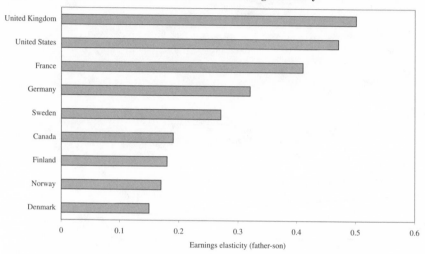

Source: Hertz (2006), citing Corak (2004).

not seem to have occurred, at least in any obvious way. So this bit of evidence would seem to undermine one aspect of my mega-hypothesis—the idea that immigration may have produced greater wage inequality.

A third piece of evidence is on social mobility in the United States compared with that in other advanced countries. This is a particular interest of mine. Figure 3 is from a paper by Tom Hertz at American University, drawing on a review of the evidence by Miles Corak.[3] What it shows is that intergenerational mobility—measured here by the size of the intergenerational earnings elasticity between fathers and sons—is pretty low in the United States. The only country that seems to do worse is the United Kingdom. It is important to note that immigrants are not in this data, so the United States' reputation for being the "land of opportunity" where immigrants are concerned may still be true. However, it is not true where native-born Americans are concerned. I make this point because it has been argued that we do not need to worry too much about growing inequality since so much opportunity is available for people to move up in American society. Rags to riches in a generation may be the myth, but it is not the reality.

How, then, should we—the citizens of the United States—weigh the good versus the bad? On the one hand, we have a strong economy that is attracting labor and capital to our shores. On the other hand, we have—partly as a result—a more

3. Hertz (2006), citing Corak (2004).

Figure 4. Happiness and Income per Capita, 1990s

Percent above neutral on life satisfaction

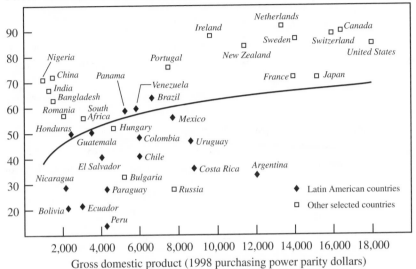

Gross domestic product (1998 purchasing power parity dollars)

Source: Graham and Pettinato (2002); Veenhoven (2002).

fragile prosperity and (although less certainly, given the evidence just reviewed) more inequality and poverty than otherwise might exist. And we do not offer a lot of opportunity for people who are born here to move up the ladder.

To add icing to this cake, I turn to still another body of evidence related to the effects of various economic developments on happiness or national well-being—research being done by my colleague Carol Graham, among others.[4] The message I take from this research is that growth is good, but, in advanced countries anyway, further growth may not produce a lot of additional happiness, unless that growth is broad based and is used to reduce inequality and insecurity and to promote mobility and opportunity. We may have been able, because of our flexible markets, to keep unemployment low and growth rates high, but underneath those aggregates there is some bad news related to the sustainability of that prosperity and its distribution. So, suppose I am a median voter in a rich country, what do I think? Would I rather live in a country with high growth and low unemployment, or would I rather live in a country that has a little less growth but also less inequality and more opportunity? One way to think about that choice is to ask which improves well-being or happiness more, being absolutely better-off or living in a society where the gaps between rich and poor

4. Graham (forthcoming).

are not so large and opportunities to move up the ladder are greater? Figure 4 provides a partial answer. It suggests that, assuming people have reached a certain threshold of income, what makes people happy is not further growth that increases their standard of living but where they are in relative terms and how they perceive future opportunities. As the figure shows, after a certain point, rising absolute incomes do not result in major increases in measured happiness.

In sum, I do not see a lot of evidence that increased immigration has produced greater inequality. Moreover, immigrants are clearly better-off here than they would be in their home countries. On the other hand, recent growth in the United States may not be sustainable. Moreover, for whatever reason, it has not been broad based and has not been accompanied by any increase in the prospects for upward mobility. This type of growth is unlikely to be highly valued by the average citizen or to improve their subjective well-being.

References

Akerlof, George A., William T. Dickens, and George L. Perry. 2001. "Options for Stabilization Policy: A New Analysis of Choices Confronting the Fed." Policy Brief 69. Brookings (February).

Autor, David H., Lawrence F. Katz, and Melissa S. Kearney. 2006. "The Polarization of the U.S. Labor Market." Working Paper 11986. Cambridge, Mass.: National Bureau of Economic Research (January).

Corak, Miles. 2004. "Do Poor Children Become Poor Adults?" Paper presented at the Colloque sur Le Devenir Des Enfants de Familles Défavourisées en France, Carré des Sciences, Ministère de la Jeunesse, de l'Éducation nationale et de la Recherche, Paris, April 1. Also published as "Do Poor Children Become Poor Adults? Lessons from a Cross Country Comparison of Generational Earnings Mobility." Bonn: Institute for the Study of Labor (March 2006).

Dickens, William. 2006. "The International Wage Flexibility Project." Presentation at the Reserve Bank of New Zealand, Wellington, March 10 (www.brookings.edu/es/research/projects/iwfp.htm).

Graham, Carol. Forthcoming. "The Economics of Happiness." In *The New Palgrave: A Dictionary of Economics*, 2d ed., edited by Steven Durlauf and Larry Blume. Basingstoke, United Kingdom: Palgrave MacMillan.

Graham, Carol, and Stefano Pettinato. 2002. *Happiness and Hardship: Opportunity and Insecurity in New Market Economies.* Brookings.

Hertz, Tom. 2006. "Understanding Mobility in America." Paper presented at "Moving on Up? Economic Mobility in America." Center for American Progress, Washington, D.C., April 26 (www.americanprogress.org/kf/hertz_mobility_analysis.pdf).

Veenhoven, Ruut. 2002. World Database of Happiness. Erasmus University, Rotterdam (www.worlddatabaseofhappiness.eur.nl).

Discussion

Carmen Reinhart asked Arvind Panagariya whether he had ever thought of creating a measure of total capital flight by combining the human capital he was talking about and the financial capital that she typically worked on. Since she believed that they tend to trend together, it might be worth integrating them. Lant Pritchett observed that no one ever suggested that U.S. banks not take deposits from Latin Americans, whereas lots of people have suggested that we not allow Latin Americans to come here. Panagariya said that, while he associates physical capital flight with crises, in his view human capital flight tends to be different and not hinged as much on crises. Reinhart responded that they were indeed correlated. During the debt crises in the 1980s, none of the Latin Americans who studied in the United States returned; they only began to do so years later, after stabilization.

Michael Kremer raised a question about the happiness slide at the end of Isabel Sawhill's presentation. He accepted that increases in income do not make people happier at the national level and that things depend on relative income. But he is not sure that necessarily implies that a more equal or mobile society creates more happiness. That would depend on concavity and relative income. However, mobility often entails losses, and behavioral economics suggests that people dislike income losses more than the pleasure that they get from income gains. With a mobile society, the people who move up will not be happy enough to compensate for the unhappiness of those who move down. From a pure happiness perspective, Kremer noted, perhaps mobility is not all that it is cracked up to be. Sawhill supported the point about loss aversion. In an ideal situation, one would have some growth combined with social mobility, so that even if the rich move down—or their children do—they are still better-off than their parents. She noted that that is what we used to have in the United States. There is indeed good reason to keep growth going. But her point was that growth alone is not enough.

251

Carol Graham added that she agreed that some mobility was desirable and at some level was essential. However, to maximize happiness requires mobility plus safety nets. She cited her own work on mobility and happiness, which suggests that even upwardly mobile people who do not have safety nets are very loss averse and worried about falling back. Volatility is very bad for happiness, and thus slower growth with less volatility is better for happiness than is rapid but unstable growth. Yet the one thing that she and her colleagues consistently find is that people who assess positively their prospects of upward mobility are, on average, happier than those who do not. Whether that is because they can predict their future or because they are just happier and more optimistic in general is not known, but there is a clear correlation between positive expectations about one's own and one's children's future and happiness.

Graham then made a last point about happiness and migrants. In her work on Latin America and Russia, she finds that those who report themselves as minorities are less happy on average than others. In the United States, though, the only minority group that is less happy than others are African Americans. In contrast, Hispanics tend to be happier. Thus, as far as this data show, we do not have a story of unhappy migrants in the United States.

Susan Collins commented that the panel presentations were ideal candidates for answering the question raised by Jeffrey Williamson: why is it that people's attitudes about migration have changed so much? She noted that one possible answer is that in countries like the United States, the average citizens' perceptions of the extent to which their children will do at least as well as they have been eroded. And it is the perception of this rather than the actual numbers that determine how people vote and act.

Collins's second point was that one of the key issues—particularly in the context of the various kinds of service activities—is that people have to have enough understanding of common language terms and how they are used to be able to work together. This large international migration of people who are going to school and then perhaps back to their countries or to other places creates a pool of somewhat more educated workers who have closer synergies and are more able to work with highly educated people in rich countries than the people they left behind in their poor countries who did not have the same opportunities. Thus there may be very important linkages between the temporary migration models that were discussed in the panel and the massive schooling flows that Mark Rosenzweig highlighted in his paper.

Gary Burtless noted that there was a great deal of consensus about the gains for migrants crossing from poor to rich countries. The question is whether those gains amount to 50 percent, 100 percent, or 110 percent of the total efficiency gains that come out of migration. Are the migrants themselves and their immediate relatives back home capturing part of, all, or more than all of the gains? For countries that are the primary destination of migration, such as the United States, Canada, and Australia, what matters is what the median voter thinks about how the gains from the migration are distributed. Thus, however distasteful, a reduction in migrants' gains through taxation, which explicitly compensates for welfare losses in the rich countries, might make a liberal immigration policy more attractive to rich-country voters.

Burtless also pointed out that the United States came very close to ending free immigration before the end of the nineteenth century. If that had happened, it would have had a huge effect on the United States. He noted that a big difference between the era before World War I and the post–World War II era is the extent of the welfare state. The concern for most people now focuses on the calculations of the gains and the losses through the tax system in terms of public services, public benefits and so forth. The big question is which is the right model for valuing whose wages, whose property income, and whose capital income is affected by the shift of people across borders. The tax and public service questions are obvious and explain the greater hostility to immigration in western Europe compared with what is felt in the United States, Canada, and Australia.

Devesh Kapur noted that the discussion could end up with the uncomfortable paradox that more liberal policies concerning the treatment of foreign labor and treating them more as citizens could lead to a reduction of global welfare by increasing resistance to labor flows. In this case, we would get fewer poor people moving across borders and lower global welfare. Thus if Europe and the United States had the kinds of migration policies that are in force in Singapore and the Middle East, it is possible (although not certain) that the resistance to the types of labor flows Pritchett suggests would be lower. That too might be an uncomfortable policy outcome.

Lant Pritchett concurred. He suggested that, perhaps what Kremer did not want to say is that Kuwaitis do not care much about Bangladeshis—either when they are in Bangladesh or in Kuwait. And because of that, Bangladeshis are enormously better off economically because the Kuwaitis let them work in Kuwait on very restrictive terms. You do not acquire any of the gains of Kuwaiti citizenship by being physically present in Kuwait to perform labor services. The difficult discussion, which is why philosophy is all the more relevant, is on what terms we are willing to have people physically present in our country to provide labor services in a way that benefits them and us but does not entitle them to all claims to citizenship. This is why Plan B is a temporary quota.

You can come to be a maid in Singapore, period. This makes Indonesian women working in Singapore enormously better off. This is proven by revealed preferences and by the queues.

Pritchett went on to argue that it may be that it makes us uncomfortable to have second-class citizens. But in his view, the point of the matter is that there is no global labor market and that we are perfectly comfortable having Nth class citizens. We are perfectly comfortable with people being absolutely destitute in Mali. However, if they happen to arrive on U.S. soil, we have to treat them as on the path to U.S. citizenship, which makes the citizens of Mali enormously worse-off than if we were to say, "look, you can come if you work for three years mowing lawns in the United States and then go back to Mali, period."

Pritchett acknowledged that this is a difficult conversation to have in a democracy. We would have to admit hard things about the world, such as that people would be enormously pleased to be second-class citizens in Germany or France—as long as the terms are clear and as long as they choose to either come or not come on those terms. This also introduces a huge domestic political problem about the implications for the disadvantaged within our own society. If it is all about relative status, how would having a group of less-privileged immigrants in society affect the status of low-skilled workers? It is not clear what direction that goes in. The key issue, though, which requires a difficult discussion, should be around the terms on which people are willing to have people physically present in their country to provide labor services and whether those terms have to include some access to citizenship.

Carmen Reinhart expressed strong disagreement. She noted that she was a second-class citizen: she came to the United States from Cuba with only three suitcases. As a Cuban-born citizen of the United States, she had serious problems with people being treated like second-class citizens and felt very strongly that immigrants should not be segregated. If they immigrate, they need to integrate into a normal distribution. Immigration should be treated very seriously; it also involves taking chances as some people never really do integrate.

Pritchett responded that there should be both temporary labor and permanent immigration tracks and that there is no question that large numbers of people should have access to the path of U.S. citizenship. He concluded by noting that the reaction to his proposal is clear proof of his point that the whole issue of global labor markets entails a very uncomfortable conversation.